The Last Real Showgirl

The Last Real Showgirl
My Sequined '70s Onstage

DIANE CHRISTIANSEN

Foreword by Barbara Beverly-Crockett

McFarland & Company, Inc., Publishers
Jefferson, North Carolina

ISBN (print) 978-1-4766-9793-2
ISBN (ebook) 978-1-4766-5570-3

Library of Congress cataloging data are available

Library of Congress Control Number 2025002352

© 2025 Diane Christiansen. All rights reserved

No part of this book may be reproduced or transmitted in any form or by any means, electronic or mechanical, including photocopying or recording, or by any information storage and retrieval system, without permission in writing from the publisher.

Front cover image: Diane in stage makeup and Tarantella costume in *Allez Lido*, Stardust, Las Vegas, 1981 (author collection).

Printed in the United States of America

*McFarland & Company, Inc., Publishers
Box 611, Jefferson, North Carolina 28640
www.mcfarlandpub.com*

For my mother, Phoebe,
who secretly dreamt of being a dancer

Acknowledgments

I am indebted to my writing coaches Marilyn Kentz and Minda Burr for their constant inspiration, endless support and loving friendship. Without them, this book would not be. To my dear friends Barrett Carol Brown, Stacey Powells, Heidi Bright and Barbara Beverly-Crockett and to my Ya Ya sisters Suzan Blanco, Louanne Harrison-Chessik for loving me and our real showgirl lives. To Katrina Steele, Jan Fowler and Simone Turner, many heartfelt thanks. To my beloveds, Max and Jessica, Tess and Matt and my glam daughters, Ripley and Gwenyth, I thank you all so very much for your precious time, encouragement and love. To Juliette Townsend, you are a genius and you helped drive this book home and I am so grateful I met you. So much gratitude to ALL who believed in this book at McFarland. Epic thanks to Kacie Newport at BAM Management who gave and gave and gave of herself even while on vacation. And last but not least, to my fully realized literary manager, at BAM Management, Mindi St. Peter, you are a goddess in my country!

Table of Contents

Acknowledgments — vi
Foreword — 1
Preface — 3

1. Rockettes or Bust, 1969 — 5
2. The Waiting Game, 1969 — 13
3. Meet My Mom and Dad, 1950–'60s — 17
4. Getting Out of Dodge, 1969 — 22
5. Conceived and Directed by Tibor Rudas, 1970 — 35
6. And 5, 6, 7, 8, 1970 — 37
7. Guardian Angels Arrive, 1970 — 41
8. Sexy Psychedelics, 1970 — 44
9. Beauty and the Beast, 1970 — 58
10. Meeting the Legendary Barbara Beverly, 1970 — 62
11. Enduring Paradise, 1970 — 71
12. Insomnia, 1971 — 77
13. Success, 1971 — 84
14. Birds with Broken Wings Can Fly, 1971 — 89
15. Elvis, Carolee and Me, 1971 — 96
16. Making the Most of Island Life, 1971 — 105
17. When You Least Expect It, 1971 — 110
18. We Were Pioneers, 1972 — 113
19. Lido de Paris, France, 1972 — 118

20. La Vie Parisienne, 1973	126
21. Recovery and Romance, 1973	137
22. Recapturing Lost Youth, 1974	144
23. The Land of Milk and Honey, 1976	148
24. Island of Tropical Breezes, 1976	153
25. My Comeback, 1976	159
26. Transforming My Life, 1976	165
27. Extra Spicy, 1976	172
28. Manifesting Love, 1976	177
29. Start Spreading the News, 1977	183
30. An Eye for an Eye, 1977	192
31. The Wild West, 1979	197
32. Let the Games Begin, 1979	206
33. Viva Las Vegas, 1979	213
34. Win-Win, 1979	218
35. Living Large in Sin City, 1979	221
36. Cha-Ching, 1980	228
37. The Big Apple or Lala Land?, 1981	235
38. The Big Move, 1981	241
Epilogue	246
Index	251

Foreword

BY BARBARA BEVERLY-CROCKETT

Meeting Diane in 1970, when we roomed together at the Britannia Beach Hotel in Nassau in the Bahamas, during rehearsals for "Casino de Paradis," was life-changing! The course of our lives intertwined regularly over the following years and to this day. Diane has great communication abilities, loyalty, dependability and encompassing love, including her instant understanding of needs in any relationship. I've been abundantly blessed throughout our friendship of adventures, acceptance and growth.

I've unceasingly admired Diane's ability to live life to the fullest, which is clearly demonstrated in this delightful book. Diane depicts the '70s and early '80s in candid and descriptive detail. Through her many transformations as a dancer, a showgirl, a Playboy Bunny, a comedienne, a clothing designer, an actor, a disco performer and a headliner, a girlfriend and a wife—searching for life's answers—she maintained a heart of gold.

Diane created diversity in her life, as her inherent lovability inevitably engaged and drew others into her sphere. Diane's story was uncannily similar to mine, and her book brought back abundant memories of that carefree era. From Diane's first introduction to French cabaret in Montreal, Canada, to the Bahamas, Paris, Atlanta, Puerto Rico, New York and Las Vegas, Diane managed to live ten lifetimes!

Always ready to embrace others, while frequently too trusting and vulnerable, she usually managed to be disappointed, succumb naively to others, and get derailed in the process. But with her eternally optimistic, hopeful and positive nature, she always picked up the pieces.

I was lucky enough to spend time with Diane in the Bahamas, Paris and Las Vegas, and in between as well. Always a creative person, Diane was endowed with diverse talents she courageously displayed, embraced and utilized. She succeeded in many different areas! But she never hesitated to adopt change at the drop of a hat and had the ability to redirect her energies and location so often; it was almost dizzying! But that's

Diane—always confident and ready to welcome new adventures. Diane captures the era with honesty, wisdom, lightheartedness and a constant willingness to take chances, leading her to a myriad of opportunities.

Diane writes with clarity, sensitivity, spirituality and an uncanny gentleness of spirit, reflecting her personality. Always ready to begin the next adventure, she never hesitates to accept each journey with an open heart and sense of discovery. Her loving nature allows others to embrace, love and protect her.

She writes with candor, without fear of exposing the juicier aspects of her journey and that long-gone era. Her friendship will always be a vital element in my life, long-lasting now for more than 50 years, and will certainly continue hereafter. It's such a gift to have a forever friend with whom to share so many of life's adventures, dramas and familial concerns. She is truly my sister in life!

This wonderful book exposes the realities of an era full of the lightheartedness of youth seeking to find their way in a simpler, more innocent time. An uncomplicated time that allowed one to grow without the constraints and confines of social media, IT, political disarray, eternal news coverage and fear of others. Unafraid to live and grow, we made our way with fearlessness and belief in others. The "disco era" will always be fondly remembered as a time of carefree energy, happiness and freedom of expression, which Diane fully captures in her story; she relates every detail with honesty, openness and vulnerability. We see a youth with compassion for herself and others, a loving soul, a nature full of acceptance, and an abundant heart. I love you, Diane!

Barbara Beverly-Crockett's dance career is legendary. She was renowned as one of the most successful principal cabaret dancers in the world.

Preface
A Retrospective

People kept saying the same thing to me everywhere I worked, in Paris, Montreal, the Bahamas, Puerto Rico, New York and Las Vegas: "You're one of the last real showgirls." At the time, I thought they meant I wasn't a very good dancer. In retrospect, I realize that it was the beginning of an era's end. What we did as showgirls was fading into non-existence. As it nearly had by 1990.

Now, in 2024, there are very few shows left in Las Vegas, the resorts and Paris that feature showgirls. All of the other outstanding international shows these days are centered on Cirque du Soleil. In fact, the last Lido de Paris show in Paris became a semi-Cirque show slash tits-and-feathers mash-up, and they closed in July 2022. I was fortunate enough to have worked at both the original Parisian Lido in the early '70s and the Siegfried & Roy Las Vegas version in the late '70s while Miss Bluebell was still living.

Once the Stardust reunions were upon me, I realized how timely this story of French cabaret-style dancing divas was. All of the research I could collect, and sharing my personal odyssey, will tell of an entire era that includes at least four decades that we cannot allow to fade away, from my early days with the Rudas dancers, then the Miller-Reich dancers, and finally as a Bluebell at the Lido de Paris in Paris and the Las Vegas Lido at the Stardust.

The first Bluebell girls arrived in Las Vegas at the Lido de Paris with Madame Bluebell in 1957, directly from Paris. In 2007, their American home, the Stardust Hotel, was imploded. It was small compared to newer resorts on the Las Vegas Strip, and revenue fell during its final years. Boyd Gaming announced in January 2006 that it would close and demolish the aging Stardust to build a new project, Echelon Place. The Stardust closed on November 1, 2006, and the two hotel towers were imploded on March 13, 2007. The resort had a popular roadside sign, which was given to the city's Neon Museum.

We lost the Dunes and the Sands several years prior. What will replace these Las Vegas landmarks? Another theme park hotel? Perhaps yet another edition of a Cirque de Soleil show? We know it will be large and corporate-owned, as the Mafia had been cleared out of town by the mid-1980s. So, either Wynn or Boyd Gaming will continue to present their latest, hottest additions to the Mega Structures already dominating the Strip.

One thing we can always count on in that town is extraordinary entertainment, including more and more Cirque shows, with talent to satisfy the new generation of thrill-seekers and excessively media-saturated audiences. We may still find a wonderful dance show in a lounge or showroom. *Jubilee* was the last to go at Bally's. The show ended its 35-year run on February 11, 2016. Even the free dance extravaganzas such as the Sirens and the Pirates al fresco at the Treasure Island are gone, replaced by another designer shopping mall or a CVS pharmacy.

But if you really want to see where the spectacles originated, you must travel to Paris, France, where the Moulin Rouge and the Crazy Horse Saloon continue to draw audiences to the original heart of cabaret. Even most island shows have disbanded in lieu of local fare, as in the Bahamas, Puerto Rico and Jamaica and even the South of France and Spain. The days of the tits-and-feathers revues are nearly extinct. The only tappers and precision dancers left are the Rockettes at New York City's Radio City Music Hall, truly an American institution that will live forever, even if they only perform the Christmas Spectacular annually, as they have done since 2021. Their creator, Russell Markert, passed in 1990.

But rather than belabor what has been lost or what remains, let us segue into my story, as my first professional audition was with that classic genius. Let's travel back to my semi-private audition at 17 years of age at Radio City Music Hall, where the birth of one ambitious young woman's career, steeped in dazzling history, will certainly amuse, arouse and enchant you. My story is a nostalgic journey down memory lane through the experiences and ups and downs of this last real showgirl who overcame the limitations of her small Midwest town and launched an international career in the entertainment industry. Some people are only referred to by their first name in the book, and other names have been changed altogether to protect the privacy of the real people who were involved in my story.

Follow this small-town girl from Illinois on a joyride as I jet-set to international success as a dancer, showgirl and actress to becoming the number-one, award-winning acting coach in Hollywood to some famous kids, teens and young adults.

1

Rockettes or Bust, 1969

A flurry of butterflies rose in my tummy as I stood side stage in the enormous, cool and overused rehearsal hall at Radio City, taking in every moment of my talented friend's audition on the expertly taped floor. I interpreted this feeling as excitement, a sensation that has always pushed me as a performer. Little doubts began to flutter through my overactive 17-year-old brain, but I immediately replaced them with my inner heart-warming smile. I developed this little trick at the age of 12 to tame even the slightest hint of beastly negativity. It helped me revert back to the confident, skilled, talented dancer I was well-trained to be! Surely, the seasoned 70-something creator of the Rockettes, Russell Markert, would see my dedicated performance on that cloudy day in April.

1969!

It was nearly my time to shine. I never sweat, no matter how hard I train or how much pressure is upon me. I never display anything that could even remotely resemble fear! Not me! I'd gotten my resourceful self here, to Radio City Music Hall in New York City, to audition for the Rockettes. Born into the confines of a limited and violent home environment, nothing could stop me now!

You'd think that five years of dance training and performing in theater for another eight would be sufficient preparation for a career with the famed Radio City Rockettes, wouldn't you? I certainly did, and so did my mentor, Mary Lou Dennhardt. I performed with my high school dance team, the Golden Girls, for two years. There were six of us, and you had to be "invited" to join the exclusive group.

I was invited to join the Golden Girls, where legs for days was a requirement. That was when I was starting my junior year, as there were several openings now that seniors were graduating. My classmate Deonna Durkee invited me to join, knowing my dance abilities. Her older sister, also a Golden Girl and about to graduate, had passed the torch to her, and only five other coveted spots were open on this six-person team.

This dance team was truly a bright part of my life at Rock Island High School. We traveled every Friday for exchange assemblies to neighboring rival high schools, in our own cars no less, and danced at weekly pep rallies. We rehearsed when we could use the gym, mornings at five a.m., once or twice a week.

We had two traditional classic numbers that we passed down year after year, a can-can and a Western hoedown number, which included costumes for both. We choreographed a splashy routine together in 1968 to the popular Herb Alpert and the Tijuana Brass hit "Spanish Flea," which had just won a Grammy for Best Pop Instrumental. We had black-, white- and red-sequined costumes and black Spanish hats trimmed with little black cha-cha balls.

Everyone loved this new addition to our tradition. Each Friday, we were let out of school to travel to a rival school's exchange assembly to perform our three numbers. This was our way of being inclusive and non-competitive with neighboring schools. We met lots of people, including many cute athletes, and we had a blast. By senior year, I also hosted and did sketch comedy at those rallies with a dynamic fellow actor, John Robinson. We took risks with our humor, much to the delight of our audiences, but not always as much with our school musical director.

We did everything from *Laugh-In* style skits to Barbra Streisand–Fanny Brice humor, which was very popular in 1969 thanks to that hit TV show and the film *Funny Girl*, respectively.

I lied about my age a few times in my senior year, claiming I was 18 in order to fill in for a good friend who worked as a go-go girl for KSTT radio events around town. I wore her white sequined mini-dress and white go-go boots and danced in a lighted cage with another girl in an adjacent cage onstage in 1969! I was paid $75 to do my groovy moves! It was Heaven; I loved it! I mean, how much performance experience could one girl possibly obtain in such a short amount of time?

I crammed to be ready for the Rockettes, knowing that most girls started dancing when they were five years old, where I had started at 13. I was forced to learn to play piano at five, taking a private lesson every Saturday. I'd practice on my dad's upright in the basement for hours while watching longingly through the window as my brother frolicked outside in our yard. It was more than I could bear. I whined and begged to be allowed to stop; it hadn't even been my idea to play piano, even though listening to my dad play was one of my favorite experiences with him. He had studied for ten years and played by ear. He was extremely talented!

I cried and begged for dance lessons because, at that time, I wanted to be a ballerina more than anything. Any time I saw a ballerina on TV or a doll in a store, my heart skipped a beat, and I longed to wear a tutu and fly through the air. But my parents said I was too young and would have to wait. By the time I was ten, I had four baby brothers, and money was tight, so I waited until I could pay for my own lessons with babysitting money when I turned 13. I made things happen, knowing that was the only way it would. I started babysitting for my little brothers at ten years old, and by 11, the whole neighborhood knew how proficient I was with little kids. I was in demand! This went on until I was 16 and I became too busy to babysit.

Once I began taking dance lessons, I was fiercely committed to learning as much as I could as fast as I could!

Before I knew it, it was April 1969. I was 17 and ready to go to New York City to audition for the Rockettes, along with my dance pal Karen Darnall and my mentor, Mary Lou Dennhardt. Mary Lou had arranged everything with the original Rockette choreographer and company manager, Emily Sherman. The legendary American Institution offered four shows daily, seven days a week.

Shows were at ten a.m., three p.m., six p.m. and ten p.m. A gigantic Wurlitzer organ had pipes covering the ceiling at the resplendent art deco venue, which filled the nearly 6000-seat theater with unimaginable sound that transported you to another world when it was played.

Karen and I, flying for the first time, enjoyed a filet mignon meal in coach on our United flight from Chicago to New York. We were only 17

Seventeen-year-old Diane perfects her eye-high kicks at her hometown dance studio, 1969.

and trembling with excitement. Mary Lou had planned quite a trip for the three of us. Mama Leone's for dinner, dance classes with Luigi and Fred Kelly (Gene's brother), *Hello Dolly!* with Pearl Bailey, Cab Calloway and an all-black cast at the St. James Theatre. *Hair* was the biggest hit on Broadway and we went to see that, too, naked actors and all! But seeing the glorious Rockettes the night before our big audition was the biggest thrill.

From the *The Great Radio City Music Hall Spectacular* program:

> Radio City Music Hall was the nation's showplace. The stage resembles a sun, setting over a red velvet ocean of seats and is the size of a full city block—144 feet long. Radio City is still considered the world's greatest showplace. On December 27, 1932, Radio City Music Hall opened its doors to the world for the first time. The Art Deco style of that era gives the showroom the effect of a long vertical illusion, with 80-foot-high ceilings.

Diane Pirmann at the pre–Rockette audition, 1969.

The Rockettes' show was beyond breathtaking. The sound of 36 girls tapping and precise eye-high kicking on the block-long stage was like thunder! We could only imagine ourselves up there, tapping and kicking with these talented beauties. It was so inspiring watching them in perfect unison, not a line out of place. They were perfection.

According to Wikipedia, "The Rockettes were formed in 1925 when Russell Markert of St. Louis selected 16 dancing girls to become the 'Sixteen Missouri Rockets.'" This precision dance team was so well-received that they began touring the country, ending up in New York City, where "Roxy" Rathafel saw them. Wanting them for his new Roxy Theatre, he doubled the size of the group and renamed them "Russell E. Markert's 32 Roxyettes." When "Roxy" moved to Radio City Music Hall, he expanded the dance line to 36 to better fit the stage. They remained the Roxyettes until 1933, when "Roxy" left, and Markert decided on a feminized version of the original name: the Rockettes. According to the *Encyclopedia Britannica*, Markert remained director of the Rockettes until his retirement in 1971.

In 1977, the City of New York honored Markert for his contributions to popular entertainment. We would be auditioning for this extraordinary man, who was in his mid–70s in 1969. The historical aspect of it all was mind-boggling!

When we auditioned to be Rockettes, all girls stood between 5'5" and 5'8", with similar bodies and, of course, legs for days. Everyone wore the same makeup and costumes. All Caucasian—there was not one woman of color in the line! I thought that was weird. Rockettes mastered eye-high kicks without leaning forward or touching the lower back of the girls next to them, where their hands landed behind one another. They made it look so easy. Kicking eye-high without bending your knees or leaning forward wasn't a simple task. For me, the real challenge was to not stand out, to be just like every other girl in the line. One of my specialties was drawing focus and shining brightly onstage with lots of personality.

Yikes, I thought! Would we be ready? Were we good enough? So many doubts filled our minds and hearts after we watched the Rockettes. This splendid show seemed too perfect for reality. We were invited backstage by company manager Emily Sherman and shown around the massive stage. It was filled with lifts and secret floors that opened with magical hydraulics. The hydraulics could hold 27 tons.

Karen Darnall at the pre–Rockette audition, 1969.

Our backstage tour included visiting the dressing room. I will never forget the heady smell of pancake and lipstick in the long, individually mirrored dressing room lined with seemingly endless racks of costumes. Pancake makeup is a cosmetic makeup made of a soluble, matte powder compressed into a thin cake and typically applied with a damp sponge for a full-coverage look.

Each girl was busy doing their own thing between shows, wearing three pairs of eyelashes glued together, tightly slicked buns, little robes covering fishnet tights, and cozy slippers soothing their overworked feet. Some were knitting, some eating, some sewing, some stretching—it was all so fascinating. They were wholesome, beautiful, talented girls who dedicated themselves to their four shows a day, seven days a week, with an income of $150 per week in 1969.

We were introduced to several of the girls. Karen and I were dumbstruck and tongue-tied, taking it all in, while Mary Lou chatted with some of the girls. (Mary Lou was a petite Ginger Rogers–esque blonde with a huge *Hello Dolly!* personality and charm.) We learned that most of them lodged at the nearby Barbizon Hotel for Women, which we also visited. It was similar to a dorm and housed mostly Rockettes. I saw that this was their whole life! The Barbizon reminded me of *Stage Door*, the old movie with Katharine Hepburn and Ginger Rogers (and, in a supporting part, Lucille Ball).

The girls often congregated after the last show at a nearby piano bar, where many sang and were scouted by talent agents. The girls performed nightly, hoping to land a Broadway show and a larger paycheck or even a day off once a week. One of Mary Lou's former students was a Rockette at that time and we went out to the posh piano bar to hear her sing.

Karen and I were like baby ducks out of water. New York beckoned us to hatch, grow, spread our wings and fly! I was drawn to the acting scene. Mary Lou had our taxi driver show us the Herbert Berghof acting studio. Many Rockettes were studying acting there, and apparently, it was the place to go if one was serious about their craft … and I was! I planned to study there once I became a Rockette. I hoped they would accept my scholarship.

The two of us made endless plans to find an apartment of our own and live together in this amazing city full of inspiration, talent, opportunity and buzz! Of course, a few weirdos, colorful hippies and freaks lurked on the streets, all on the outskirts of this fascinating world of talent and ambition. It felt terrifying and fabulous at the same time.

We somehow rested in our hotel room the night before our big audition, with lots of laughing and Mary Lou taking photos of us with her Instamatic camera. Mary Lou finally insisted we retire to prepare for our audition the next day. I don't know how we slept that night, but we did somehow.

Upon rising that misty April morning, Mary Lou insisted we have a light breakfast with protein, but who could eat? I managed a hard-boiled egg and some toast. We showered and did our makeup and hair, Mary Lou directing us to wear just the right amount of makeup for our audition. We donned leotards and fishnet tights. We packed our tap shoes in tote bags and covered our leotards with tasteful dresses and trench coats. Karen and I were ready!

Silliness ensued; we laughed all the way to the Music Hall in our taxi. It was certainly a side effect of our nervousness. We came in through Radio City Music Hall's backstage door, ready to show Emily Sherman and the infamous Russell Markert what we were made of.

We were led backstage by a stagehand and met Miss Sherman, who then showed us a place in the Rockette dressing room where we could change. Then she took us deeper backstage to a huge rehearsal room where the auditions were held. We had time to stretch. I felt very self-conscious as several Rockettes were milling about backstage. It was between their ten a.m. and three p.m. shows. Warmup completed and tap shoes donned, we entered the rehearsal area and met Mr. Markert, who was waiting to see our individual routines.

There was a record player there, and Mary Lou offered our 45s to Emily. Karen went first. I was glad because I was not keen to go first. Karen was a dynamic tapper and exquisite dancer, having trained with Mary Lou and Larry Dennhardt since she was three. She was one of the best dancers I have ever known. My ticket was my ability to perform like a charismatic diva. I hoped that this would distract from the fact that my routine was not quite as elaborate as Karen's, dance-wise. Each of us had something special to bring to this job. I was very confident in my performance abilities and excellent kicks. Mary Lou always supported me.

We performed our eye-high kicks for them. I trembled on the inside, yet felt extremely excited to be there. I pounded the taps on my shoes into the wooden boards that had been graced by some of the world's finest dancers. I had given a stellar audition.

And then it was over ... our much-awaited audition complete.

We celebrated with dinner at Mary Lou's favorite Italian restaurant in New York, Mama Leone's. Karen and I devoured the food like ravenous athletes. Finally, we could eat and not worry about our tummies! We laughed a lot, and through that momentous evening, we really let loose. At one point, we got so giggly and silly that Mary Lou had to remind us we were in a nice public place.

The following morning, we squeezed in a visit to the garment district where Mary Lou bought beautiful Swarovski crystal beads for our upcoming recital back home. She and Larry always graced us with a performance for the finale.

We were heading back to Illinois, waiting for the results of our immense efforts, like all performers do after auditions.

2

The Waiting Game, 1969

Flying home from New York, I felt uncommonly numb. I was not ready to leave New York City, struggling to accept that I was leaving behind all that stimulation, excitement and opportunity ... not to mention how incredibly alive it had made me feel. I belonged there; everything in that city felt like pure show business to me. I needed all that New York had to offer, like the ill need a good physician. It had quenched my parched soul like an endless fountain of inspiration and had given me a glimpse of the reality to all my dreams of becoming a great dancer and actress. Now I had to go back to Rock Island, to complete high school in two months, which felt like an eternity. How could I do that knowing Radio City Music Hall and Broadway and the life I'd dreamed of was nearly mine?

I began to conjure images of my survival back in Rock Island in the coming months. With my Summer Productions, I had dream roles to look forward to at Music Guild. *West Side Story* in June—I had been cast as Anita! *Oklahoma!* was set for August, and I was cast in the one role I'd longed for since the third grade, Ado Annie. I was so excited and shivered with delight just thinking about playing those two divinely written divas!

Graduation was coming up, and there was the senior prom to look forward to. I had all that to submerge my restless spirit while awaiting word from the Rockettes.

Mary Lou and I felt confident about my audition. I would hold onto that with the fiercest positive thoughts and vibes. Diane Pirmann, the Rockette! It wasn't easy because so much of me felt intimidated by it all, yet New York still felt like a proper home for me. I chose to keep imagining myself kicking away in perfect precision on that glorious stage. "I belong there" was my new mantra. That is where my superpower revealed itself—my determination, ambition and ability to manifest a life I loved. Positive self-talk creates the affirmative!

During our flight, Mary Lou lit up a cigarette (yes, it was still legal to smoke on planes in 1969). Knowing she was in relaxation mode, I asked, "What do we do now?"

"We wait," she replied. "Keep on training, stay in class to make sure you keep growing as a dancer." I'd certainly keep doing my three classes a week.

"When will we know if we made it or not?" I inquired.

"We should know within the month," she guessed. A month seemed like an eternity, requiring more patience than I had. Seventeen-year-old me felt burdened by that albatross. Patience. When would this career I'd dreamed of for so long jump start? Where would I muster all the patience I needed? Probably in the same place I'd found it when I began learning tap at 13.

I'd had no dance training a short four years ago, and here I was, auditioning for the Rockettes. I began to look at all I'd accomplished in the last four years and was able to acknowledge the achievements I'd rendered possible. I calmed down, took a deep breath and relaxed. I felt proud of myself.

I was able to break away from the destructive household created by my chaotic parents, and begin to pursue the life I'd imagined for myself. As I nodded off, I was grateful to my mom and dad for supporting my ambitions and lofty goals, and for paying for this trip. I knew it hadn't been an easy task, but they'd done it. I felt loved; it was the greatest act of love they had ever bestowed upon me, apart from keeping me and giving me life at their extremely young age of 18. I was a lucky girl indeed! With that thought, I dozed for the rest of my flight headed home.

I settled into my routine once we were back in Rock Island. Feeling excited about everything happening in my busy teenage life. Possibilities flooded my thoughts. I was kept busy finishing high school and preparing for senior prom and plays.

I was most excited about rehearsals for my summer shows. The Quad City Music Guild even provided complimentary voice lessons for me for the role of Anita in *West Side Story*. This wonderful community organization served a lot of young talent and was led by cream-of-the-crop directors, choreographers and musical directors. It included many Equity performers.

The Quad City Music Guild did three shows each month of summer as it was a seasonal organization.

We had just started dance rehearsals for *West Side Story*. I loved the original Jerome Robbins choreography for my big number, "America." It felt like the role of Anita had been written for me, with lots of dancing and acting. Embodying her was exhilarating, an electrically charged mission for my talents! Plus, the song "America" was a trio featuring Anita, the girls and Bernardo; it was inspiring for me to perform this role alongside a very talented cast. And with dialogue like, "If you were bleeding in the street, I would walk by, and I would spit on you!" It was pure Heaven.

2. The Waiting Game, 1969

With senior prom coming up in May, I designed my own prom gown. I loved choosing the fabric and trim, as I've always been a fashion designer at heart.

My dear friend Alma had a mother who was a fantastic dressmaker, and she tailored the gown to my exact specifications and measurements. Alma was going to the prom with our set designer friend Jim Reed, and it all felt a little like *West Side Story*. Anita and Maria were dressmakers in that show. Art has always imitated life, and life always imitates art in my world.

I was on the brink of blossoming, like a lotus flower blooming in a calm and tranquil pond. Was my discipline paying off? So many of the seeds of who I would grow to be in the world were planted during this time. Little did I know that in the years to come, I would have a professional career in dance, drama and design.

One spring evening, Mary Lou called and announced that Emily Sherman had accepted me and Karen. We were to be Rockettes! This news flooded me with joy. It was real: Karen Darnall and I were to be summer replacements as soon as any current Rockettes left, as many did after the summer ended. Many went back to college. We were now officially "on call" and needed to be ready to leave at a moment's notice when those calls came. Karen would be the first one to go, and I would go next. I was thrilled because I still had my shows to do. We now had to prepare ourselves for actually going to New York.

Mary Lou gave very specific instructions: "You'll need to stay in class, keep working, and continue to fine-tune your dance skills."

"Will we possibly be called before graduation?" I inquired.

"No, they did say most likely you'd be called late summer or early fall as that is when more girls leave."

"So I can still go to prom?"

"Oh, yes, of course. But you will have to give up your commitments at Music Guild this summer."

"Both lead roles?" I gasped.

"Yes, honey, you could officially be called at any time starting in June," Mary Lou explained. "You'll have to let the understudies take both roles. You can't take the chance of not being here and leave them hanging at Music Guild." She was the choreographer of both shows, she would know.

My heart was simultaneously breaking a little and thumping out of my chest with excitement.

"These are the kinds of professional decisions performers make throughout their careers, sweetheart," Mary Lou said. "You have to choose."

"I choose to go to New York City to be a Rockette, naturally, I'm just sad that I must surrender my two dream roles," I insisted.

"I'll let your directors know at Music Guild," Mary Lou replied.

"Thank you," I said, sobbing until my new reality sunk in. "I'm going to be a Radio City Rockette!"

3

Meet My Mom and Dad, 1950–'60s

In the local newspaper, Jerry Pirmann was called "one of the greats" when he passed at age 63. Much too young for such an athletic legend. He was almost an all-state basketball player. He was also the star quarterback on his high school football team and an astounding golfer. Many hole-in-one plaques graced our walls. He had indeed been gifted with athletic prowess.

I was conceived in the back seat of his New Pontiac, some time in January 1951. How Americana. I learned to temper and parent my alcoholic father simultaneously. It was instinct, like survival mentality. I don't think children should be subjected to that, yet they are. Protecting children became part of my livelihood and life, especially in the entertainment industry. I must have been guided to it by my higher self. I was capable.

Jerry Pirmann and Phoebe Shull were seniors at rival high schools when they met at 16—rivals in the world of sports, which was their world. Jerry was a handsome, popular basketball star who helped put Rock Island High School on the map in Illinois in 1951, the year I was born. The youngest of 13 children, Phoebe was a darling blonde cheerleader from Rocky's rival, Moline High School. They met at the games, and these two good-looking kids fell in love at 16.

At 30, I was curious about my conception. My mother confided in me that they had only "done it" once and she wound up pregnant with me. My parents came from a generation that tried very hard to separate their interpretation of reality from the concrete truth in order to keep themselves in control, or perhaps more innocent than they actually were, at least in their children's eyes. I decided to go the other way with my kids and be upfront about who and what I actually am—in other words, *human*, with faults and shortcomings. But I am a child of the '60s, and hiding wasn't our thing. "Know Thyself" was a motto for our generation.

By the time spring rolled around, 36 full basketball scholarship offers had come streaming in for my father. They were free rides from countless Big Ten schools across the country, including UCLA. So even though my parents had only "done it once," they found themselves "with child."

In the '50s, teenagers didn't attend college on full scholarships along with their pregnant teenage wives. My grandparents convinced them to stay home. I can only imagine how disappointed my father was. He was a rising star in the athletic world, on the brink of becoming a college basketball legend, now facing the responsibilities of fatherhood at the age of 17. My mother lost her dad at 12 and had a much older widowed mother. She felt unable to discuss her current condition with anyone but Albert Pirmann, my paternal grandfather. Together, they labored over what to do.

"Do you love each other?" Albert had asked the frightened young couple when they came to him for his calming wisdom.

"Yes, we do," they confirmed.

"Then I don't see a problem. You can get married, have your baby, and come live with me and Lois and work for me."

Problem solved, or at least swept under the rug. Jerry and Phoebe eloped to Chicago, secretly marrying on March 25, 1951, in a Court of Law with a justice of the peace. I think I saw one photo over the years of their innocent teenage faces on the day of the sacred event. They were to attend their upcoming proms and graduations in June, which would put the secret newlyweds at six months with child (me).

The reality was that they were fiercely driven by the fact that they didn't want people to know that my mom was pregnant. Yet, bam! Baby out of nowhere. How do you explain that to people? The '50s were so secretive.

Upon my delivery a month early, I was told that a disappointed Jerry stated, "I wish it was a boy." Out loud!

I'm lucky I was born at all. Primarily because my mom didn't eat while she was pregnant; she told me she felt too shy around her in-laws to just go to the fridge! And my grandmother was a chef! She said she ate apple pie. She also confessed to me that her primary reason for not eating was not wanting anyone to know she was pregnant.

Two weeks before my father's passing, my kids and I were at my parents' home. My dad started drinking and said to me, "I know why I was put on Earth. It was to have you."

Wow! I guess having four boys changed his tune, or possibly he discovered I really was something special after all? By this time, I knew my dad thought I was pretty special after going off and making my dreams come true in the world. Still, it felt good to hear since he originally wished I'd been born a boy!

His drinking began when I was eight years old, just after he had

3. Meet My Mom and Dad, 1950–'60s

designed and built the most incredible demo home with one of his best contractor friends. They were so excited to begin their newly combined contracting business. My dad was not only a gifted athlete, he also had an abundance of other talents. He had easily glided into his father's successful painting and contracting business and had added his own special flair to everything they did. His ambitions were high when he and his friend constructed the ideal '50s home to demo what they could create. We're talking pink appliances and a weathered slate exterior ranch-style home on a gorgeous hill with a stunning view. It was spectacular. When I walked into that house, I felt like I was in a fantasy. I marveled at his talents.

My mom couldn't understand going into debt to create a business. She couldn't grasp doing anything but paying in cash. Her fear of credit was a real thing. After all, she was a Depression baby from a poor family.

We had just moved into a gorgeous new tract home in a newly developed neighborhood. Dad had also decorated this home beautifully. He had given everything to her, yet her inability to support him in this new endeavor, especially after his first basketball dream was shattered, left him feeling completely diminished. Her lack of belief in his talents and gifts or ability to see his potential future of success and creativity hurt him deeply. He began to drink and became a philanderer. I know that because they fought loudly about these things when he would come home late, drunk. Even my innocent little eight-year-old soul knew that his heart was breaking. Mine broke, too. I wanted him to become great as much as he did.

After that, everything in our lives spiraled out of control. Nothing would ever be the same. Jerry, who had been making incredible money as a contractor, was unable to handle his newfound success without Phoebe's support. She was fearful of Jerry's growth, and once again, he was stopped in his tracks.

The bitterness, disappointment, lack of support and overwhelming responsibility threw him into the deep end and he started drinking heavily. We lost our beautiful new home, and my mom lost all trust and divorced him. I couldn't believe this was happening to us. Back then, divorce was the exception, not the rule.

Believe it or not, it got much worse after that. My parents remarried. Yep! Six weeks after they divorced, they went to Chicago to tie the knot again. He moved into our apartment. That's when the real hell began.

His alcoholism accelerated, and the tormented soul that he was began taking it all out on my mom. The beatings she endured while he was drunk landed her in the hospital several times. The ambulances would arrive in the middle of the night. It was all so humiliating and scary to ten-year-old me.

I guess they finally worked something out in marriage counseling because they made up and accidentally had another baby! Brilliant. My youngest brother was born. Totaling five kids!

We soon moved to a lovely new home. Things were looking up again, sort of. Dad still drank, but not as much. They both worked quite a bit, and Dad seemed to stay out on the nights Mom worked in a restaurant, leaving me in charge of my four little brothers!

The out-of-control abuse of my mom ended after their counseling. His drinking was still an appalling, gaping wound in our lives at this point. I eventually made a speedy exit into the local community theaters. I took my dance classes and found relief from the chaos. The theater became my refuge. I'm certain it saved me.

My siblings and I were becoming teenagers when my dad finally stepped up for us. He knew how important our dreams were. He matched the acting scholarship I won at 17 to send me to New York with my mentor to audition for the Rockettes. He made sure I had beautiful prom dresses. I still paid for my own dance lessons.

When my oldest brother, Tom, was a senior, Dad made the call to move to a nearby city so that Tom would be in the right school to earn a full basketball scholarship when the scouts came looking. It worked, and my 6'9" brother played basketball for the University of Texas for five years and then went on to play pro. That move was critical for Tom.

My therapist said the best thing I ever did was remove myself from my family. I remained very close to all of them; I simply never moved back to Illinois. I loved my family despite the chaos. I was extremely close to my paternal grandmother and felt somewhat responsible for my four younger brothers.

Dad was eaten up by his inability to live up to his potential. Maintaining his skills as a golfer, he remained an extremely gifted athlete on the golf courses. After all that we went through, ups and downs and horrors, I still grieved terribly when he unexpectedly passed from an aneurysm at 63. I grieved a little less when my mom passed because at least she loved being a mom. She had something that made her happy, even if she spent much of her motherhood vexed with five kids and Jerry Pirmann to deal with. Dad was never fulfilled as a person.

There was an annual Jerry Pirmann Open Golf Tournament in his honor after he passed. It was held in our hometown of Rock Island and a considerable number of golfers participated for years. After all, he was "one of the greats."

Phoebe was a good mom. She liked being a mom and her own brood seemed small compared to her parents' super-sized family. My mom did all she could to make our lives as smooth as possible, including working at many restaurant jobs once I was old enough to babysit at ten. She tried

3. Meet My Mom and Dad, 1950–'60s

to supplement the family income, which went out before it reached home thanks to my dad's frequent nights playing piano in the local bars. He always claimed he was "working," meaning he was booking painting and decorating jobs for his contracting business. Networking, so to speak.

Mom worked as a hostess in a restaurant a few nights a week. My dad kept drinking and philandering, causing my mom to become extremely co-dependent. I became the caregiver of everyone, especially to my brothers! Even though I escaped often to the theater and the dance studio, I still contributed heartily to the family by babysitting.

When I was in my 40s, I asked Mom if she had had any dreams or goals as a young woman. She claimed she had always wanted to be a dancer! She and Dad were great jitterbug dancers! But I'd never heard this until much later in her life. I was surprised. She told me she wished she could have done what I did—become a professional dancer. Little did I know these dreams lived inside her soul. She'd never told me she loved dancing.

One thing I can credit my mom with is being very strong, stable, strict and reliable. She encouraged us in anything we decided to do and showed up for everything. She drove us to anything we did and supported us as much as possible. Although she and my dad were miserable most of the time, fighting and struggling to make ends meet, she still loved him. She loved all of us. What she lacked in creativity and organizational skills, she made up for in her efforts to be a loving mom.

But for a woman who wasn't a planner or a manifester and was afraid of many things, she did teach me strength. I don't think I could have accomplished my goals without her encouragement. I love her for that most of all.

* * *

When I stayed at my grandmother's house, I went to Bingo with her and her friends on weekends. It was 1958 and Grandma would give me nickels and I would go upstairs where the jukebox was and dance the night away with the other kids.

Grandma and her friends would come up after the Bingo games and watch us dance 'til we dropped! I loved that. I guess the gift of dancing was passed through the gene pool of Mom and Dad. For that, I am eternally grateful!

4

Getting Out of Dodge, 1969

Mary Lou consoled me over the lost lead roles in the Music Guild productions.

"Yes darling, you are now a Rockette. All of your dedication is beginning to pay off and now the real work begins," she reminded me. "More waiting and more training."

My mentor fully understood priorities from her own career as a professional dancer.

"I'm going to go tell my mom and dad," I interjected with gusto.

"You go tell them, and I'll see you in class next week, honey." Mary Lou hung up, and I screamed with excitement, "I'm going to New York City!"

My entire household came running to me to revel in the joy of this announcement. I'm certain my parents were just as delighted as I was and feeling just as conflicted. The realization that their 17-year-old, first-born, would be leaving for New York City broke their hearts a little. When I relinquished my lead roles of Anita and Ado Annie to my understudies at the Quad City Music Guild, they knew I was really going to New York.

I would soon leave Rock Island, Illinois, my hometown, commitments, family and friends for a much larger life. I had succeeded! I made it! Just like my first love, Blase Krogman, had predicted for me before he moved to Hollywood a year earlier when I was 16. Before long, I would be eye-high-kicking in perfect unison on the largest stage in American history! Radio City Music Hall, here I come! This was May of 1969.

* * *

Blase left our hometown in 1968 at the age of 20 to pursue his dream of being a model and actor in Tinsel Town.

In 1966, Blase was my mom's good friend from work. Mom was a hostess at a popular dinner club called Marando's where Blase was also a host. He was a gorgeous 19-year-old local male model when they met.

There weren't many of those in our town. I was 15, and although I had my share of male friends at school, the dance studio and in the theater, none of them looked or acted like Blase.

He just seemed so interested in me. He'd drop by the house on his evenings off every few weeks since Phoebe believed we would be great friends. He loved fashion, and my mom would invite him over to see the costumes and fashions I designed in my spare time. He was fascinated with my drawings and designs, and for two years, he would drop by to see my latest illustrations.

No other male had ever taken an interest in me like Blase. Many cute boys my age had pursued me, but none were anything like the exceptional Blase. He came over frequently to see how I was and what I was up to. He'd ask what play I was in, where I was performing, or what I was designing. I loved his attention. He made me feel like the most special person on Earth.

In my junior year of high school, he announced that he was Hollywood-bound. I thought my 16-year-old heart would break into a million pieces. We had begun spending lots of time on the phone each week, laughing, being creative, sharing our lives. He insisted we go out on a date before he left.

It was winter, and basketball season was in full tilt. When my high school and Blase's former high school played each other, he said we had to get dressed up and go to UTHS, his old campus, to the big game! I was 16, he was 19, and we dressed to the nines! I'll never forget his three-piece suit and my mod, plaid, wool, Chanel-like, double-breasted mini-dress with neon green tights and boots. When Blase and I strolled past bleachers filled with my classmates, their jaws dropped. Even the guys I'd had crushes on couldn't take their eyes off us. My girlfriends swooned. We turned every head in the UTHS gym that night. He made me feel like Cinderella.

Blase insisted we leave early to avoid the traffic to make our dinner reservation at a trendy gourmet restaurant, the Gay '90s. People generally patronized that establishment for celebrations. Yet there we were, on a Friday night in Rock Island, dining on filet mignon in our fabulous fashions.

That entire evening felt like a fantasy to me, a date I'll never forget; a date that changed me forever. The things I wanted in life emerged gently, like a newborn dove. After dinner, he drove me home and parked outside our large, rambling house. He popped a stick of Juicy Fruit gum into his perfect mouth, offered me a piece and then turned on the radio. "Happy Together" was playing.

Ahhhh, I thought, the Turtles, perfect.

I couldn't have conjured up a more perfect moment if I'd been writing a romance novel.

As we listened to the music, he paused momentarily, chuckling his precious laugh. He smiled and then took me in his arms and kissed me. His lips were soft, full and tender, with a yummy Juicy Fruit finish. I melted a little and whispered, "I've waited a long time for that."

He smiled again and asked, "You have?"

I waited for another kiss, but it didn't come. He seemed sad suddenly, which made me think he was struggling with something … but what could it be? Ah, of course, he was leaving for Los Angeles, to pursue a modeling and acting career. God! I adored this man, his beauty, grace, class, fun-loving spirit, his kindness and his sweet Gemini soul.

I finally broke the silence, "Well, I guess this is it, you're off to L.A. next week."

"You will be, too, one day," he assured me, "and I'll be there waiting for you and I will introduce you to everyone."

"I love that," I said. "Thank you, Blase." I meant it, and so did he.

He opened the car door, got out, came around and opened mine as I stepped onto the glistening, snowy sidewalk. He wrapped my coat around my shoulders and came in to see Mom, Dad and the boys. We all loved him so much. It was obviously midnight for Cinderella, with the fantasy slowly ending. When the clock struck 12, I would return to my life, and off he'd go to find success in Hollywood.

Upon his arrival in 1968, he met Otto Preminger and became very close with Ann-Margret, making movies with both. He also modeled with the best of them and appeared on *The Dating Game*. He wrote me five- and six-page letters in his impeccable handwriting monthly. He filled me in on all things Hollywood and continued to make me feel that all my dreams of becoming an actress, dancer and model could happen. I cherished his letters and read and reread them daily. I carried his new photos with me; my girlfriends continued to swoon over him along with me. Until the letters became fewer and fewer, shorter and shorter. They began to feel rushed, and I gathered he had a very full life in Los Angeles.

Sinking into a deep depression, I was not eating, losing interest in nearly everything.

Finally, one Sunday afternoon, my dad stopped me in the dining room when no one else was around and said, "Diane, you need to snap out of this mood. Blase is queer."

"How dare you say that about him!" I shouted. I burst into tears and ran to my room, where I sobbed into my pillow for hours. I had known it deep down, but it burst my bubble of a love life to hear my dad say it aloud. I needed to hang onto the fantasy of me and Blase just a little longer, at least until I had my own Hollywood or New York stories to share. It broke my 17-year-old heart to hear the truth. How could I ever date high school boys after Blase?

4. Getting Out of Dodge, 1969

Once Blase had gone to L.A., I realized he was living his fabulous, new, gay life there. Eventually, I somehow got over him and began dating several high school boys again, having a good time while planning my escape.

Even though we hadn't spoken since I was 18, when I finally moved to L.A. at age 31, Blase was one of the first people to introduce me to everyone as he had promised he would, forever ago. He took me out on dates, even though he had a live-in beau whom I never met. Through Blase, I met the Stallone brothers and many other incredible people. He had become a very popular hair stylist on Rodeo Drive. Shortly after we reunited as friends, he moved to the East Coast and died on Fire Island of AIDS at age 44. Gone in a Blase of glory, much too young.

Blase was my first love. He taught me so much and was so loving. He was often very jealous when we dated in L.A. if I brought up my latest crush. I would chuckle and exclaim, "You have a boyfriend!"

"It doesn't mean I don't love you," he'd reply. He was the first of three gay men in my life who fell in love with me. I loved them all, and though only one had become intimate, none of them were ever like Blase. He was undeniably the most exquisite, unrequited love I've ever known.

* * *

I vividly remember early winter approaching in 1970 and that desperate feeling of really wanting to leave. I could hardly believe a new season was unfolding, with winter's crystals sparkling on every branch. I was dangerously close to going mad from living at home with my chaotic parents, dangerously close to getting high on LSD with my friends, dangerously close to perhaps losing my virginity to some unworthy, long-haired local boy. I fought off those temptations, but I had begun smoking a little marijuana with my best girlfriends on the weekends.

Nothing even began to fulfill my ambitions. I was drowning in a sea of local limitations, both artistically and emotionally. My hometown felt oppressive, and I was certain the world was just waiting for me. Yet here I was, stuck.

It had been eight months since I auditioned for the Rockettes, and after my acceptance call, I waited and waited for the call to replace someone, but it never came. Karen was called in the late summer. The holidays came and went, and I was still there.

I corresponded regularly with Karen Darnall in New York, getting updates on the Rockettes. No one had left since she joined. Ugh! How long did I have to wait for a spot in that coveted line of lovelies?

Early that winter, I had been asked by another local community theater company to audition for the lead role of Barbara Allen in the play

Dark of the Moon. The Playcrafters Barn Theatre had been aware of my skills as I had already done two shows there, both in leading roles. This was also where I had won my scholarship for acting.

I decided to audition. I was sick of giving up everything for the Rockettes! Forget the Rockettes, I needed to live my life!

I landed the lead role and one of my best friends, Corky Laurin, was cast in another role. I had persuaded her to join me at auditions and, sure enough, she was cast.

We had such an exciting time doing this show together in the round at the Barn Theatre. All of our friends came to see us several times, it was *that* good! We worked with a great director and cast. I was the star once again! In *Dark of the Moon*, Barbara Allen falls in love with a witch boy in the Ozarks! What a role! I knew I was taking a risk doing the play, knowing the Rockettes could call at any time, and I alerted the director to that fact. Being the consummate professional that he was, he assigned an understudy to learn my role.

March 1970 arrived … and still no call. I was disappointed beyond measure.

Frustrated and erupting with ambition, I finally asked my mentor to help me get out of town. She knew I had been patient with Radio City and that I had been a dedicated performer. I still religiously studied dance and obviously kept performing locally as an actress. With many of my friends away at either college or in Vietnam, I felt trapped and wondered how I'd make my escape from the mediocre existence that had long ago lost its allure. This bird needed to fly.

And I did. I convinced my adored mentor, Mary Lou, to help me get outta Dodge. Since many of her students were acrobats, she was directly linked to the Rudas Dance Troupe. We had dance photos from my Rockette audition and she submitted several of those along with a pitch to Colin Wilson, the Rudas Dancers' company manager, in Montreal. I guess they liked what they saw because I was hired on my photo, résumé, mentor's pitch, and the fact that the famed Rockettes had accepted me.

Another deciding factor in this industry, I've recognized, is that timing is everything. The Rudas Dancers were preparing for two new shows and had productions in three major locations: Montreal, Paradise Island in the Bahamas, and Las Vegas' Tropicana Hotel. At last, I had my ticket out, and I couldn't wait to take flight. Mary Lou's parting words were, "Don't let them talk you into wearing pasties. You'll stop growing as a dancer." I wasn't sure exactly what she meant. I was a skilled dancer and would never dance topless!

Once in Montreal, seeing the girls in G-strings, feathers, pasties, fishnets and huge headdresses up close was the first and most shocking experience I would have as a professional dancer.

4. Getting Out of Dodge, 1969

I joined the Rudas Dancers in the early spring of 1970, but I didn't meet Tibor Rudas when I arrived in Montreal. I met him a few months later.

Fortunately, the show, showroom, choreography and most of the dancers were awe-inspiring to me. I'll never forget turning to Bobbi, the Australian line captain who showed me around the backstage area my first night in Montreal, and asking, "Does everyone wear the same bikini bottom?" She looked at me as curiously as I had her and said, "Do you mean the G-strings?" I innocently responded with, "What's a G-string?"

She chuckled slightly and said, "The jeweled bikini bottom worn over the fishnets. Yes, you'll wear that too." I gave a little grin.

In my mind I was thinking, "Hell no, I most certainly will not."

But I nodded, knowing I already appeared quite green and didn't want to admit I could not see myself onstage with my bum out like that. I'll never know how we made it through the ranks, yet some of the most delightful memories come from the new kids' stories. Some take it all in stride, some of us freak out inside, some cry or leave, but most adapt and conform to the laws of the land.

Being a brand-new hotel, the Chateau Champlain was indescribably beautiful and elegant. It was the most modern building in Montreal in 1970. The entry to Le Caf Conc cabaret was ground level. Once inside, you ascended several wide, red-carpeted staircases to the grand tiered showroom, with arched velvet boxes and tiny twinkling lights everywhere. Very Paris, circa 1929. Gay Paree and the Moulin Rouge inspired this exquisite showroom that looked down upon a rounded proscenium stage.

When I think back to the backstage and dressing room areas in Montreal, I vividly recall the scent. It was a combination of delightful French cuisine wafting through the dressing rooms from the showroom's kitchen, mixed with fresh paint, pancake makeup and cigarettes. Dunhills were quite popular due to their enticing aroma in 1970 and were still permitted in dinner venues. They were unlike American cigarettes. I regrettably inhaled Winstons and Salems my entire childhood living with two smoking parents.

That same heady scent followed me throughout my dancing days, with slight variations of the same theme in places like Paris, the islands and Las Vegas. Dressing rooms these days are much more sterile thanks to the banning of cigarettes.

Rehearsals began early the next morning at Le Caf Conc. The showroom took on a different aroma, vibe and essence at nine a.m. when we came in to rehearse. It was dark and cold. We rehearsed on the third floor balcony on the carpet once the dining tables and chairs were moved to the sides. None of this equaled the warm fuzzies the sparkling

Diane doing the Can-Can in Montreal in 1970.

evenings offered, full of light, music, champagne, laughter and glamorous warmth.

I began training to become a covered dancer, and it was work! Those rehearsals were long (15- to 18-hour days), painful, exhausting and emotionally draining. A lot of this was because I was inexperienced and transitioning from small-time hometown star to a working professional.

Every evening, I would go up into an empty balcony box and watch the show and try to imagine becoming a professional. When I watched the skilled international dancers before me, I could barely imagine being one of them in a month. The energy level alone was nearly beyond my "girl from Illinois" comprehension. I really thought I was hot stuff at home, a place I longed to be right then for comfort. I would collect-call my mother daily at one point from the phone booth outside my dear roommate's flat and cry in pain. Feeling tortured, I cried to my mom, "I don't think I can do this. It's too hard, Mom."

She'd reply tearfully, "Honey, if you want to come home, you always can, but I do think you can do this."

Her encouragement helped me believe in myself—but hearing my mom weep always impaled me. I would cry some more and say, "They hate me here. The choreographer makes me stay hours after everyone else has gone, and he's mad at me because he has to work harder."

"You are good, Diane. I know you can learn to do this."

"But Mom, I can't even walk or sleep. I have hot water bottles and ice on my aching muscles, and I can't even fall asleep. I can't live like this."

By this time my dad was on the phone: "You just come home tomorrow. I'll send you a ticket. You do not need to do this." He couldn't stand to see his wife and daughter so distraught.

Something in his demanding tone made me stay put. I loved my parents, and I appreciated my mom's support, knowing how much she missed me, but had I somehow, through the breaking-down process, become stronger, more independent and more determined. Could I really ever go back to amateur status? To the destructive home life my mom and dad had? I realized then that I couldn't.

* * *

I decided to make friends with the detached girls who really couldn't give a rat's ass if I were to fail or succeed. I needed a friend badly. One of the Czechoslovakian girls had already crumbled and returned home. That would not be me. I had no desire to go back to the Pirmann house of horrors.

Our exhausted choreographer, or possibly Mr. Rudas, convinced our new principal dancer, lovely Pearl Ho, to help me after everyone else left daytime rehearsals. She was more patient than Ron Walker, the choreographer, and stayed to work overtime with me. Tibor Rudas was probably not paying her extra, so she must have been doing this out of kindness and sympathy. I could tell she resented it at first, as she seemed annoyed. But eventually, she and her boyfriend, a darling Canadian lawyer, began taking me out to the underground jazz clubs and brand-new French-inspired discothèques in Old Montreal. They were such a sophisticated couple. I felt like I had a mentor, friends and new pseudo-parents in them.

The generosity of compassionate Pearl Ho kept me there. Call it divine intervention, if you will. I was blessed, I had a beautiful Japanese guardian angel who had certainly earned her star status.

There was another angel in my life then, my temporary roommate Julianna, a dynamic 19-year-old dancer from Baltimore, one of the best dancers in the show. She had generously offered to put up the three new girls for a month.

Those three new girls were me, an 18-year-old from Rock Island, Illinois; a 16-year-old from Perth, Australia, named Carolee, and an 18-year-old ski fanatic from Modesto, California, named Madonna. The Aussies finished high school at 15, so Carolee was already college age and working age by Australian standards. We bonded while staying at Julianna's apartment in Montreal. I think we all matured a lot that month.

Julianna was a sweet, talented girl. The understudy for Pearl Ho, she had a kind of Liza Minnelli–ish quality, except blonde. She was quiet, almost shy.

Carolee, Madonna and I switched night to night from floor to sofa bed, depending on who was the sorest from our 15-hour rehearsals. About two weeks into our stay, we were asked to keep a secret for our generous hostess, Julianna. She was pregnant. She had been dating several guys, and none were as important to her as her career. So she was planning a trip to Baltimore to have an abortion. An abortion! This was the first person I knew to plan on having an abortion. Was it wrong of me to go along with her secret to travel alone to Baltimore, have an abortion on her day off, fly back and return to work? Could that possibly be okay? What about her safety, her health, her baby, her body?

I had so many questions, yet I was too inexperienced, too naïve (a virgin no less) and too exhausted to ask. Madonna couldn't handle any of it and left that first month. Too bad; she was a great girl whom I really liked, but during rehearsals she cried even more than I did. She opted to go back to California, her boyfriend and her family.

Julianna didn't want Mr. Rudas or company manager Colin Wilson to find out about her pregnancy. Our line captain, Bobbi, was aware of it. Bobbi was a warm Australian girl in her late 20s. She really helped Juli. Carolee helped me. Aussie girls grew up fast.

With these circumstances, I emerged from my cocoon of inexperience and confusion. I quickly accepted the way things were done in this world of driven young women who had coveted careers that many dancers worldwide only dream of, but few manage to grasp. We had it all. Very few departed along the way, and when they did, it was usually for love or because they were fired. There were always many replacements waiting on that assembly line.

I learned something about show business very quickly: Do not make waves or trouble, never gossip backstage, and definitely do not draw too much attention to yourself. Do your job well, collect your pay, and have a little fun while consistently improving your skills. This was especially good advice for young dancers who had a future with a dance company and places to go. It's essential to keep taking classes, to grow, and to keep getting better. Keep your private life to yourself. Keeping Julianna's abortion secret was a teachable moment for me, it really drove home how important keeping private lives quiet backstage can be.

I was learning to juggle being a professional, manage living in a one-bedroom apartment with two other people, and handle my own paycheck at 18. It kept me humble while forcing me to grow.

4. Getting Out of Dodge, 1969

* * *

I enjoyed the perks of being a Rudas dancer, especially when people like Liberace came to the show. He sent the entire cast buckets of champagne backstage and sat so close to the stage that he was engulfed in our feathers like one of the girls. He loved it! We loved Liberace. He was the first celebrity to attend one of my shows and it felt marvelously glamorous!

Just when I was beginning to have fun, Tibor Rudas showed up, like God. All the dancers knew he was in the house watching the show. We were several months into the illustrious new French spectacular "Le Caf Conc" (the same name as the theater). It was the dazzling and modern version of a typical French revue, *à la* Toulouse-Lautrec of 1929, in pure Parisian style. It included the can-can, several modern dance numbers and a comical star reminiscent of Señor Wences, the famous ventriloquist. The stars of our shows were often great plate spinners, flying Wallendas or something similar to Las Vegas, where the likes of Siegfried & Roy, Wayne Newton, Elvis and the Argentinian Gauchos were the reigning headliners.

I remember everyone being on their toes the night Tibor Rudas arrived, giving their most energetic performances. I was suffering from a pulled hamstring due to our can-can. We all pushed ourselves to the max that night. We were not honored with Tibor's presence backstage that evening, as he and his consort Lee were weary from traveling and retired early. There was a company meeting–rehearsal called for the following morning.

Le Caf Conc theater, Chateau Champlain, Montreal, 1970.

We all arrived around ten the next morning, ready to rehearse. We gathered on stage, where Mr. Rudas and his precious Lee gave notes to the company. Notes are the critiques or constructive criticisms in the theater. Or flat-out insults, depending on the producer, choreographer or line captain. Mr. Rudas was rather comical in his own way. I'm not sure if he meant to be or if his Hungarian, Jewish and Australian demeanor was simply entertaining. He often gave notes to our mentors instead of us or sent notes indirectly through the line captain. I don't recall any notes that day; all I remember is that he wanted a meeting with Eva, another 5'9" Czech showgirl who had recently come into the show, and me. Bobbi came up to me and asked if I could stay a bit longer to meet Mr. Rudas in the dressing room after company rehearsal.

Oh my God, I thought, what did I do? Surely he wasn't going to fire me just when I had settled into my role. Carolee and I had our first apartment in one of the hippest cities in the world in 1970.

We had Sunday off each week, days of "free love" in this magnificent city. We met the real people of Montreal and the flower children. We could be weekend hippies and trip around in the mountains, smoke pot and be free here. This could not end; it was just getting started. Carolee had met a radio D.J. and was dating him. Of course, she was 16, and he was 10 or 12 years older! That's where Carolee and I differed; she wanted to do all the grown-up things. I just wanted to be 18.

Meeting Mr. Rudas face to face was obviously freaking me out. All the girls seemed a little intimidated by him. I arrived backstage and there he was, with Lee, his concubine, and Colin Wilson and Bobbi. Thank God Bobbi was there! She was everyone's rock.

Mr. Rudas was trying to be light and comical. He liked me, I could tell. I had a sense of humor and could make him laugh. I'd learned well, having grown up with an alcoholic father, how to humor men. I fancied myself the equivalent of a modern-day Fanny Brice and Mr. Rudas my Florenz Ziegfeld. I would spew out funny remarks here and there, and he would chuckle. I liked making him laugh.

I was a bold teenager and skilled in comedy. However, I was still vulnerable, sensitive and insecure. Colin reported that my skills were not strong enough for the can-can now that I had pulled my hamstring; also, I was taller than most of the covered dancers. Colin pointed out, "Diane would make a better dancing nude. She's tall, and now that she's hurt, she can rest her hamstring."

"Nude" was the modern word in the dance world for showgirl.

"But ... but..." I stuttered, my mind racing back to my mentor's final words to me: "Do not dance topless!" Her voice filled my soul: "You won't become the dancer you can be if you are a showgirl."

4. Getting Out of Dodge, 1969

The horror must have shown on my face because then Colin delivered the final blow, "The only way we can keep you in the show is if you become a nude." He embodied zero endearing qualities as a human.

Lee chimed in with her bougie Australian accent, "Darling, you're tall. You have so much natural charisma onstage. You really are an actress out there, a performer more than a technician!"

My ears perked up. Had I heard her correctly? Actress?

"Oh, yes!" I lit up as only a naïve 18-year-old could. That is what I am, an actress.

I felt surprised knowing someone saw me for who I actually was.

Bobbi added, "You sell the numbers better than any girl on that stage!"

The compliment felt soothing, like an ointment, and it helped me feel a little better, but then someone delivered the punchline. I don't remember who said it. I was in an alternate reality in my head where the planet had cracked loudly. I felt afraid, afraid of becoming one of "them."

Someone said, "So, let's take a look at your breasts."

"What...?" I murmured, "Who, me?" Everything started moving in slow motion at this point and I only heard about every fifth or sixth word people were saying.

Bobbi quickly and sweetly interjected, "Let's go try on some pasties."

The nudes wore silvery, star-shaped, sequined pasties that covered most of the breast. They knew I was completely freaked out. Tibor kept walking around with one arm tightly tucked under his armpit, the other covering his mouth, pacing.

I don't remember anything from this point on. I returned from the dressing room with Bobbi, in shock. I disrobed from the waist up and stood before him like a statue. This would be the first man to ever look at my bare breasts. He was polite, quick and professional.

Lee hastily said, "Very nice."

Colin may have glanced; I couldn't tell. That was it! They left and spoke with Bobbi on the way out as I pulled my robe up. Bobbi came back and calmly told me I would be a dancing nude opposite Eva, the Czech showgirl with the first boob job I'd ever seen; she was a gorgeous blonde with rocks for boobs. We would ride down from the ceiling in giant lighted stars to open the show, and I would learn all of the dancing nude parts of the girl who was leaving.

Bobbi asked me to report early the next day; she would personally train me. I believe I continued protesting because Bobbi reassured me it was no big deal. I had never revealed my breasts to anyone before today.

Not only did Mary Lou's words haunt me, but the mere thought of going onstage topless horrified me.

Bobbi and Pearl Ho had danced topless in the show, and I loved the two of them most of all. That was about all I could hang onto at that moment.

5

Conceived and Directed by Tibor Rudas, 1970

I would make more money now and work less. No more pulling muscles in the can-can.

But was I selling my soul? How would I tell my mom, dad or Mary Lou? Especially Mary Lou. How could I bring myself to show 1000 people my tits every night?

Damn it, I thought, why didn't I start dancing at five years old like every other dancer in the show? I began at 13, and although I took three dance classes a week and performed with the high school Golden Girls, it wasn't enough.

"*I* wasn't enough" was all I could feel, hear or believe. Little did I know that destiny was playing its tune in my life. Divine orchestration was being composed. My life changed dramatically that day.

That was the day I knew I couldn't ever go back home. I couldn't live the life my parents had so carelessly created for their children. Although I knew they loved us, they were just so young.

I made the ultimate sacrifice, to bare my chest to stay in the show and Montreal. That choice was not easily made, and Tibor Rudas knew it. I was unknowingly being prepared for a much different role in his productions. They found me to be difficult to manipulate but still naïve enough to gobble up whatever they dished out. In this case, a much larger picture was about to be revealed that I certainly couldn't see at the time.

I was 18, and my world had just closed in on me. My vision was blurred. Who was I? What was I? The only way I could cope with this transition would be to continue fantasizing that Tibor Rudas was Florenz Ziegfeld and I was Fanny Brice on her way to stardom. Oh, the power of denial.

Like every other young, ambitious performer, I needed to be loved and accepted. In the world of Rudas Dancers, I received the love of thousands each night. I needed that much adoration. Why? Probably because the two people who didn't clap, cheer, support or show up for me enough left a hole, a deep cavern in my soul that needed filling up.

The large audiences came to see and love me. Some of us didn't get what we needed from the people who were supposed to love us and protect us unconditionally. We needed more love from many people: hundreds, thousands, millions. Some of us need millions of people to applaud us and love us. I then became aware of the fact that I was one of them.

6

And 5, 6, 7, 8, 1970

There were many recreational forms of denial available to us in 1970, including marijuana, LSD and fantasy. We hippies indulged our inner fantasy lives to the max in so many creative ways. The hippie movement was alive and well in Montreal that summer. I was about to turn 19 in August, and I had just found my very own furnished brownstone studio apartment on Lincoln Avenue. It was a fashionable, artsy, well-kept, clean neighborhood within walking distance of everything I could wish for: the park, restaurants, boutiques and the rapidly emerging underground discotheques, the Chateau Champlain.

Montreal was both a French and English city. What a glorious, desirable and hip place to live! The streets were lined with shoes from France and head shops galore, filled with drug paraphernalia and boutiques offering sparkling mirrored items from India. Incense and patchouli oil permeated the air. A walk to the park produced offers of pot, free love and flowers from saffron-robed Krishna devotees. Everything was there. Montreal had it all!

I adapted to wearing sequined pasties, enormous feather headdresses and wings in the show. While it was not an easy transition, I began designing a life I loved. It took me a long time to accept that I was actually becoming a showgirl! I went along with it, but I was not fully engaged at all. I felt I had compromised myself somehow. Sold out.

Once I agreed to become a dancing nude, I began to rehearse with Bobbi for my new spot. There were only two nudes in the show. It was a piece of cake compared to the rigorous work of the covered dancers. It appealed to me on a performance level. I felt relieved to give my previously pulled hamstring a rest. Those leg lifts, jump splits and kicks in the can-can were really hard on everyone. It was extremely rigorous, including 36 back bend kicks by the acrobats and another 36 reverse pirouettes for we dancers, twice nightly.

I would miss the trendy choreography of the opening and a few of the other dance numbers in the show. I would also miss frolicking and screaming out French phrases when we ran into the audience during the traditional can-can. Now that was vivacity!

My opening night was fast approaching. Carolee and I were still very close, although we had parted ways as roommates six months after we shared our two-bedroom flat. She had found a boyfriend to live with. He was a D.J.

I was still a virgin, growing ever more curious about sex. It was inevitable, of course, caught somewhere between the free love of the times and the more experienced dancers, not to mention the hormones pulsating through me. As my life transitioned, so did my interest in men.

When opening night as a showgirl finally arrived, everyone was very supportive, especially wonderful Bobbi. Without her, I doubt my legs would have carried me from the theater's wings to the stage that night.

Very few moments stand out vividly in life. Putting on my star-shaped pasties with white adhesive tape was one of them. They were large enough to cover the nipples and a bit of the surrounding breast. What a sight: gorgeous fishnet-ed, long legs, silver jeweled G-string, a headdress made of a jeweled silver cap and tall pink plumes jetting straight up, silver heels, long white gloves that reached my mid-upper arm. The stagehands slipped heavy, pink-plumed backpacks onto our shoulders in the wings.

I was trembling and could barely manage to fight back tears. I covered myself with a towel. This was it: the first reveal. I was numb. I reached out to put on the wings and realized I would have to drop the towel. I heard a whispered apology in my head: "Sorry, Mary Lou." I felt I had let down my mentor. Bobbi, Carolee and Pearl Ho were all there in the wings saying, "C'mon, Diane, you can do it."

The stagehand was very polite and wasn't staring, just supportive. Just before handing the towel to Bobbi, tears began slowly streaming down my face. I managed to dry them with the corner of the towel before an eyelash drowned on my cheek. I surrendered the towel, and the feathered wings were lifted onto my back.

"Smile!" was all I heard from the dancers. The girls knew how hard this was for me. I knew Mr. Rudas, Lee and Colin were in the sound booth, I couldn't turn back now. I somehow slipped onto the stage. The lights had never felt brighter. I tried to muster my usual beaming smile, but it was lost amidst a steady stream of tears and panic. The whole world now sat peering at my breasts. Here I was, out on stage, dancing with pasties, showing the audience and my co-workers my virginal breasts. I was still a virgin, miraculously, especially during the era of free love. But it was my choice to wait to have sex. Wearing pasties was not really my choice.

It was unsettling to know that I had revealed my breasts to over a thousand sets of glaring eyes before I'd revealed them to any man in my life.

6. And 5, 6, 7, 8, 1970

This was perhaps one of the most difficult nights I'd ever experienced. I was officially and entirely depressed. No one could console me. I felt as though I was letting down my mentor and my parents. I wasn't sure if my own disapproval got to me or if it was the potential disapproval of others.

Lord knows, in one of the most dazzling settings in the world, I was feeling insecure and very self-conscious, to say the least. I not only broke my promise to my mentor, but I also had not told my parents I had become a showgirl. I would eventually, but not yet.

The stairway to the Le Caf Conc theater, Montreal, 1970.

Bobbi took me aside a week into my new role and told me that she had just had a meeting with Mr. Rudas. He would be leaving for Nassau, Bahamas, to oversee his show on Paradise Island the next day.

"I'm supposed to tell you this," Bobbi said. "In my meeting with Mr. Rudas, he commented on your first week as a showgirl."

"What did he say?" I asked, anxious to know.

"He said once you stop crying, you will be one of the best showgirls he's ever had in any of his shows."

I couldn't believe it. "Really?" I asked.

"Absolutely," said Bobbi, "and I agree. You really know how to sell a number. You are a true performer. These other girls are primarily technicians. So many of them are great dancers, but you know how to work an audience in these numbers. You are a real showgirl!"

"I am an actress first, you know," I added.

"You're going to be great," Bobbi said in her rich Aussie accent, giving me a warm, maternal hug.

Wow, I thought, this isn't punishment for not being good enough after all. Maybe Rudas did see my real talent. I left Le Caf Conc with a new sense of myself that night and a paycheck, which included $25 more per week. Checks for $175 looked better than $150. By 1970 standards, that was good pay for a professional dancer who had Sunday off each week. This was certainly better than being a Rockette in New York City. They had to work four shows a day, seven days a week for $150.

I was feeling successful. I was acting more now. I decided to really own those critiques. I never cried onstage again. Life took on more ease. I worked less and I made more. I was acting more than dancing, which was my first love, and Mr. Rudas said I was one of the best. This, topped with the extra pay, gave me a new sense of accomplishment.

I decided to celebrate. After the show, I went out with Julianna to our favorite all-night deli-steakhouse and we had filet mignon, baked potatoes, vanilla shakes and lots of bread and butter. One of the things I failed to see at the age of 18 was that less dancing equals less exercise. More money meant spending more and going out to dine more often. Within the month, I had gained 10 or 12 pounds. Duh!

Add Kahlua and creams at the clubs and very little outside exercise and what do you get? A fat showgirl. Hello?

Upon Mr. Rudas' return from the Bahamas a few months later, his first comment to me was, "What are you doing? Drinking buttermilk?"

I choked, "I do drink a lot of shakes, and I love Chinese food!"

"Well, I need you to lose ten pounds!" Mr. Rudas requested. "No more butter, bread, milk, or spaghetti."

"I'll watch it!" I added playfully.

"Okay," he answered in a raised voice. "Otherwise, you are beautiful, and a great example to these girls who have forgotten that I pay them to smile onstage!"

Ouch, I thought. The dancers glared at me. I could feel their brains plotting against me. Bitch, she comes in here, a pain in the ass, cries like a baby onstage, needy, needy, needy, and now she's better than we are?

I was needy, young and extremely naïve. Quite a juxtaposition to my life just six months ago in Illinois. I had won the most coveted acting scholarship in the state, starred in all of the plays, danced for all assemblies, and was pretty much small-town hot stuff. Now, in this professional life, you were damned if you do and damned if you don't. Those girls may not have cared about me, but I was in favor with our producer Mr. Rudas, and I liked it.

7

Guardian Angels Arrive, 1970

I lost ten pounds, and with my weekend dose of pot smoking, this was not easy. I needed something to replace food. I needed a boyfriend. There sure were some cuties roaming around this city. On my day off, a Sunday, I moved into my very own, new, darling furnished brownstone apartment on Lincoln Avenue. I was there alone, hanging beaded curtains, when, after dark, I heard lots of noise below my third-floor window.

It was late June, and with my living room window open and tepid summer breezes sweeping through the apartment, I was drawn to the sound of laughter outside. I went to the window and sat on the sill to enjoy the breeze. I saw dozens of gorgeous young guys streaming into my building. Three floors up, I saw them clearly, although they could not see me. Wow! Wherever they were going was where I wanted to be.

This continued for over an hour. I kept watching, feeling like a voyeur and frustrated at not being seen by them.

As the second hour went by, I heard more of what sounded like one heck of a party on the fourth floor, just above me. I was wide awake, I had nowhere to go, and I wanted to be at that party.

I started brainstorming to find a creative way to go to the door, knock, go in and party—but it needed to be clever or I'd just be a party crasher. They all looked friendly, and I was dying to get to know my new neighbors. That is the difference between the innocence and energy of youth and the jaded solitude of age.

What to do? How do I get in? Hmmm. Then I saw it: the empty crystal sugar bowl and creamer. My thoughts raced. That's it. I had found my ticket to party-land! I'll go ask for a cup of sugar! I was dead serious. Not an ounce of me thought of this as anything but reasonable.

I got ready, put on a cute top and bell bottom jeans, fluffed my hair, added a bit of mascara and sprayed on a dash of White Shoulders. With prop in hand, I headed for the party palace. The party was in full swing:

music blasting, singing, whooping it up! "Hey Jude" blared through the door, which bolstered my courage. The Beatles played on, and I was ready.

I knocked at the door. I don't think they heard me. I rapped harder. This time, the music stopped and the partygoers quieted down significantly. A moment or two went by until, finally, the door opened slightly. A young man with a surprisingly friendly face peered through the crack at me with a jolly smile. "Yes?" he asked.

"I'm so sorry to interrupt," I said politely, "but I am your new neighbor, and I just moved in and wondered if I could borrow a cup of sugar?" I held out my crystal sugar bowl, and he smiled again.

"Ahhhh," he squealed, "a cup of sugar?" He began to laugh, then turned to his guests. "A cup of sugar," he said again as he swept the door open to present me. I felt like Loretta Young! Screeches of laughter could be heard blocks away. The next thing I knew, I was being hugged, loved and swept into the fray with rounds of laughter and wafts of marijuana, flowers and wine. Someone put a joint in my mouth, and bam! Instant love!

Our hosts, Leo and Larry, were so relieved that I was anything but the police. Not only was I not the police, they claimed I was something out of a dream. Keep in mind, they were all stoned!

Straight out of a Mae West movie, it became an instant love fest. I was the darling, beautiful hippie blonde showgirl neighbor who had delighted them all with the "cup of sugar" line. The party boys all danced with me, embraced, loved and fed me. They gently and delightfully welcomed me into the fold. I had never felt so much mass love. Oh, to be 18 again. Life was wonderful. A dash of creativity and a heaping dose of courage produced two lifelong friends.

Destiny has a fabulous way of uniting kindred spirits, and that night, when asked my name, I delightfully cajoled, "Shoiley Lipshitz."

Several more rounds of uproarious laughter spilled from the party walls—screeches of enchantment. Not only did they love me, but they also laughed at all the silliness I could muster. I mean, they were all high, but I felt like the queen of a great comedic fantasy, embraced by the beautiful people. I had an instant family. Leo Savoie and Larry Peace (his real name) are still my friends.

I was offered apple pie by a large Italian opera singer with an endless curly Italian 'fro who lived on the second floor and was affectionately referred to as "Mother." It was about that time that it dawned on me, through my marijuana-induced haze, that there wasn't one woman at the party. Not one girl, just wall-to-wall guys: gorgeous, and all in love with cute, young, clever me. Then it hit me: Oh my God! How fun, they are all gay.

Disappointing? On a romantic level, yes, but on nearly every other

7. Guardian Angels Arrive, 1970

level, it was one of the best nights I'd had in my entire life. I can't remember ever feeling more loved and appreciated for just being me. I made friends for life that night as we all partied into the wee hours, laughing all the way.

The very next night, who did I find in the audience sitting down front, sipping champagne watching my show? You got it! My new best friends, Leo and Larry. Whooping it up in our audience—my latest, greatest support system. I was so touched. I was so in love with my new family.

From that day forward, they truly filled my "sugar bowl" with love and care. They looked out for every phase I went through and ensured that I enjoyed the ride. We spent every Sunday having "Mother"'s apple pie in the morning, then going to the park for pot or a little LSD. We went hiking in the beautiful Laurentian mountains, seeing all the notable sights in the most vivid states of mind. We were weekend hippies. Complete hippies for one day each week and then back to business by Monday.

8

Sexy Psychedelics, 1970

In August of 1970, my 19th birthday was fast approaching, and my desire to consummate a relationship with a physical conclusion was washing over me in waves of pulsating hormones. There were several "offers." The most distinct offer came from the star comedian in our show, Barry Lee. I liked Barry. He always made me laugh and encouraged the comic in me. We hung out many nights after our shows.

He managed to find all the entertainment spots that kept late hours in Montreal. He often took me and several dancers out for fun nights on the town. He was a very short, bulky and wildly successful Jewish New York City comedian.

Being surrounded by his entourage of leggy young showgirls when out and about was one of Barry's favorite things. He made all of us laugh, and he also did "comedic" magic, so he was "on" wherever we went, making people laugh. Everyone loved Barry. However, he never let me forget he wanted to be my "first." Eventually it became annoying, and I had to inform him that I liked a different "type" of guy. Namely, rock star types. Barry knew lots of them, and the clubs were a constant with him.

It seemed other girls in our show liked Barry "in that way." My greatest desire was to fix him up with someone gorgeous whom he liked and at least get this guy laid. Being horny was more than part of his act. It was his way of being, and as much as he liked me, even taking my mom and me to lunch when she was visiting, I didn't want my "first" to be my funny buddy. Eventually, he hit it off with my first roommate Julianna, and they finally connected. They had this lusty drive in common.

Although I had dated interesting guys in Montreal, I just hadn't met "the one." "The one" didn't mean the one I'd fall in love with; the "one" consisted of something unexplainable. It would be someone I had chemistry and electricity with. Some hip, good-looking and, most importantly,

7. Guardian Angels Arrive, 1970

level, it was one of the best nights I'd had in my entire life. I can't remember ever feeling more loved and appreciated for just being me. I made friends for life that night as we all partied into the wee hours, laughing all the way.

The very next night, who did I find in the audience sitting down front, sipping champagne watching my show? You got it! My new best friends, Leo and Larry. Whooping it up in our audience—my latest, greatest support system. I was so touched. I was so in love with my new family.

From that day forward, they truly filled my "sugar bowl" with love and care. They looked out for every phase I went through and ensured that I enjoyed the ride. We spent every Sunday having "Mother"'s apple pie in the morning, then going to the park for pot or a little LSD. We went hiking in the beautiful Laurentian mountains, seeing all the notable sights in the most vivid states of mind. We were weekend hippies. Complete hippies for one day each week and then back to business by Monday.

8

Sexy Psychedelics, 1970

In August of 1970, my 19th birthday was fast approaching, and my desire to consummate a relationship with a physical conclusion was washing over me in waves of pulsating hormones. There were several "offers." The most distinct offer came from the star comedian in our show, Barry Lee. I liked Barry. He always made me laugh and encouraged the comic in me. We hung out many nights after our shows.

He managed to find all the entertainment spots that kept late hours in Montreal. He often took me and several dancers out for fun nights on the town. He was a very short, bulky and wildly successful Jewish New York City comedian.

Being surrounded by his entourage of leggy young showgirls when out and about was one of Barry's favorite things. He made all of us laugh, and he also did "comedic" magic, so he was "on" wherever we went, making people laugh. Everyone loved Barry. However, he never let me forget he wanted to be my "first." Eventually it became annoying, and I had to inform him that I liked a different "type" of guy. Namely, rock star types. Barry knew lots of them, and the clubs were a constant with him.

It seemed other girls in our show liked Barry "in that way." My greatest desire was to fix him up with someone gorgeous whom he liked and at least get this guy laid. Being horny was more than part of his act. It was his way of being, and as much as he liked me, even taking my mom and me to lunch when she was visiting, I didn't want my "first" to be my funny buddy. Eventually, he hit it off with my first roommate Julianna, and they finally connected. They had this lusty drive in common.

Although I had dated interesting guys in Montreal, I just hadn't met "the one." "The one" didn't mean the one I'd fall in love with; the "one" consisted of something unexplainable. It would be someone I had chemistry and electricity with. Some hip, good-looking and, most importantly,

8. Sexy Psychedelics, 1970   45

talented guy was out there. I just hadn't met him yet. It didn't matter how badly I wanted to surrender my virginity—it all had to line up.

Barry seemed the most determined to make that happen. It became his mission. He even talked about the "virgin" showgirl in his comedy act. It became embarrassing. I did not find it funny at all. Thank God he didn't mention my name. It also came with a certain degree of peer pressure.

On the other hand, while Leo and Larry were all for it happening, they were very protective of my wishes. They were cautious yet full of love and wonder over the prospect. So I had the Devil on my shoulder (Barry) and two guardian angels (Leo and Larry) on the other.

Regardless of all this divine intervention, I was closer than they knew to being ready. I simply had to be the one to choose the lucky guy.

We came across a club we loved in old Montreal. It featured many top bands, including Chicago. At the time, they were #1 in the world.

Between headliners, the club featured bands with hits at the top of the charts. They had late-night sets I was able to attend after my performances.

Nearly every other night, I was there with Barry, the girls and my angels Leo and Larry, listening to music, dancing and eating lots of Chinese food at the restaurant next door. Many musicians met inside that 24-hour restaurant. I shared many egg rolls with cute young guys my age. Alas, none of them was "the one."

I loved my life of partying after work and sleeping into the day. I had lots of friends, fun and love. I felt I had it all. I lived in one of the hippest cities on the planet. Montreal had copious amounts of personality, and the Canadian people are the original party people! Canadians are wonderful, fun, happy-go-lucky!

Montreal was an international gateway for people from everywhere. The styles, trends, diversity and the music-entertainment scene were all there.

One balmy night in August, several of us went to the club to hear a very popular band. They had a very charismatic lead singer who reminded me of Jimi Hendrix, whom I'd seen in person in Iowa in the summer of '69 for $5. His name was Don. He had a band with a full horn section, and they played their hits and did Chicago covers nightly. They were popular!

Clubgoers filled the venue for their late-night sets every night for the weeks they were in town. By the time we got there at one a.m., it was impossible to get a table. But good old Barry Lee knew everyone and always brought his entourage of tall showgirls with him, so we always got a table down front. A little fame, a big tip and a few pretty girls went a long way.

Club owners wanted us there. It was one of the perks of being in the industry. We not only got into the club easily, but we were often escorted backstage afterward with Barry leading the way. We would get invited to the green room to have some fun with the musicians. For me, the real fun was the music.

I became transfixed with this band's talent. They had their finger on the pulse of rock and roll, and the music always moved me. I secretly became interested in the Filipino trumpet player. He was also a backup singer-dancer. Horn sections dancing behind the lead singer was a big thing then. They had a very hip, funky style, combining Sly and the Family Stone and Chicago. I loved every element of it. This was some of the best live music I'd ever heard. It would seem the entire city agreed. Every night, the club was packed.

My secret swooning over the trumpet player soon came out. Once Barry got wind of my fixation on Flip the trumpet player, he insisted we try to meet up with them after the last set.

We hung around the Chinese restaurant, knowing the band came in each night. But Flip never did. The other guys did, especially Don, the lead singer. Girls would be waiting for him with his leather pants, fringed vests and larger-than-life Afro. He was one sexy guy and looked so much like the amazing Jimi. We became friends. He liked me. Many young hippie girls or hot worldly chicks were always hanging on Don, and that was not my thing. I needed to be special, the only one!

Don did become our buddy, though, and Barry held court every night, making everyone laugh. He was not only generous in spirit, he was also generous in general and often treated everyone to drinks. He tipped everyone very well, and everyone loved him. I chose him as one of my new best friends. Life was carte blanche with Barry around, full of laughs and good times.

I don't know what he said to Don, but Barry organized a trek to the club for our crew, and we were ushered down front to a table stage left, right in front of Flip. I managed to make eye contact with him several times.

Although he was a very focused performer, he did seem to be checking me out. My crazy comedian buddy, Barry, didn't seem to miss a beat or a glance. He was with Julianna that night, and they were in lust, but it was obvious that he was on a mission to hook me and Flip up.

I didn't really know to what degree Barry was operating, but after the show, he went to the dressing room entrance where a bouncer proudly protected the door. He somehow got in … probably slipped him a hundy.

Barry rushed back to our table and insisted the girls and I come backstage with him. He was trying to be cool, but there was an urgency beneath the surface that was tangible.

Butterflies fluttered in my stomach. We were whisked backstage. We headed to the band's green room area. I felt shy and awkward. This seems

8. Sexy Psychedelics, 1970

to have been my pattern around cool guys who were semi-famous. There we were, meeting for real for the first time. We were finally face to face.

Barry grinned. I could tell he was delighted with himself.

Flip was gorgeous. He was American Filipino, with rock star good looks and a body to die for. A dancer. He was shy, and for a 27-year-old man, that seemed cute. I liked it, in a way. To me, he was the sexiest man alive. I couldn't remember ever feeling like this. I was all aflutter with the newness of lust! I was a virgin approaching the ripe old age of 19 this week! Electricity and pheromones pulsed beneath the shyness and coy glances. We chatted for a while. Eventually, our friends readied themselves to depart. Barry, Julianna and the others began to leave.

When I stood to join them, Barry said to Flip, "You'll get my best friend Diane home safely, won't you?"

"Of course, no problem." Flip smiled reassuringly at me.

Whoa, I thought. No backing out now. I panicked for a second, and Flip took my hand. I had anticipated having sex for so long that now, on the threshold of this momentous occasion, I was nervous.

Barry winked at me. "Have fun!" he exclaimed on his way out the door.

We bid Barry and the girls good night and I relaxed a bit.

Now, it was just me and the band. I was trying to be cool, but cannot even describe how many different things were racing through my teenage brain. I wasn't good at this. So the actress in me took over. I decided to enjoy the ride, which literally turned into a ride in their van to the hotel. Don drove. He had a girl with him, too. He and Flip seemed very close. The other band members went their merry way.

We drove through the early morning hours to a lovely hotel. They were staying at a Hilton or Sheraton. It had a beautiful lobby and they all had their own rooms.

Flip and I had a nice rapport, but then again, what did I know? He seemed like the strong, silent type. I found out he was from California, near Los Angeles. He had had a two-year stint as a dancer on *Shindig*, one of my favorite TV shows during the '60s. I watched it primarily for the music and the dancers. I loved that he was a successful musician and dancer—you don't find that combination every day. He had taken a shot at acting but said it really wasn't his thing. He loved playing trumpet and sax but didn't love being on the road. He missed L.A. and missed dancing but made more money on tour.

The conversation did eventually segue to me, and the fact that I was still a virgin did come up. He knew already!

"How did you know that?" I asked, knowing full well how he knew.

"Oh, just a guess," he claimed.

"Can you tell from just talking to me?" I asked bluntly.

"Well, it sort of came up," he added gently.

"Leave it to Barry," I guessed.

God only knows what the crazy comedian told him and there I was thinking Flip was simply hot for moi! Oh well, I doubt if it would have mattered. I chose this man, this hot exotic guy, to be my first. And he was sexy! What did I get out of this affair? Several things I will never forget: an excellent, experienced and gentle first lover. He was very careful and even toasted the event afterwards with Pepsi from the minibar.

He even stated, and I will never forget this, "I wish we had champagne." I thought that was so cute. When I look back now, that night was amazing. The greatest learning tool that I collected that night was self-knowledge. I was with someone much more experienced than the two or three high school boys I almost made it with. This says something about how I value myself. I needed a man who was experienced, gentle, gorgeous and sexy!

For me, in spite of everything he really was, he was perfect for this particular event. The most exciting feeling was finally feeling safe enough to let go and go with my desire and let it happen. This was sex! I was timid and scared, but I felt ready. It felt good to have cared enough about myself to have waited. I just wasn't one of those girls who would give it up to some fumbling high school boyfriend! I was glad it was here, with Flip.

Flip and I spent a week together. He was my sexual teacher, my first lover. I was smitten. He taught me lots of things about myself and life. I learned about orgasms, douching, birth control pills and oral sex. He asked for a blow job, so I blew softly and sensually on his penis. I knew nothing! God! Virgins must be so boring. When he taught me about oral sex, he made me squeal with delight. Afterward, he showed me how to properly give him pleasure orally.

"Ohhh, I see!" I exclaimed. Flip also taught me how to get stoned on a lazy Sunday afternoon and order Chinese food and have it delivered. It was my first taste of nesting with a man. It was new and fun! I went to his show nearly every night for the remainder of his stay. They were on tour and would soon be traveling to Quebec City, a quaint French-Canadian village set in the most exquisite mountain resort.

I went by on his last night to see him off. He was very focused on packing, preparing the vans for their departure. We had a quick goodbye. I said farewell to the band, the wives and lovers with promises to keep in touch. Someone said, "Come see the show if you can."

"Where is it?" I asked.

Flip had not offered anything but a nonchalant, "I'll call you!"

Someone gave me the address, and I gave Flip my home number and the number to the backstage dressing room pay phone. With a kiss, lots of hugs and a deep, sensual gaze, we said goodbye.

8. Sexy Psychedelics, 1970

I was heartbroken. I am a Leo, after all. I am a fixed sign! Leos tend to be loyal to a fault. I don't let go that easily. I was attached. I had to see him again. One week after he left Montreal, I decided to do just that.

* * *

The girls in the dressing room became my protectors. They looked out for me in my vulnerable yet graduated state. They made sure I had a gynecologist to visit, birth control, and lots of comfort. I needed these women. Like a tribe, these experienced elders took my exposed soul under their wing. I belonged. I smoked with them, but I didn't want to eat. I started losing weight, much to the delight of Mr. Rudas.

I moped about, waiting for Flip's call. When it didn't come all week, I tried calling him at the club in Quebec City, to no avail. According to Barry Lee, the only thing to do was go out and have some fun. Feeling somewhat responsible for my situation, he took me to the club where I met Flip to see a new band. They were quite good. They were younger, not quite as popular as the last, but talented and cute.

I met Michael, a darling hippie guitar player from Arizona, a 19-year-old with long hair. He was crazy about me. He called me "Sunshine" and phoned me every day and night. We hung out and made out while he listened attentively to my tale of woe. He was committed to being my hero. He even came to my show on his night off. He was everything I wanted Flip to be. I wasn't ready to be his lover yet, even though I found him attractive.

I wanted to see Flip in Quebec City. Michael was patient and willing to wait until I worked out my angst with Flip, but he only had one month in Montreal. He never pressured me in any way; he only comforted me. The Universe brought me living guardian angels, and Michael was one of many to be there for me in the years to come. But the truth was that bad boys did it for me and I had grown up learning that love was painful. Sad, but true.

Michael was probably the guy I should have loved; he was sweet, sensitive, down-to-earth and wonderful.

* * *

After our three shows on a Saturday night, I made the journey by train with a French-Canadian girl, Jeanne Marie, who I'd befriended. She had dated Don in Montreal, and when he invited her to Quebec City, she invited me to go with her to see them at their lodge in the Laurentian mountains. I tried calling Flip again, but no luck. So I would surprise him! Why not?

The Canadian countryside and mountain resorts were among the most beautiful places I'd ever seen. I meant to sleep on the train that morning, but the sunrise over the Laurentians was too divine to miss. The lakes surrounding the charming village of Quebec City were majestic in the summer dawn. Sparkling lakes shimmering as a hint of sunshine whispered to the sleepy, quiet town when we arrived.

Once let off at the train station, we grabbed our overnight bags and stumbled through the cobblestone village, seeking any establishment that might be open. We needed information to get to our destination, and we needed coffee. I didn't even drink coffee, but today, I needed to be awake!

We shuffled about, smoking cigarettes, Canadian Dunhills, waiting for any place to open. As dawn broke at six, we finally heard the sounds of life on this quiet morning. A bakery opened its doors, and the smell of freshly baked bread and croissants invited us to breakfast. The village was over 300 years old. We felt as though we had traveled back in time. Perfect for two hippie girls from different countries. It was most fortunate, again, that I traveled with Jeanne Marie because this region was completely French. The baker only spoke French, and this establishment was the only business open early on a Sunday morning. We ordered our *café* and were served warm, fresh croissants and *du beurre*.

Ahh! The essence of France right here in Quebec City. The refreshment helped wake us for the next portion of the journey. Apparently, the only way to the secluded lodge was by taxi. We called the cab, and three coffees later, it arrived to take us to our sweeties.

This lodge was huge and housed the entire band; many of the wives and girlfriends had joined them here. The taxi driver gave us a tour of the land and some history as we drove. All in French, once again, I was grateful for my French companion. I honestly do not know how I would have managed without her. Our excitement mounted as we drove for nearly an hour before the taxi pulled onto a road leading to the mansion.

We arrived at around eight a.m. It was a gigantic old Swiss lodge alongside a magnificent lake and majestic mountains. A long wooden dock led to boats on the lake. It was unreal. Quintessential nature at its most beautiful. Quiet and serene. We paid the taxi driver and stumbled out into the exquisite grayish morning.

Here came the sun. We wandered to the lake's edge and welcomed the morning through chattering teeth. Jeanne Marie was anxious to go inside and embrace her sweetheart Don. He must have felt the same way because as we turned to go into the lodge, a sleepy Don came down to the dock to greet us, seeming happy to see his girl. I could tell he was surprised to see me, but he put his arms around both of us and dragged us into "Heidi-Land." With its vast, open living room that greets you with a giant stone fireplace complete with a moose head, it had all of the trappings of a Canadian mountain chalet.

8. Sexy Psychedelics, 1970

A knotty pine staircase framed the great room on either side of the fireplace, leading to separate wings. The cathedral pine ceilings were carved and painted à la Swiss Chalet style. Don showed us to the quiet yellow kitchen. Tea began to brew when Linda, one of the band member's wives, appeared. I recognized her from Montreal; she seemed nice enough, through her early morning haze, but also reserved. She briefly exchanged some information with Don about driving to the airport to pick up band member Danny's wife Debbie (from the States), who would be arriving for their last week in Canada. Linda went upstairs to dress for her journey.

I asked Don where Flip was. He answered, "sleeping," as he magically produced two "Blue Cheer" tabs from his pocket of his jeans. His eyes lit up when he did this, and he added, "It's everybody's day off. Let's party!"

I knew what "Blue Cheer" was. It was 1970, and the LSD with any credibility at the time was "Yellow Sunshine" and "Blue Cheer." I asked how potent it was, never having taken more than a quarter of a tab myself. The one time I did, in my hometown, I enjoyed it very much, but it was only a tiny amount. It was very psychedelic.

He said it was good shit, and this place was the perfect place to drop acid. "Look around, ladies," he chimed as he drew back the yellow gingham kitchen curtains.

The sun had come to greet us at last. I felt a warm rush.

Jeanne Marie said, "Why not?"

I hesitated for a second when Don handed me an entire tab. I wondered what it would be like.

Something made me throw caution to the wind when I asked, "Will I be able to work tomorrow night?"

"Absolutely," he assured me.

So, with tepid tea in hand, I popped an entire tab of acid for the first time.

"That's going to kick in in about an hour. Let's go to the lake and do this right," Don suggested. We threw on sweaters and lounged on the long dock and sipped peppermint tea, laughing and basking in the splendor of the morning. As we began to get off on the acid, Don started fucking with our heads. He was our pilot, and we were taking flight. We watched the sun on the shimmering lake become gliding streams of fish, merging with the purple shadows cast by the mountains. The breeze of the pine trees danced and nodded, turning into an electric kaleidoscope of colors, all joining into one great natural visual concert.

I was enthralled, submerged in my mind-blown state. Linda came down to take the van to the airport and saw the state we were in. Linda told me to enjoy it and stay connected to nature as much as possible during my trip. Don walked them to the van, and Jeanne Marie and I giggled at how very stoned we were. I told her I couldn't wait to be with Flip this stoned.

"Sex would be great like this," she stated through giggles.

"Yeah, I bet!" I added as if I knew anything.

When Don returned, he was definitely tripping! We hung out and were enamored with how magnificent nature was here. It seemed like a never-ending concert, all sounds, movements and colors perfectly choreographed for our entertainment. Eventually Don and Jeanne Marie were overcome with waves of passion and decided to take their own personal party inside. They asked if I would be okay and I replied, "Do you think Flip is awake yet?"

Don assured me he would send him to me if he was. I believed him. Denial is a powerful tool, especially in this lovely altered state. I decided to bask in the glory of the day. I stretched out on my sweater and embraced the glistening sun. I felt the sun was my ruler and my God-Goddess-life force. The breeze knew how to entertain me as it whistled through the scenic view and made all of nature dance her mystical dance. Even the grass danced in motion to her music, embellished with colors and patterns, bright and beautiful.

Several of the guys came to check on me. I remember Linda and Debbie coming down when they returned from the airport.

Linda brought me orange juice and said I had been down here a long time, the clouds were coming, and it looked like rain. She wanted me to come inside and eat something. It was now nearly two in the afternoon. Where had the time gone? I couldn't even stand up, so she and I hung out for a while, I tried to focus on her face, but I felt she was too concerned about me.

"I want to feel the rain," I laughed as the first droplet made its arrival on my head. Something, perhaps nature, perhaps my higher self, told me not to go into the house. Linda said she'd go wake up Flip and tell him to come out. She left, and I again laid down and enjoyed the darling little raindrops as they fell upon my face. I was fascinated.

I had never realized how much life there was in a single droplet of iridescent rain. Time passed as I studied the new lead dancer in Mother Nature's spectacular show. Eventually, a large, foreboding black cloud covered the lake. It frightened me with its growling thunder. The Earth seemed to quiver. The dock was bouncing in angry waves and snapping at me. Frightened, I decided to go inside.

The lodge was aflutter with life. A few of the guys were in the great room. I vaguely recall a gangly band member. He must have realized how high I was. It seemed like everyone was trippin' that Sunday afternoon in the lodge. I still hadn't seen the man I came to see!

8. Sexy Psychedelics, 1970   53

"Where is Flip?" I asked Steven. He giggled in response. He was definitely high.

Everyone who had been wandering around left the room.

Steven offered, "Why? I'm here!"

"Steven," I said, staring directly at him, "I came to see Flip."

"Okay," he said, "that's cool. He's upstairs. Just at the top of the stairs, second door on the left." He pointed at the right-hand staircase leading to a wing with Flip's room.

The second door on the left seemed like a lot to remember in my current state. Once I figured it out, I hesitated before I opened his door. I really needed a hug from Flip. I knocked gently, feeling he might be asleep still.

"Come in," he called out.

Thank God he's awake, I thought. Oh, how I longed to hold him! I opened the door to a partially lit room. The afternoon rain had made the room somewhat dark with its shades pulled. I glanced at his bed and there he was, sitting up in the corner, smoking a cigarette. The reddish glow burned in the dim room, and my eyes fell directly on the skinny, beautiful brunette lounging next to him, covered in only a sheet.

Flip greeted me awkwardly: "Oh, hey. I'll be down in a sec." My LSD trip took a sharp left turn.

"Who the hell is she?" I wondered. I quickly shut the door.

Oh my God, how could he? Is this why he hasn't called me? Who was the girl? My practical, logical self was trying to grasp some reality and ground me into some rational thought process. I felt tears rushing to the surface. I struggled with this new reality.

I wondered, "How could I be so stupid?" I began to feel like Alice, shrinking very rapidly. I ran down the hall to the staircase. When I reached the top of it, I froze.

How can I go back downstairs and face these people? They must think I'm an idiot. Why did Steven send me to Flip's room? Did he know? I was overwhelmed. I couldn't move. Don came from the kitchen and into the great room. He had to have seen me. Jeanne Marie must have been in the kitchen because Don went after her from the crossover hallway. Debbie came from her room. At this point, I had found a step to sit on at the top of the staircase. I hung onto the railing for dear life. Debbie knew.

"Here, honey, come here." She offered a motherly hug. "Are you tripping?"

I nodded, eyes full of tears. I was sure Debbie was a golden Earth mother angel sent to help me stay in one piece. All the colors and nirvana that the acid had provided turned a muted shade of green. She saw my dilemma.

"Here, sweetie, let's get you downstairs where you can sit down." She guided me down the stairs to a large chair. I sat down, trying hard not to cry.

Jeanne Marie came in and sat down, holding my hand. "Are you okay?" she asked.

"I don't think so," I answered honestly.

Debbie launched upstairs. Don brought me orange juice. As I drank, they all began to turn into cartoon-like characters. Inner chaos emerged. Suddenly, I heard Debbie banging on Flip's door, shouting at him. I remember a portion of her scolding that has stayed with me.

"She's only 18 years old, and she was a virgin. Do you have any idea what she is feeling?" she shouted at him.

He shouted back, "I didn't invite her!"

Jeanne Marie was sweet. "I am so sorry," she whispered.

Then the whole room became very surreal. Each person in it not only became a cartoon-like, animated character, but they also sounded like they spoke in slow motion and at light-speed simultaneously. It was all gibberish. At this point, I just let it all unravel. I was now having a bad trip! This was weird and scary.

Flip and Don appeared in the room. Everyone was mad at Flip. He appeared to me as a jittery rat. Don was a sly wolf. They had boy banter, all in gibberish. Debbie was the lioness, and Jeanne Marie was a kitten.

Oh dear, I thought, I am lost in Cartoon Land. But it wasn't funny. I looked at my hands; they were rubbery, limp, and made of patterns. Each time the cartoon played out before me, many colorful trails followed. This was the circus of the absurd. Very Salvador Dali–driven, and I was lost in the maze of it all.

Flip never spoke to me. We never connected again. Somehow, that reality was the wave that washed over me, making me tumble to the ground emotionally. I had to leave! There was no place for me here. I had made one gigantic mistake, and I must go home. Don, Jeanne Marie and Debbie saw me hastily grab my overnight case. I said goodbye. I told Don and Jeanne Marie I had to go; I couldn't stay any longer.

"Are you sure?" Jeanne Marie asked me delicately, "Do you want me to come with you?"

"No," I stated, making my way down to the main road from the lodge, still stoned. I was trembling and crashing quickly back to Earth.

As I began my trek to God knows where, I heard Don, outside, say out loud, "Strong little chick!"

I felt his admiration for me. I knew with certainty that he was right. Leaving was the one thing I was destined to become good at, but it was the opposite of what my mother excelled in, which was staying! It wasn't until years later, after my second divorce, that I figured out why I leave when things are too hard for me to deal with.

Walking along the road, overnight case in hand, tears flowing, feeling stupid, I was oblivious to the amount of time that had passed. Struggling to stay grounded, I was shaking and quivering. It was the absolute worst time to be stoned. It wasn't the first bad trip I'd had, but it certainly was the worst; I had taken a whole tab rather than a half, as I had before.

A noisy, familiar sound caught my attention. A vehicle was approaching on the rural road behind me. Before I could decide whether to hitchhike, the van stopped on my left. Debbie insisted I get in. It was sweet, maternal Debbie, the American mother-wife who seemed to keep the whole damn band together.

"Come on, sweetie, you shouldn't be walking alone out here in your condition." I got into the van.

"I have to leave," I announced.

"I know. I just don't want you out here walking when the sun sets."

I suddenly noticed that this day was drawing to an end.

She spilled the beans on Flip the rest of the drive to Quebec City. "He has numerous girls in every port. He also has a wife and two kids back in Los Angeles. How dare he take your virginity and not be more responsible?" She was angry with him.

"Is his wife your friend?" I asked.

She answered, "I know her, but she's not around much."

"I had no idea he was married," I told her. "He hadn't told me."

"Check your phone bills when they come because Flip is famous for using his girlfriend's dime to call his wife," she snarled.

Great.

Debbie reassured me, "It is only your innocence that kept you from knowing what he was really like. You're gonna be fine; you're a smart girl."

She was an angel—another staple I could count on in my life, a guardian angel in a crucial moment. I needed her. God must have a soft spot for me.

Sure enough, lengthy, expensive calls had been made to L.A. when I checked my phone bill. He'd spent over $35 to call his wife on two separate Sundays at my place.

Once Debbie let me off at the train station, I assured her I would be fine. I thought I would be, anyway, until I tried to purchase a ticket and couldn't read the sign with the fares listed or count out the Canadian money. I was still tripping. This was not easy. It took me a long time to sort out something simple. Eventually, I asked a young, cute guy to help me. He did. I didn't expound on my condition. I got the ticket and found a pay phone.

I called Leo and Larry. The minute I heard Leo's voice, I burst into tears again.

"I'll be arriving at 6:30, and I will tell you what happened," I told them. "I'm too high on LSD right now and too upset because Flip was with another girl and I found them in his bed." I wept. "Can you pick me up at the train station in Montreal?"

"Yes, darling, of course we will! Is there anything else you need?"

"I need Mike," I said. I only wanted to see my sweet new beau who called me "Sunshine." They asked for his number, and I gave them the name of his hotel.

That two-hour train ride in the Canadian sunset was one of the weirdest journeys of my life. I smoked an entire pack of Dunhills. I was crashing hard, and those cigarettes were the only things keeping me grounded. They tasted awful, but my soul was slipping with the sunset. I was internally speeding, my heart and mind racing, crashing. I was flitting here and there. It was exhausting. Was this a metaphor for my life? I was so afraid that I would slip away somehow if I didn't smoke.

The combination of no sleep, crashing from my LSD trip, the devastating emotional journey, and the loss of my virginity to a chump was just too much. It was more than I could handle. I needed something to touch, something familiar, safe. It wasn't until I saw Leo and Larry's shining faces at the Montreal train station that I began to fold. A fractured girl, I stumbled off that train into the arms of my two best friends. Once their strong arms were around me, I nearly swooned. Tears spilled over from all of us.

They hailed a cab and we made our way back home. They held me while I cried, gave me lemonade, and lovingly listened while I recapped the day's events through choking and tears. They insisted we get some soup and that I get some sleep. They were two of the most loving human beings ever. When we reached our comforting brownstone there was Mike. When I stumbled out of the cab, I fell into yet another solid set of arms.

"Hey, Sunshine," he said, "it'll be okay. I'm here." And he was.

After having soup with us, Mike stayed at my apartment until I fell asleep. He set my alarm clock before he left for the club to play, and I woke up somewhere around three the next afternoon. I felt like hell! My soul was immediately renewed when I awoke to find croissants in a bakery box on the coffee table, along with a little note from Leo, Larry and "Mother."

"The croissants are from Mother, but we will have fresh coffee for you when you wake up. Come on up!" the note read.

"Do these guys ever work?" I wondered.

I felt so loved. I showered, dressed and went up. Leo was there with coffee and dinner. We hugged and talked. We ate, and I felt better. The love these guys showed me represented the amazing grace that lit every dark

8. Sexy Psychedelics, 1970

turn of my life's journey. No matter what I went through, someone was always there for me immediately.

Feeling blessed, not cursed, I was able to pull myself together and go to work at six and do two shows. Backstage felt safe to me, familiar. I had become much closer to three of the sweetest, older girls in the show: one American, one Canadian, one British. I had bonded with them on a whole new level. They had rallied behind me and made sure I had a doctor, birth control, knowledge about sex and womanly life lessons. We didn't just bitch about our injuries from the can-can any more. We had quiet, grown-up conversations about men, love and sex. I'd graduated into the world of womanhood that had not been there when I had arrived, a virgin. I guess I have Flip to thank for that. And Barry Lee, of course.

9

Beauty and the Beast, 1970

Comforts and cuddles filled my next few days with Mike. My desire to have sex didn't emerge with my affections. I guess I needed some time. He was always okay with whatever I needed.

With the sameness of the show and the newness of my quickly approaching nineteenth birthday, I found contentment, even though the heartbreak of lost innocence was upon me.

I awoke the following morning to yet another gift from the magical elves in my building. Two dozen rainbow-colored carnations, with a card from Leo, Larry and "Mother" wishing me a happy birthday! Calls came from my folks, brothers and grandma back home. The girls in the show brought me a cake and gifts.

I loved it all. This day helped calm the beast living inside me: anger. It lurked around each corner and occasionally brought bursts of tears with it, keeping me on edge. But for now, it was soothed.

For another week, I was dating Mike. He was the sweetest guy and placed no physical demands on me. I couldn't. He knew that. I wasn't a seasoned enough sexual being yet. My virginity was gone, and there was an adjustment period that I needed to experience before I could move on to the next lover. With Mike from Arizona, I returned to innocence.

Our relationship lasted a few weeks, and then he was gone, back out on the road. My birthday was over, and there I was, alone with my phone bill. I decided to call Flip. Those $35 worth of phone calls to L.A. were a lot of money in 1970. I'm not sure what the plan was when I dialed his number. I simply called, not knowing where this would go or what I would say. He must have figured I'd never notice, or even worse, that I'd never call the number on the phone bill! How dare he think I was such a doormat? Who the hell did he think I was?

I picked up that phone, I would reach Flip's wife and tell her about her seedy husband and his shenanigans in Canada! Not to mention their balance due on my phone tab.

It took me a long time. I smoked a few puffs of a joint. I dialed the number on the phone bill to L.A. The phone rang as I held my breath and covered the receiver.

"Hello," a sweet, maternal voice answered, laden with all the divinity of motherhood and simple human kindness.

I unexpectedly thought of my mom, betrayed for years by my dad—the womanizer. I felt no more anger. The beast was silent. I hung up the receiver, suddenly feeling like "the other woman." Oh, please, God. *No!* That was the last thing I ever wanted to be. How had my relationship with Flip led me to all these feelings about my mom and who I didn't want to be?

The beast growled; I let it roar. As it growled its soft, angry growl deep down inside the center of my being, I began to cry softly. I allowed my tears to soften the angry monster, and I vowed never to be a victim again!

* * *

It was the end of the summer of free Love, or simply the summer I lost my virginity. Sex and love were two different things, but not in 1970. I had been living in Montreal since early spring. The blossoms were in full bloom. There were blossoms in my hair. My body and talents as a dancer were blossoming, just as my virginity had been in full bloom, ready for the plucking! Being a consummate professional, I devoured my job and slipped away for frolicking only after I put in a minimum of 13 performances per week.

I had worked in Montreal for nearly seven months when the company manager Colin Wilson called me in for a meeting one warm September morning. Being the paranoid child of 19 that I was, I thought I had to be in trouble for something. But what?

Approaching the opening of the new fall spectacular, the show was designed around our new principal dancer, Pearl Ho, the exquisite Asian beauty who was some ridiculous height, like 5'5". Which meant that the two 5'9" showgirls in the production, me being one of them, were being shipped off to one of the world's most exclusive resorts: Paradise Island, Bahamas. Tibor Rudas decided the Czechoslovakian blonde Eva and I were just too tall for the new Montreal show. We were going to perform in his largest show to date, "Casino de Paradis"!

I was pissed off! I had just signed another six-month lease on my luscious brownstone on Lincoln Avenue. Being young, uninformed, inexperienced and a bit of a drama queen, I said, "No, thank you. I'll stay here!" Whoa! That was unheard of. No one said no to Tibor Rudas or Colin Wilson.

Colin looked deep into my wide, innocent eyes and proclaimed, "Then perhaps you'd like to go home?"

Oh, I saw how it was! It was their way or the highway. I felt as though he was unfeeling and cruel. I sat stunned, unable to speak. They had actually been plotting this all along.

"We'll send your landlord a letter," Colin added calmly. "You'll leave in two weeks for Paradise Island in the Bahamas."

"But my friends are here, now...."

He looked at me coldly and said without flinching, "That's show biz."

Oh my God! I thought, This man is heartless. How could he treat my newfound happy life with such disdain?

"Can you at least give me a few days to go see my family in Illinois? Please?" I asked.

"Oh, all right," he said, "three days!"

I don't know where that request came from, but I had to get something out of this raw deal.

I simultaneously learned to negotiate and become accustomed to very short visits home.

Little did I know what lay before me.

The hilarious thing about being sent to the Bahamas in 1970 was that I actually resisted moving to an exclusive island resort. Hello? Who knew about the "path of least resistance" at 19? Certainly not me! I guess at that age, things were just so new and novel; they simply had to be laden with drama. Each new experience carried so much weight and responsibility, I couldn't help but react.

I packed, said my goodbyes, cried leaving a few dear friends, and traveled to Illinois for a much-needed three-day family reunion. After which, I finally embarked on my journey to exquisite Nassau, Bahamas. I don't think I could have possibly fathomed what I was about to experience.

As the little plane I boarded in Fort Lauderdale approached the Bahamian Islands, with every mile of aqua-teal sea that lay beneath me glistening in the sun, I magically released the past. So much so that once we prepared for landing, Montreal and any ties to my life there were never pined for again. By the time we landed, I was sure I had died and was being delivered to Heaven.

The airplane door opened and I descended onto the tiny airport grounds. The tropical breeze gently lifted my hair. I was utterly smitten, immediately. The lazy palm trees, the sparkling eyes and bright smiles of the Bahamian people filled my soul with warmth and familiarity.

I distinctly remember the way the island air smelled as I passed through customs. This island had an aroma like warm tide and tropical shellfish. Like tropical breezes with a steamy portion of humidity on the side. I loved it. This weather suited my soul.

I followed the instructions given to me by my line captain, Bobbi, and

9. Beauty and the Beast, 1970

Colin Wilson in Montreal. I hired a taxi to transport me to the Britannia Beach Hotel. The cab was an open jeep, military, rustic and rugged. I felt like I was on safari, rolling down dirt roads through lush tropics.

Since the Bahamas was a British Commonwealth, my driver pointed out several landmarks en route to our destination, combining his native tongue and a bit of a British sound to his dialect. I was not in Canada any longer. I allowed myself to sink into the essence of the island. It was calm, balmy and beautiful beyond my wildest imaginings. This had to be Heaven, or another planet. Not yet the busy tourist trap it has become in later years, but a rich and densely tropical oasis.

Perhaps the natural route from the remote airport to my destination was the Universe's way of welcoming me into this Heaven on earth. Although we passed several huts where Bahamian women were strolling while balancing baskets on their heads, the poverty didn't seem to equal unhappiness. The Bahamian people seemed peaceful and proud.

Could this really be the setting for my new life? How would I fare in this tropical culture? Would I fit in? Would I love it? Could I adapt to the heat? So many questions began to emerge, but I was rapidly brought back to the present moment with each turn of the bumpy road. I felt at home, like I had finally discovered my natural habitat. I had known my whole childhood that the climate of Illinois was not a good fit for my soul or my health. Montreal had been a wonderful place in the spring and summer, but I'm doubtful I would have liked another intense winter. I had always pondered life in a tropical, subtropical or coastal setting.

* * *

Several years ago, my daughter and I stayed at the RIU Hotel, adjacent to the Atlantis Hotel on Paradise Island. While vacationing there, I asked around and found out that the Atlantis Coral Towers were once part of the Britannia Beach Hotel, and our hotel, the RIU, was the Paradise Island Sheraton in the early 1970s.

Back to 1970! I took tennis lessons at the Sheraton courts weekly; the players who had a weekly game together just before my lesson were none other than Sidney Poitier and Harry Belafonte! The first time I saw them coming off the court, I was astonished at how extremely handsome they were. I recognized them immediately and swooned inside a little. At that time, they were vibrant 40-something celebrities and Nassau was their home. When I arrived for lessons, they would smile and nod. I'd say, "Hi." They were charming. I was melting and fan-girling inside.

10

Meeting the Legendary Barbara Beverly, 1970

Rarely are we conscious enough at a young age to know we are meeting a lifelong friend at the moment it is occurring. In retrospect, I can see the Divine intervention the instant I met my dearest friend, Barbara Beverly. When we met, Barbara was 20 and I was 19. We had both just arrived on Paradise Island to dance in the all-new multi-million dollar Tibor Rudas spectacular "Casino de Paradis."

As soon as my jeep arrived at the Britannia Beach Hotel, our Australian line captain Mikey (Bobbi's older sister) met me in the luxe lobby and said, "Welcome to Paradise. Mr. Rudas is going to have you watch the show tonight, and you can leave your luggage backstage until we sort out your lodging. The show starts in half an hour, and we have several dancers arriving tonight, so let's get you settled in to watch."

"I can't wait," I replied excitedly.

Backstage, Mikey tucked my bags into her office.

"Let me introduce you to the girl who just flew in from Los Angeles, and you two can watch the show together in the showroom in the casino."

"Okay, thank you," I replied, eager to see the current show. We walked briskly through the gorgeous Britannia Beach lobby down a long, balmy hotel hallway. We took a shortcut through the immense kitchen to the backstage dressing rooms. I was beyond excited to meet the dancers.

Mikey said, "I have to leave you here until the show starts because I have to go meet another girl coming in, so let's go get you settled before it starts." I loved how delightfully efficient she was! Off we went, back through the backstage wings into the kitchen, to the maître d's area. The elegant maître d' was charming in his tuxedo.

"You will be in good hands," Mikey told me. "Have fun. I'll come collect you after the show." She was off in a rush, unlike everyone else I had encountered thus far on this slow-moving island.

10. Meeting the Legendary Barbara Beverly, 1970

The maître d' said, "I have you in a booth near the podium and I will have a waiter stop by. Are you hungry?"

"Oh, no, thanks, I just ate on the airplane, but I will have a 7-Up please." He escorted me to the large booth at the back of the sparkling 1000-seat showroom theater where a very tall, thin, beautiful young blonde girl sat alone.

"Thank you," I smiled at the maître d', sliding into the booth, with the exceptionally beautiful blonde girl across from me. Immediately, a waiter came by and took our order for soft drinks and the blonde girl looked away, coolly. I got the feeling she wanted to ignore me, and then I realized she might be shy. As we waited for the curtain to go up, I wondered who she was.

After a moment, I asked, "Have you seen the show before?"

"No, I just got here. I just flew in from L.A.," she answered.

"Oh, you must be going into the new show, just like me!"

"Yes," she answered in a detached manner, "I am."

"So am I," I replied warmly. "I just flew in from Montreal. My name is Diane."

"Hi, I'm Barbara. I auditioned for Mr. Rudas in Las Vegas. You too?"

"No, I didn't. I have been a Rudas dancer for the last six months in Montreal, in the Caf Conc show."

"Oh, how was that?" Barbara asked, warming up.

"Good," I answered, "I was a covered dancer and recently became a nude. Mr. Rudas thought I was too tall for our show in Montreal, so he offered me a featured spot if I came down here to work in this new show. What about you?"

She replied, "He hired me to be the principal dancer in the new show. I was working in Vegas in a show with Gene Kelly, called 'Wonderful World of 30 Girls,' before I auditioned for the Rudas Dancers."

"Wow, Gene Kelly, what was that like?" I had to know. After all, Gene and I were born on the same day, and he was an idol of mine!

"Great, Gene was so nice to us. It was really fun. It was my first job," she told me.

"Oh, really? This is my second dance job, too! The Rudas show in Montreal was my first. I have been a showgirl in the show there for the last few months."

Suddenly the orchestra struck up the overture. Our attention was immediately diverted to the large stage as the showgirls came out. They looked outstanding when they pulled back the curtains and introduced the show, doing a French lip sync. It was a huge stage, and the theater was nearly full. Filling the seats were elegant-looking travelers who obviously had the means to attend a multimillion-dollar Vegas-like spectacular. It all felt glamorous and exclusive.

The show was good; it included the Rudas Acro-Ballet, basically dancing acrobats and showgirls and specialty acts with a touch of Vegas. There was a bit of Europe with some island flair. There was a fire eater who did the Limbo and danced to Bahamian Junkanoo music. The orchestra was great and the show was dynamic. I was impressed and felt the range of what the Rudas Dancers demonstrated in this show far surpassed the more intimate, artsy Toulouse-Lautrec style of "Le Caf Conc." The show in Montreal was extraordinary, but it simply wasn't this big.

Barbara and I drank our sodas and devoured every beat of the show. We studied and analyzed our new surroundings, completely enthralled. I am sure we were both imagining ourselves on that great stage in this exotic resort, wondering what our spots in the show would be. I was excited and grateful to have another new person here to start rehearsing and share the excitement with.

Once the show was over, Mikey came to collect us and took us backstage to discuss the plan for the evening. We were to go to the Britannia Beach Concierge and check into the hotel. Typically, Tibor Rudas provided charming trailers on Paradise Island, within walking distance of the hotel and casino; that was standard housing for the dancers until they found more personalized lodgings. Since the old show was still in progress and new girls were still arriving for the next production, we would have to wait for the current dancers to depart before a trailer would open up. A few other new dancers had already arrived from around the world and taken the last few rooms open in the trailers.

So, lo and behold, Barbara and I would have to become roomies in the Britannia Beach Hotel on the Rudas dime. Poor us … *not!* The hotel was pure luxury and we were situated three floors below its primary owner, Howard Hughes. He was right upstairs!

I really had discovered nirvana.

We were escorted to our hotel room on the sixth floor. Mikey had instructed us to report for rehearsal the next morning at 11 to meet the choreographer, new cast and crew. Naturally, many of the dancers in the existing show were staying on for the new one.

That night, Barbara and I truly bonded. I shared pictures of me in Montreal, and she showed me drop-dead gorgeous photos from her portfolio that she had shopped around in Los Angeles. We talked all night long, sharing stories of the boys we left behind. I talked about my first love, Blase, my first lover, Flip, and my sweet knight in shining armor, Michael. She told me about dating Dean, of Jan and Dean, in Los Angeles. Jan and Dean was a popular 1960s "surf music" singing duo, with such chart successes as "Surf City," "Little Old Lady from Pasadena," "Popsicle," "Dead Man's Curve," "Drag City," and "Ride the Wild Surf."

10. Meeting the Legendary Barbara Beverly, 1970

Barbara broke Dean's heart when she went to Vegas to work on the Gene Kelly show. She struggled with telling me the story.

"I felt so bad, mostly because he had not only lost *me*..." Barbara choked, barely able to keep from crying. "...But also his partner Jan, who lost mobility in a bad car accident in Los Angeles."

She went on, "I had a more current boyfriend in L.A. named Jimmy whom I left to come here to pursue my own career." She cried a bit, then she seemed to recover with, "Why do you fall for guys with weird names?"

We laughed. Her timing was hilarious. I liked Barbara. She was sensitive and funny! We chatted well into the night.

The next morning, on the balcony of our hotel, we gazed down at the beautiful Shangri-La before us. We chuckled over possibly having died and gone to Heaven. We pinched one another to confirm we were actually alive in this amazing place.

We didn't discuss Jimmy, Flip, Montreal or Vegas again. Our new life in Paradise consumed and thrilled us. We became best friends after living in three countries and four cities together, and I can honestly say we never had reason to look back at those first loves we lost. We became jet-setters and met the most extraordinary people. We had the most glamorous international experiences two girls could ever dream of.

I'll refer to Barbara many times throughout this book. I might also mention that we both reside in Southern California currently and still see our dancer friends from our escapades as often as possible.

We will always be friends. Nothing will ever alter that. How often can one attest to that in a lifetime? Barbara is my touchstone. All perspectives and timelines in my life since 1970 refer back to Barbara. She is the only person in this memoir whose private life I asked permission to discuss.

After all, that is what life with legends is about. You will learn for yourselves what I mean by the legend known as Barbara Beverly as we continue on this path of friendship, dancing, hijinks and folly!

* * *

Since our producer had lodged us in the Britannia Beach Hotel, we decided to partake of their complimentary Continental breakfast before heading to our first rehearsal at 11 a.m. with Ron Walker. Ron was well known for his work in Vegas and on the Caf Conc show I had just concluded.

It was a beautiful tropical morning, and the hotel dining room was exquisite. It overlooked the Caribbean, swathed in turquoise, coral and white linens with real silver. Everything was very posh, untouched by the tourist traffic of today, void of theme park consciousness. We were immersed in Caribbean dynasty.

To my amazement, twig-like Barbara Beverly could eat like a strapping lumberjack. She consumed a four-course breakfast with ease.

I had tea and a fruit cup.

How could she be that thin after downing half the breakfast menu? I was officially jealous because I wished I could eat the delicious omelets, bacon, muffins with jam, croissants with butter, and fruit!

When we left the restaurant and stepped into the elevator, we were joined by a very unusual-looking elderly man. He leaned against the elevator's corner, looking down at the floor. He looked slightly off, with long, brittle white hair nearly covering his face. Barbara pressed the button for our destination. I noticed the only other button glowing was the ninth floor. Sneaking a look from the corner of my eye, I noticed the man's extremely long fingernails, summer suit and white canvas shoes. Nothing seemed out of place, except perhaps the unusual odor in the elevator. I'm not even sure what I smelled. I was still adjusting to the environment, having only arrived yesterday. I dismissed the musty odor, since many of the hotel hallways were filled with a rich "beachy" scent. It was soggy and salty, especially the ones at the lower level where we boarded the elevator.

Arriving on our floor, we exited the elevator. I was about to laugh out loud at the oddity of the moment when I felt Barbara's hand grab my arm.

"What?" I asked.

She was aghast when she exclaimed, "Do you know who that was?"

"No, do you?" I answered.

"That was Howard Hughes," she gushed. "He lives on the ninth floor. I read it in the papers in Los Angeles."

"*The* Howard Hughes?" I inquired, flabbergasted.

"Yes! Yes!" she added urgently.

"Wow!" I was aware of who he was. I just didn't realize he was here. Ironically, two or three days later, I got a letter and newspaper clipping from my dad stating that the infamous Howard Hughes had taken up residence on the entire ninth floor of the Britannia Beach Hotel as he struggled with his disease.

Mr. Hughes spent the more significant part of his last five years of life on Paradise Island, which means he had probably watched the show in the showroom at some point. He liked showgirls, too. Well, he preferred actresses, ultimately. Although, by now, I am sure he was beyond his playboy days.

I rode the elevator with Howard Hughes in the Britannia Beach Hotel on an island owned primarily by him and Huntington Hartford, heir to the A&P fortune. In their heyday, they were kings. To me, they were just weird old rich guys. Barbara saw them slightly differently, but I was entirely too self-absorbed at 19 to give old rich guys the time of day.

10. Meeting the Legendary Barbara Beverly, 1970

Once Barbara and I arrived at our first rehearsal for the new show, all of the dancers, new and old, assembled onstage. Mr. Rudas was there, with Lee and Ron Walker. The company was a combination of acrobats, covered dancers and showgirls or dancing nudes. Mikey, our line captain, greeted us and said that Mr. Rudas would announce each of our roles in the new show soon. They were waiting for one more girl to arrive before starting the meeting and announcements. Mikey was just as adorable and charismatic as her younger sister Bobbi. I wondered, what's with the boy names? Did Australian fathers want boys? Or were boys' names common for girls in Australia?

These sisters had grown up in the Rudas dance studios in Perth and had trained to become professional acrobats. Mikey was nearly 40 and both she and Bobby were covered dancers. Their acrobatic days were over and they had taken on the role of line captain. They were responsible for keeping the show details and performers up to par once the choreography was completed and the show had opened. They were also responsible for all company details and communications with dancers regarding their overall professional status, weight, health and weekly rehearsals. They sometimes trained dancers who came in to replace girls who had left after the show had opened.

A tall, attractive young redhead arrived with luggage in tow and joined us onstage. Her name was Tracy. Her flight had been delayed. Mikey escorted her into the fold and Mr. Rudas began to discuss the new show.

Barbara was the principal dancer, and Tracy was a featured dancer. The featured dancer would have one solo in the show and be one of four dancing nudes. Her solo was a Jean Harlow number, and she would lip sync "I Can't Give You Anything But Love." The nudes would wrap up that number by becoming an entire line of Jean Harlows, who joined her onstage in a diva-driven dance routine with cigarette holders, platinum wigs and furs.

The remainder of the new show included a space number, a Russian number and the Magic Screen. There was a traditional can-can with the acrobats doing amazing gymnastic feats like triple backflips, backbend kicks and high-energy acrobatic tricks. This was all challenging work. Most of those girls were extremely petite, like Leah, a young acrobat from my hometown who had been hired at an audition that Mary Lou had arranged.

We learned that, once rehearsals were underway, we would shoot a film on the beach that would play on the all-new "Magic Screen." The Magic Screen was Mr. Rudas' big vision for the show. It worked like this: A movie screen as wide as the stage would descend silently between numbers. It was made of heavy-duty elastic strips about four inches wide. The screen strips opened, and the movie projected onto the large screen.

We started out as beautiful mermaids sunning ourselves on the Paradise Island beach. Suddenly, something magical happens: Tropical winds begin to blow, we mermaids start to retreat and we lose our tails, finding ourselves with legs. We were nymphs frolicking by the sea in flowered pasties, G-strings and new legs. We ran toward the audience and vivaciously popped through the Magic Screen onto the stage, where we completed our romp with a lively island nymphette dance number.

Diane on Paradise Island shooting the Magic Screen movie for the Casino de Paradis show, 1970.

The beauty of this ridiculousness was that we were the girls in the movie *and* the girls onstage. Five of us, Barbara and the four nudes. We didn't begin shooting the movie until rehearsals for the rest of the show were completed and the Magic Screen had arrived and been assembled.

One or two days into rehearsals, Tracy decided to leave the show. She wasn't happy. Mr. Rudas allegedly had given her the impression she would be the principal dancer in this production, but she was actually a nude with one featured number and no extra pay. She would be making the same money the other nudes made. The principal dancer does more work and makes $25 more per week.

I remember speaking with Tracy that first day of rehearsals. I guess she knew that Barbara and I were roommates and she asked me lots of questions like, "Was Barbara hired in Vegas to be the principal dancer in this show?" "Has she been a lead before?" "Where else has she danced?" And on and on. Awkward!

I suggested she ask Barbara these questions. According to Tracy, Mr. Rudas had promised them both the principal spot. I could see she was disappointed once he assigned her the understudy position for Barbara. Tracy was a nice person who had been duped by the organization. I didn't blame her for being upset. Barbara and I both empathized with her.

10. Meeting the Legendary Barbara Beverly, 1970

The situation put Barbara in an even more awkward spot. She shut down a little after that, not knowing who to trust. She disappeared into historical novels for a time. I reassured her she was too fabulous to be replaced! Mr. Rudas rarely played the bad cop; he had Lee do it. She had no problem giving critiques to people in our shows or even manipulating them emotionally. At least, that's how she came across to me.

I don't know what actually went down or how Tracy left, but there we were, about to begin rehearsing the Jean Harlow number, when Mr. Rudas announced to Mikey that Tracy had left. He didn't know what to do about the empty spot in the show. Having been downwind of that conversation with Mikey, my very bold, young, ambitious self stepped into that moment with, "I know the number and would be happy to fill in while you decide what to do, Mr. Rudas."

I had already learned the choreography and lip sync. I knew the entire song and most of the choreography she'd been given.

"Wonderful, of course," Mr. Rudas replied. "Diane will fill in; let's go."

Here was my opportunity to show him what I was made of. I would do it like Tracy had never done it. Although she had been a masterful technician, I prepared to blow their minds. I would serve my best Jean Harlow impersonation with a little Fanny Brice chaser!

Mr. Rudas and Ron Walker went to the sound booth to watch. I was trembling but not scared. This, in my mind, was me stepping into my destiny as an actress. I took the bull by the horns!

The orchestra began, and I took my place outside the set door of the 1920s club entrance.

I emerged in the dark and posed in the doorway. The hot, close-up spotlight hit my face, and the song began. I started lip-syncing perfectly, cigarette holder in hand. I dazzled them. Everyone backstage was watching from the wings, and dancers were scattered in the audience. They knew I was a ballsy girl, but they didn't know how much I loved this number and what I could do with my acting skills.

I performed most of the choreography Ron had given Tracy until the other three girls came on behind me, merging into the dance routine. Instead of doing the original choreography, I sexily dropped the sequined pink coat with black fur trim and dragged it behind me on the stage floor. We performed with coats and props over our leotards and tights during rehearsal. But for the actual show, we'd wear a black sequined jumpsuit. I moved in precision with the other dancers until they exited stage left, leaving me there for the final eight counts. I grabbed the curtain's edge when exiting the stage, adding a sexy slide through the two black velvet curtains separating the wings. Then I returned and winked into the spotlight before exiting with a blown kiss and a little back kick! The improvised bits were my own, and I knew they were a risk. Yet it flowed better and was sexier and cuter than anything Ron Walker had given Tracy to do.

Oh my God, did that ever feel good. This felt better than anything I had done as a professional! My heart was pumping. I was winded yet elated.

Barbara popped on and completed her darling Charleston number in her bright blue, fringed flapper costume. When the sequence wrapped up, for the first time ever, I heard thunderous applause clapping into a microphone in the booth. Everyone onstage and backstage joined in, and the dancers in the audience stood up. Tibor Rudas spoke into the microphone, "That's the best Jean Harlow we've ever seen. Diane is our new Jean Harlow."

Diane backstage in Casino de Paradis as Jean Harlow, 1970.

11

Enduring Paradise, 1970

Performing that Jean Harlow number 13 times a week kept me going strong for a good four months. I was happy, fulfilled and excited to do the show each night. After a while, I began to understand why the girls who had been on the island for years kept telling the newbies, "Find a boyfriend, or you'll be bored out of your mind here."

Paradise Island in 1970 wasn't designed for ambitious chicks (like me) who liked to fill their days with creativity and fun, advancing dreams and channeling a never-ending reservoir of ideas. This island was captivating for relaxation. Perfect for chilling with your beloved. I had no beloved at this point. There were no classes to attend, no auditions, no clubs with bands playing aside from the shows in the hotel lounges.

So I started crocheting, decorating, eating, taking piano and tennis lessons, eating, going shopping, doing decoupage, eating, writing letters to everyone, going out to dance after the shows to private clubs, eating, going to the various lounge shows between my shows, collecting shells on the beach, trying health food for the first time, and did I mention eating?

Health was a major driving force in 1970; everyone was into it. I think the counterculture wanted to change the way everyone ate. That influence was upon us, especially with early macrobiotics. People would get off LSD or stop smoking pot. They'd do the brown rice diet to purify themselves. A lot of people converted to vegetarianism after doing acid: Feeling a sense of oneness with the universe made them want to stop eating animals.

Unlike my roommates, I didn't find the casino's Italian croupiers that interesting. They were far too short and a bit too machismo for me to date. But I did become friends with many of them. There were a lot of English croupiers and pit bosses. The good ones were taken, mainly by the dancers who got there before me. The island hadn't become commercialized yet. It was exclusive. Finding interesting people to date seemed daunting.

We lived amongst the tourists, winter international jet-setters, luxury cruisers and huge celebrities constantly coming and going. We spent a lot of time on the beach during the balmy days.

Australian pirates annually invited us to come party on their ship while in port in Nassau. Some of the Aussie girls went and had a blast. Just the word "pirate" scared me a bit. The Australian girls who did go described them more like "party pals." Think drinkers, adventurers and stoners. But what the heck is a girl to do with dudes who live on the high seas for a living?

We met the musicians who came in every few months to play the casino's two lounges while we headlined in the main showroom. Artistic and talented types drew me in. In retrospect, I fell in love with talent.

The cruise ships arrived on Tuesdays and Saturdays, and we were off on Mondays. I took a taxi with Barbara across the bridge from Paradise Island to the only movie theater in Nassau to see *Klute* starring Jane Fonda and Donald Sutherland. We settled into our seats in the small theater, snacks in tow. I had popcorn and a drink. Barbara had a half dozen snacks, as usual. We looked around the theater between the Junior Mints and Milk Duds, realizing we were the only white people in the place. This was the first time we found ourselves the minority in our entire lives. It was a Bahamian island, so it made sense, but it was interesting to experience for the first time.

Once the film was over, we went outside to catch a taxi back to Paradise Island. We had no luck, so we decided to walk to the bridge and maybe hitch a ride with someone we knew. That's how small the island was then. Everyone knew everyone. The walk to the bridge was a bit of a trek, and a few blocks before we reached the bridge, a black convertible MG pulled up with one of the cute Italian croupiers from the casino. In his Italian accent, he said, "Please let me give you both a lift to the island. You shouldn't be out walking alone at night. You stand out too much."

He swung the door open, and Barb and I looked at one another knowing we were Amazons compared to this tiny man.

"Thanks, we will," I replied.

"I am Piero." He smiled between drags of his cigarette. "I've seen you both in the new show; you are both very good, bella, bella. What are your names?"

Piero and Barbara began dating shortly after that.

Now that Barb had Piero, we still went out with a few friends and his extended social circle of croupiers and casino employees. But Barb and I didn't spend as much one-on-one time as we had. The brunette Australian showgirl Cheryl and I began to frequent the beaches and clubs quite a bit to sow some oats.

I must have sown too many oats: I was living La Dolce Vita and before you knew it, I was 15 pounds heavier! All of that Dolce caught up with me just as Mikey retired and Mr. Rudas recruited a new line captain-company

11. Enduring Paradise, 1970

manager and her husband. Gina and George moved there from Hungary (she was originally from New Jersey). They had married while in the Hungarian Circus as a featured act. At one time, they had been an adagio-acrobatic team. Now they had two small children.

Gina was an intense lass, nearly 40, and a working acrobat herself. She would manage the acrobats and the rest of the company. She had a way of delivering notes that had no filter. You need a better strategy than just saying whatever pops out of your mouth. I didn't respect her or want to work for her. I did because I liked my job.

One day, Gina said directly to me and loudly in front of everyone in the dressing room, "People don't pay good money to see fat girls." How could she? I mean, seriously? As if I didn't know my scale was tipping toward 140? Geez, Gina, you couldn't do that in private?

In addition to her rudeness, she was quick to send the acrobats to a doctor who prescribed large doses of pain meds, which they took while working night after night. This camouflaged their pain so they could keep delivering triple backflips twice nightly. Talk about *Valley of the Dolls*! That's the film that this scenario reminded me of.

"You're fat," Gina said. "If you don't lose ten pounds, you'll have to go to the fat doctor."

She continued to pierce through my psyche and demolish my self-esteem with every derogatory word. When I caught my breath, I hesitantly asked, "What will he do?"

"He'll give you diet pills," she spat out.

Harsh. Wow!

"I'll take his number, please," I insisted, "I'll just go now."

"Tell him Mr. Rudas sent you," Gina directed.

I did. It always felt shady, although the doctor was a young, handsome Bahamian man with a very upscale office and he presented himself professionally. Apparently, the rich and famous on the island (or visiting) also went to him. Including a very handsome leading man, Bahamian film and TV actor Calvin Lockhart, of *Cotton Comes to Harlem* and *Myra Breckinridge* fame.

I had a close encounter with him in the popular doctor's lobby. He was like a magnet, and I felt so pulled into whatever his force field was that I barely remember our introduction or words. After we had chatted a bit, he said he'd see me around the casino sometime as he was there often and now had a reason to visit more frequently.

This man was all swag and gorgeousness and charm. I hadn't been in the presence of someone like this since Blase. His sexual energy was so gigantic that I had to try hard not to swoon or drool when I saw him. He put a spell on me! I wanted this man with every fiber of my being. This was a new emotion for me. The connection was beyond my 19-year-old experience, but I certainly wanted to expand my knowledge with him. I felt like Calvin was Zeus sent from all the gods and goddesses to restore my feminine wiles after Gina's demeaning comments about my body.

I was prescribed two Black Beauties (a combination amphetamine drug) a day and one sleeping pill for nighttime, and told to come back in eight weeks for a checkup. Black Beauties are prescribed under the trade name Biphetamine 20 and contain ten milligrams of amphetamine and ten milligrams of dextroamphetamine. They gained popularity as diet pills. Although this did seem practical to some extent, the use of the drug gradually shifted. Misuse of amphetamines can have serious health consequences, including addiction, cardiovascular problems and mental health issues. Therefore, it is essential to use amphetamine drugs only under a healthcare professional's guidance and to follow the prescribed dosage. The combination of amphetamines and dextroamphetamine is potentially dangerous without proper medical supervision as both are stimulants and can be responsible for elevating the heart rate and blood pressure.

Black Beauties gained a whole new level of popularity during the 1960s and '70s. The appetite-suppressing pill became well-known among those looking to experience a sense of euphoria or to increase their alertness. In 1965, it became illegal except when prescribed, and with the passage of the Controlled Substances Act in 1970, its usage started to decline. According to the website drugs.com, Biphetamine 20 was removed from the market in 1998.

I began this regimen and set out to lose some weight. I stopped eating completely. My appetite disappeared. I lost weight rapidly and I was speeding nearly every day, accomplishing a lot! Gina was happy, not nice or anything, just happy that I wasn't "fat" anymore. She didn't even say it, but I asked her after a month how I looked onstage. "Oh, fine," she replied.

"I lost ten pounds in a month," I mentioned.

"Good, keep going!" she exclaimed.

"I will!"

Although it was becoming harder to sleep each night, still, I was determined to be very thin. It felt great. For the time being, anyway.

I needed new outlets for my newfound energy! So I began frequenting the lounge shows between my nightly performances. I met the current lounge singer, Clint Holmes, his amazing band and his manager Ziggy. I became friends with Smith, his keyboard player, and we discovered we had a lot in common. We began smoking some weed together on the beach on our day off. He also went to a yoga camp with me. Yes, I learned yoga in 1970 while speeding on Black Beauties. Talk about an oxymoron.

The Paradise Island yoga camp was cool back then. I often saw Peter

11. Enduring Paradise, 1970

Max's psychedelically painted plane parked on the property. From time to time, the Beatles stopped by to take yoga classes with Swami Ken. I wasn't fortunate enough to run into any of them, but I heard stories from the swami and others. There was nothing formal or organized about the yoga camp. Jet-setters and wealthy hippies stopped by any time, just like Smith and I did, all searching for a spiritual path. I loved yoga, even if I was speeding while exploring hatha yoga. Even the Beatles were tripping on acid when they visited the Maharishi in India.

I began growing a crush on Smitty. He was so cute, definitely my type. He was from San Francisco, making him even more attractive to me! We occasionally shared my Black Beauties. We had fun doing just about anything. Once we were speeding on the Black Beauties, we would color in my coloring books for fun or romp on the beach and laugh. But it seemed like he had the hots for Cheryl, the gorgeous, brunette Australian showgirl. She was my good friend, so Smitty and I stayed friends, although we spent a lot of time together. I wondered why Cheryl refused to go out with him. After all, she was single, and he was hot.

Barbara and I were about to move from the trailers to new apartments. We decided to have a big party on a Sunday night at the beach trailer park for everyone. We each made our go-to party dishes. The pot luck included our cast, crew and new friends.

Shortly after the party started, Smith asked if I wanted to go smoke a joint with him. I did. We wandered down the beach to do just that. Upon our return, Cheryl was fuming. When I asked her what was wrong, she said that Smith had hit on her, and she told him she didn't date guys who only wanted one thing and who had no intention of taking her on a proper date! "And now he's going off getting stoned with you!" she exploded on me.

Wow! Cheryl had it all figured out! She tried to make me feel bad.

In typical Cheryl fashion, she wanted to leave the party and go home. I adored her, but she was in a snit, and off she went.

I felt bad and asked Smith what had happened. He said, "She's not fun like you."

Whoa! Okay, so yeah, we did have fun. But Cheryl was my friend.

He proceeded to tell me that what he wanted was a girlfriend like me, who was fun, cool, and sexy. Girlfriend? Who knew? So my first love affair began on the island. I fell for him, and we had a good time together for two whole weeks. At first, it didn't dawn on me that I was his second choice. Once I let that sink in, it hurt me. I knew so little about relationships at that point that I had excused his bad behavior.

I decided I wouldn't sleep with him. I wanted to prove to Cheryl that she was wrong. He wasn't a player, and he wanted me for me! Keep in mind that I was 19 and very high on diet pills.

My rationale was not up to snuff during that time, and Smitty was not a mature guy. He was a 25-year-old who loved the chase. The more he had to wait for what he wanted, the more he wanted it. He had been talking about "us" being "us" after he went back home to Washington D.C., and I was up for the long game.

12

Insomnia, 1971

Before Smith left the island, he came to see my show, along with Clint's manager Ziggy. We gathered for cocktails after the show. I was sad and teary saying goodbye to Smith. I didn't have any control over my emotions in those days. I did perk up when Ziggy mentioned how funny he thought I was in the Jean Harlow number. He said I had excellent comedic timing onstage. I appreciated the compliment.

"I adore comedy," I told him. "It's my thing."

Ziggy said, "I manage several female stand-up comedians in DC."

Impressive, I thought.

"Do you do stand-up?"

"No, I've done a lot of comedy in the theater and studied brilliant talents like Barbra Streisand and Shirley MacLaine, but I hadn't considered stand-up."

"If you do come to D.C., let me know. Female stand-up comics are big business there." He handed me his business card.

I thought to myself, with so many free hours on my hands, this island would be a great place to write an act. It would also burn some of the endless nervous energy I had from the Black Beauties. He had sparked my interest.

Smitty and I pulled an all-nighter that night on the beach. We watched the sunrise over the magnificent Caribbean. I still hadn't had sex with him; something had happened to my libido. I surmised it was the diet pills. In retrospect, I know it was, because I was very attracted to beautiful Smith. He understood and seemed okay with it. We found other fun ways to stimulate one another aside from intercourse. It was disturbing to know the pills were having this effect on me, yet I was still so new to sex that it didn't bother me. I wanted to wait to have sex, I didn't want to rush. I did enjoy the foreplay, however.

We'd only had two weeks of glorious fun. But their time on the island was complete. Smith returned to Washington, D.C., to play in Georgetown for the summer. We made plans to continue our relationship despite the distance. That was my first experience having a long-distance relationship. It felt like dating a ghost.

I was entirely lost when he left. The island suddenly seemed desolate. I was still speeding on diet pills, and I was quite thin. I'd never been that skinny in my adult life. At 5'9", I weighed in at 118 pounds a few weeks after Smitty left. I was gaunt, but my body looked stunning. It was becoming nearly impossible to fall asleep at night. I was struggling with the wretched medication.

Mr. Rudas came to check in on the show and saw me. He was thrilled and told me to stay thin for the show. "You have never looked better!" he exclaimed.

Right! No worries, I'll just keep jeopardizing my health for you, Tibor! Ugh. I'm not even certain I understood that I was choosing his show over my health. The diet pill regimen was approaching its sixth week, and

Diane, very thin, in the opening number at Casino de Paradis.

I wondered if I would ever sleep again. The stress of insomnia and missing Smith was genuinely overwhelming. How would I go on like this? I felt completely fragile and didn't recognize myself any more. It felt like I had abandoned my own soul.

Smith called me backstage about once a week and wrote occasionally. He missed me, too. Or so he said.

Barbara had been packing her things in our trailer, preparing to move in with Piero, when she became extremely concerned with my condition. Tearfully, she confronted me on a night when I was suffering from insomnia: "I'm worried about you, Di. You just aren't yourself anymore. I think you need to stop taking these pills."

I was touched by how much she cared, but I wasn't ready to stop them yet. I wanted to complete the eight weeks the doctor had prescribed.

Barbara cried softly, "I feel like flushing all your diet pills. I don't want to move away and leave you here like this."

The lack of sleep made me react irrationally. I got mad at her and insisted I would be finished with the prescription in a week or so. But I did hear her, and when I went to my room that night, I too wept. I knew this prescription had taken a toll on me mentally, physically and emotionally. I wanted to be thin more than I wanted to be healthy. The naivety of a 19-year-old was alive and well in me.

I had to find a way to sleep! I took an extra sleeping pill that night (well, early morning, actually), and finally fell asleep around dawn. My friend cared more about me than I cared for myself.

* * *

I was depressed and high, speeding, and feeling disconnected from everyone and everything. I only felt alive when I performed on stage. It certainly wasn't enough to call it a life. I missed Smitty so much!

They say Hemingway was depressed and drunk most of the time as he forged his brilliant novels. The only thing found in my journals from that distorted period of my life were dismal, suicidal tendencies. Anyone who really knows me knows I am naturally very upbeat, positive, goal-oriented and fun! But I wasn't then, not at all. I was a hot mess.

Once I had completed the eight-week prescription of diet and sleeping pills, the fat doctor told me to stay on it for one more month to maintain my weight and then come back. He also added another sleeping pill nightly. Oh my God. Seriously? How? Why? What would I do? I hoped that it would help me sleep, but what would another month of this do to me?

I slept a bit more, but not enough to unearth my real personality. I managed to crochet an entire dress, glue millions of tiny seashells I had spent hours collecting on the beach onto cigar boxes, creating fetching jewelry boxes for my friends and relatives. I even wallpapered my bathroom. Still, I was horribly depressed and out of it in daily life.

One night in the dressing room, we were informed by the showroom maître d' that Mick Jagger and Bianca were seated down front for the dinner show. You certainly couldn't miss him in his white tuxedo with large plastic baby blue polka dots and bow tie. That lifted my spirits a bit until Tina (a 19-year-old British dancer) and I saw him between shows in the casino. We waited patiently to approach him until he finished his game at the otherwise empty craps table. We had our stage makeup on, and we weren't gushing at all. We were quite civilized and polite when we asked for his autograph.

"I really don't want to start anything," he said in his wry, thick-lipped British accent. Tina and I looked around; there were no more than three or four elderly couples in the whole casino. Not one of them was looking our way. Bianca smiled as Mick led her away from us!

Why? He didn't like our show or what? I haven't asked for an autograph since.

I was walking back to the dressing room in the hallway backstage, when I noticed flyers posted on each door announcing a workshop for performers. I grabbed one, shoved it in my dance bag and read it the following morning:

> Calling all performers! Join us for a four-week workshop featuring Singers, Dancers, Actors, Comedians, and Specialty Acts. Master Instructor, Prentice Minner, guides you to the performances of your life! Final performance and showcase in the Paradise Island Hotel Lounge. If interested, meet in the Lounge next Thursday afternoon.

At the bottom of the flyer, I read, "See Prentice Minner nightly in the lounge at 9:00 and 11:30 p.m."

The following Sunday night, I saw his show. It was really good. I'd never heard of him, but he seemed popular. I introduced myself to him after the show. He was extremely engaging. I liked him.

"What are you doing on the island?" he inquired.

"I'm a showgirl in the main room show 'Casino de Paradis.'"

"That's exciting. What other talents do you possess?"

"I'm an actress, and I love comedy," I told him. "I'm very interested in learning stand-up comedy, although I haven't done it."

"Then I think you will love this upcoming workshop and showcase. We can help you write your act."

We had an instant connection. I also liked his stage manager and we all chatted extensively. I asked more about his workshop. He broke it all down for me. It sounded intriguing, and it was only $100 for two afternoon classes per week for the next four weeks until showcase night. He confirmed that agents and managers from New York, Miami and D.C. would be there.

"Sounds great to me," I said excitedly. I liked Prentice; he had wonderful energy.

Ziggy had said that he'd love to see me do stand-up. I could do this, and then I'd have two reasons to go to D.C. Smitty and I had been debating the possibility on our weekly phone calls.

Prentice said, "I look forward to seeing you Thursday."

There it was. I finally had something to sink my teeth into, something creative. There were new people that I had something more in common with than just dance. I wanted to do stand-up comedy, and I had ideas for it and was desperate for a creative outlet. I joined the workshop and created my stand-up act.

"Who was I?" was the first prompt I was given. Prentice was good. My act unfolded. I began creating jokes that explained what it was like being an international showgirl and a real girl ... with a parrot. I created an entire persona. I also performed impersonations of the tourists we met regularly. Mostly retired, heavily bejeweled Jewish Princesses from Miami and New York, and their Princes. My act was coming together. It was consuming all of my waking hours!

Prentice, his stage manager and I became very good friends. I had fun, creative, supportive friends and felt happy again. Prentice provided a light during a dark time. He was wonderful.

Our showcase night was quickly approaching. The colorful cast and I were anticipating it with excitement. Close to dress rehearsal, I decided on a very cool wig, a big curly 'fro the same color as my hair. I found the sexiest dress at a plush boutique in the hotel, where we received discounts: a light, nearly sheer midi-dress in black with a shimmering silver sparkle that picked up the lights and made me look drenched in diamonds. It had a deep, plunging V-neck.

I weighed about 115 pounds at 5'9" and I think it was the sexiest I've ever looked or felt in my life. I was still only 19 and still speeding. My act had a palpable rhythm when I presented it to our guests at dress rehearsal. Prentice nearly fainted. He said to me afterward, "Your dress is just slightly see-through, and watching you is like watching fireworks. I love it all!"

"Are you sure I should do this?" I asked, unsure.

"Oh, my darling, you were born to do this! You will generate a lot of excitement in many areas on showcase night."

"Okay, I trust you, coach," I surrendered. "Let's do this!"

"I want you to meet someone, a dear friend of mine who was here watching dress rehearsal with our guest audience today, and he asked about you." Prentice led me to the casino bar. "Who is it?" I questioned. I had no idea who could be asking for me, that Prentice knew.

"Oh, my darling," said Prentice, "he claims you've met, and he's an old friend of mine. You'll see!"

Oh, a surprise! A mystery! I was excited, and I like surprises.

As we entered the opulent, elevated round bar area, a very handsome, Bahamian man in his late 30s approached, dressed very elegantly. He looked familiar, but where had I met this arresting human being before?

Once he was in front of me, I immediately knew who he was. I had met the actor Calvin Lockhart in the fat doctor's lobby and recognized him from his films. His pheromones came rushing to meet me. He embraced me with every fiber of his being. I could barely breathe. I felt like he had ethereally entered my private space and positioned himself inside my solar plexus. All my chakras were spinning. He didn't let go of me; he held on.

"You are brilliant and beautiful, and I want you!" he whispered into my ear. I could barely speak,

"Hi, Calvin," I managed to respond. "You were in the audience at dress rehearsal today?" I grinned.

"I was, and I couldn't take my eyes off you. You are a star, you've changed, and you were so funny!" He whispered like a lover as he looked me over head to toe. He added, "Let's get you a drink. What would you like?"

"Dubonnet on the rocks with a twist, please," I whispered back. I was trembling. I was warm. I knew I had to sleep with this man. Calvin proceeded to the bar to get me a drink, escorting me by the hand. My libido had returned. I was under his spell and enchanted, to say the least. He had to be the sexiest man I'd ever met. I was aroused like never before.

I realized that Calvin was already a little drunk. I also suddenly remembered Smith. I had a boyfriend! How could I forget that? What just happened to me? Where had I been transported to?

"Why don't we go to my place and really see what the island is all about?" he suggested dreamily.

"I'm afraid I can't tonight, Calvin," I pouted. "I wish I could. May I take a raincheck?"

"Any time, but at least let me take you home. My driver is just outside the casino," he insisted.

"Of course, thank you," I smiled. I said goodbye to Prentice, who was grinning like a Cheshire cat.

How would I do this? I had minimal sexual experience, and I had a boyfriend. A boyfriend in Washington, D.C., for God's sake! Calvin Lockhart sexually frightened me in a way that no other man before or since has managed to do, frightened me in a way that turned me on. Was it because

12. Insomnia, 1971

he was so cocky and sensual, and I was so young? Or was it because he was famous, gorgeous, talented and rich? My mind was spiraling on that drive home. I did not want to say no to this man, but I had to be true to Smith in D.C., I had to; we were making plans for our future together. I couldn't just cheat on him. That is certainly not who I was, no matter how high I was on Black Beauties. I loved Smitty.

Calvin dropped me off at the dancer trailers and begged to come in. Those trailers had four separate entrances to each girl's room, and he now knew where I lived. I had a hard time saying goodbye. He was a gentleman and only kissed me, but it was a deep and hungry kiss. Oh my God. I was melting. I couldn't think. I might have enjoyed that kiss much more, but I was suddenly thinking of Smith and cheating wasn't seductive. I took myself right up to the edge with Calvin, to my door, with him caressing me suggestively. He leaned us into the door.

"I'm leaving for New York on Tuesday," he told me. "I won't be around for months. I'm shooting a film, and this can't wait." He glanced at his enormous erection, which was apparent in his tapered slacks.

"I can't, Calvin," I murmured breathlessly. "I have to go."

I extracted myself from his embrace and attempted to go inside. He fiercely pulled me back very close to him so that I could feel how aroused he was, hoping it would change my mind. I felt like we were in a movie—a very erotic one.

I somehow plucked myself from his embrace and we withdrew from one another, both of us aching with desire.

13

Success, 1971

There's something about comics who do their stand-up acts while they're high. Lenny Bruce did it. Many others were high on prescription and recreational drugs; it added a certain flavor to their act. Especially during the early '70s, the raunchy, uninhibited, hilarious Richard Pryor was stoned all the time. He had his own special sauce! His drug use became quite well known while on a freebasing binge during the making of a film. Pryor doused himself in rum and set himself on fire. He incorporated a description of the incident into his comedy show, *Richard Pryor: Live on the Sunset Strip* in 1982.

Several of the quirky and funny personality traits of comedians at that time were due to their recreational drug use. Many of them became more comic with the help of uppers.

I took an extra Black Beauty on showcase night. I wanted to make sure I could dance in my two shows on Thursday night and do my new act in between. Using the prescription drugs also offered me a speedy rush and a boost of confidence

Once the finale curtain came down on my first show, I rushed to change for the showcase. I made an announcement in the dressing room: "I want to invite everyone to my stand-up comedy showcase between shows, over in the Paradise Island lounge. It's free, and drinks are discounted for hotel employees." The girls said, "We'll be there, Di!"

"I had no idea you did this, too, Diane," Jeri, the assistant line captain, commented.

"It's the first time ever for me."

"Wow! That takes a lot of courage!" Jeri was always supportive.

They said they would dress between shows and be there! I wanted everyone to see my act. I was excited.

I touched up my stage makeup and put on red lip gloss. My wig in place, I slipped into the slinky black midi-dress and sexy heels that made me look six feet tall. I was ready. But where the heck were my boobs? They were disappearing. That couldn't be good for a showgirl! On the other hand, my mini-boobs did look outstanding in this dress!

The showcase had begun just a few minutes before our first show ended. Prentice had promised to have me go up late in the show since I had to manage this between my main room performances.

When I arrived in the lounge, I was dumbfounded; I had never seen the lounge filled. There were people in about 150 seats plus quite a sizable standing-room-only crowd. Incredible! I slipped through the crowd to stage left, where I saw Prentice. He introduced each performer before we went up. Most were singers, and his show band accompanied them. Everyone was presented very professionally that night. Some were actors, some were Junkanoo dancers, and there was even a Bahamian comedy duo who did magic.

Prentice smiled and hugged me before saying, "You will go on next to last, in the next 20 minutes."

Perfect. I looked around and saw that most of the room was full of well-heeled tourists and wealthy New Yorkers dressed to the nines. The rest were the families and friends of the artists in the showcase. Prentice whispered, "Everyone is loving this. They have been the best audience ever!"

"I am so excited. Thank you, Prentice!" I hugged him.

He added, "You will be out of here long before your second show starts!"

"I so appreciate that!" I whispered as I gripped his hand for courage.

Within minutes, my fellow showgirls began filling the small spaces still available around the room. Barbara and Joey, Jeri and Tina, Sandy, Teri, Gail, Cheryl and so many of the acrobats were there.

Prentice was right; this crowd was laying on the love to every performer going up to do their thing! Enjoying this as much as we were! Nurturing young talent had to be extremely rewarding for Prentice.

I got nervous and immediately turned it into excitement as Prentice introduced me: "The showgirl from the main room show, Diane Pirmann!"

Good God, I need a better name! My real name lacked pizzazz and felt flat to me. I didn't like it. I wanted a new stage name.

I ran up and performed perfectly. Was I good? At least it seemed like it! Most importantly, everyone laughed! Every joke seemed to land. What an amazing way to introduce my stand-up act. Everyone was so engaged. My fellow dancers were laughing, too! I even got a standing ovation after my set! I guess I did something right. I can't remember ever feeling more at home than I did here! Despite my foggy state of mind, I knew this could be my ticket off the island. My dreams ignited on that stage.

After the show, I mingled with several show biz people from Miami and New York, chatting and schmoozing for a while. A gentleman gave me his card and asked me to perform in the Catskills that summer. Geez! I enjoyed receiving all the accolades for my hard work, and then duty called. I had to get ready for our second "Casino de Paradis" show.

As Barbara and I dashed to the dressing room, she was completely mind-blown. "I can't believe you did stand-up. It was like watching another person. You were so funny! I could never get up and be funny and talk to people. That was incredible, Di!"

There's a reason she was my best friend.

"It felt good, but a bit of a blur. These diet pills alter my personality, for sure!"

"It sure worked for comedy," Barb replied. "Will you keep doing it?"

"I might, I suppose. I might go do it in D.C. I've been offered help by Smitty's manager."

"I don't want you to go, Di," Barb pouted. "Can't you do it here somewhere?"

"I need to get off this island, Barb. It's just not enough for me. I want to pursue an acting career, and I want to be with Smith! I need to go!"

My contract would end in about four months. I decided that night to go to D.C. as soon as it was up. I had to.

As we walked through the corridor between the lounge and the main showroom, people who had seen the showcase started congratulating me and encouraging me to keep up the good work. They were mostly strangers who were adorable, generous and complimentary. I loved receiving that from them.

* * *

The next few weeks were brutal. I couldn't keep taking these pills. I was losing it. I wasn't getting any thinner. I had stopped dropping weight at 115 pounds and my personality was deeply confused and spacey. I couldn't concentrate on more than my two shows a night. I gave a two-month notice to Gina and Mr. Rudas just before my contract was up. Smith had promised to find us an apartment in Georgetown. Clint Holmes and his band were on fire! Smitty and I stayed in touch, making plans for our future there. Ziggy asked for my résumé and headshot before I came. He also asked me to create three or four sets of my stand-up act.

I couldn't write comedy, though. My heart and soul felt heavy, not light and funny. I simply couldn't take these pills anymore! I was at my wits' end and desperately wanted myself and my clarity back. I wanted that to happen before I left for D.C. So, I flushed all my remaining diet pills down the toilet about a month before I was to leave. I had to end it, cold turkey!

13. Success, 1971

I had no idea how that would affect my sanity and immune system. I was clouded, fatigued, incoherent at times, moody and emotional beyond belief. One night, I was so annoyed with Gina's incessant complaining that I shouted at her. She shouted back, "It doesn't matter where you go; you'll still take yourself with you!"

"No shit, Gina." I couldn't deal with her dime store counsel.

They hired a new girl named Johnette to replace me. I was to teach her my part in the show. Teri asked to do my Jean Harlow number, and having been another long-time Australian showgirl for Rudas, he gave it to her. She was hilarious! I loved Teri. She had taken Barb's room in our trailer, so we were also roomies for a while. Teri made me laugh every day. Once I had decided to leave the island, I also decided to stay in the trailer instead of moving into an apartment.

Johnette was a warm soul, so adorable, and a great dancer. We became quick friends, so much so that I regretted not having more time to get to know her. The time for my departure was quickly approaching.

I was strung out detoxing from the *Valley of the Dolls* lifestyle I had lived for nearly three months. The nightmare was with me each night as I did my best to regain normal consciousness. I was mostly sleepless and when I did fall asleep, I wanted to sleep forever.

On one of those particularly sleepless nights, Teri knocked on my bedroom door around 1:30 and said, "There's a bloody good-looking, drunk Bahamian man knocking on all the trailer doors and calling your name!"

"Oh, God, no! Not Calvin, not now!" I whined. The next thing I knew, he was banging on my bedroom door from the outside. "It's a friend of mine," I told Teri. She asked if she should stick around, and I told her I'd be fine. Would I be?

Little ol' strung-out me had to deal with drunk, strong, arrogant, sexy Calvin Lockhart again. I was not looking forward to this and certainly did not need his drama right now.

I tried to keep him at the door, but he was quite drunk. He said he had to see me. He said he missed me the whole time he was in New York. Yeah, right. When people miss you, they stay in touch. I wasn't ready to wrangle with a drunk right now. It wasn't a turn-on. I didn't want to be with him in my state and certainly not in his.

I had to shock him. I shouted, "I am leaving the island in a week and moving to D.C.!" It was the only thing I could think to do to stop his aggressive nature.

"That's okay," he slurred, "This is now!"

"No. No, I can't, Calvin," I bellowed. "Now go, you can't just show up here whenever you want. I have a boyfriend!"

"Is he here right now?" he garbled.

"Just go! Get out!" I cried. I pushed him out of my doorway and slammed and locked my door. I seriously didn't care at that moment what he did. I vowed to myself never to be with a drunk, let alone sleep with one. I ran around, locked our doors, and eventually heard his car leave the trailer park.

I spent the rest of that exhausting night in a weepy haze, wondering if I would ever feel normal again. I had to get my shit together and start a new life away from this island.

14

Birds with Broken Wings Can Fly, 1971

I wanted my last week on Paradise Island to be special. The girls threw a little going-away party for me. Most of them knew what a rollercoaster ride I'd been on with the diet pills and no sleep. Many of them were struggling with similar situations.

My incessant foggy brain began to lift slightly, but the fatigue was still incredibly real. I decided to go to the yoga camp and see what it was like without prescription drugs being involved. I managed to get there several days each week and take yoga classes with Swami Ken. They were so rewarding. One day, he taught us to meditate. This was something that helped me the most. I wish I had learned this before 1971; it lifted me into a spiritual state I had longed for, something I had been seeking since age 13. This was the real connecting point for my healing.

I began to meditate daily while my consciousness took on an elevated level of awareness.

My dreams were sprinkled with higher consciousness lessons and images, and I began rising with the sun. Renewed. No matter what time I had gone to bed the night prior. We grasp little bits of enlightenment along the way. If all self-realization occurred at once, we would be overwhelmed. My true spiritual path began unfolding.

I awoke two mornings before my departure to D.C. at around six to what sounded like my mother's voice calling my name. I rose groggily and noticed a woman standing in my bedroom doorway. She had long dark hair and the sweetest smile.

She was glowing as she said, "I will be with you."

Wait? What? I wiped the sleep from my eyes, looked again and she was gone! What had I just experienced? Who was she? Why did she rouse me from my slumber? Whatever it was, it left me with an incredibly protected feeling. I found myself elevated beyond my five senses. This gentle interaction was from my lifetime guardian angel. I knew this beyond the shadow of a doubt. Was this the result of doing yoga and meditation every day? Years into my spiritual quest, I can wholeheartedly say, "Yes." This was a guardian angel showing me I was not alone on my journey.

It was my last night in the show. There were lots of tears shed backstage with my beloved dancers and friends. Especially Barbara. Oh, how I'd miss her.

Mr. Rudas called me on the backstage phone and said, "You are always welcome back, and if you ever need a job, please call me." He gave me his personal numbers. That was very generous. Maybe he appreciated my work ethic. Or maybe he shared my father's opinion of my plan.

A few days earlier, my dad and I had spoken on the phone and it went something like this:

"Dad, I want you to know that I have a boyfriend who lives in Washington, D.C., and his talent manager Ziggy has offered to possibly sign me and promote me doing stand-up comedy there. So I am leaving the show to go to D.C. this week."

"Do you have a contract with this manager?"

"Not yet. But he's very interested, and I have been doing stand-up comedy on the island in the lounge to a great response!"

"Where are you going to live and work?" he asked.

"I am going to live with my boyfriend Smith, and find work, possibly as a comedienne or an actress."

"What does this Smith do, and how old is he? I hope you aren't mixed up with some musician!"

"He plays keyboards for a well-known recording artist."

"Didn't I tell you to never get involved with musicians?"

Silence. I wasn't sure how to respond. Yes, he had warned me when I left Illinois. The last thing he said to me was a warning, "Don't get involved with musicians!"

My first thought was, "*You're* a musician." I felt he was a hypocrite.

"Jesus Christ, Diane. What the hell kind of plan is that when you already have a good job? Do you have money?"

"Of course I've saved money, Dad. I'm not an idiot," I sighed.

"You're only 19 years old. You don't know everything, and this just doesn't make sense to me."

"You're going to have to trust me, Dad. I know what I'm doing!" I groaned.

"I hope so. Just call home if you need anything, but I don't think this is a smart move."

There it was! Dad's fear of taking risks rears its head. That was the difference between us. I was destined to live a risk-taking life, and he and my mom were taught to believe that you had to play it safe. Have your ducks in a row!

14. Birds with Broken Wings Can Fly, 1971

Smith picked me up at the airport on a Monday evening. He was off that night. We embraced, kissed and gazed deeply into one another's eyes. It was so wonderful to see him again. It had been nearly four months. He'd grown a mustache. But I had changed a lot!

"Wow, look at you. You're so thin!" he exclaimed as he gave me the once-over.

"But no more diet pills!" I assured him.

The guitar player from Clint's band and his wife had offered us their guest room for the night since Smitty hadn't procured an apartment for us yet. We spent that night and most of the next day there. We made love. I still felt like a virgin, this being only the second time I had been with someone intimately. This time, it was someone I cared for, and he was sweet and gentle. We nested as long as we could, making sweet love one more time before he had to get ready for work. It was everything I'd dreamed of.

We packed, and he said to bring my luggage to the club. I asked where he had been staying this whole time.

"I've been crashing at a friend's studio apartment in Georgetown. But we can't stay there, so I think I have something worked out for us. I'll know tonight."

I believed him. We showered, dressed and went to the club where they were playing. A large dinner club venue, yet cozy at the same time. It was so good to see everyone. I was thrilled to see the drummer Dave and his wife Geri. We had shared cocktails and laughs several times in the Bahamas when Geri visited. We had really hit it off.

The first show was great. I sat in a booth with my 7-Up with Geri. Dave joined us for a bit between shows. He seemed a little stressed.

"Where is Smith?" I inquired.

"Ziggy is having an emergency meeting with him in the dressing room right now. I'm not sure when Smitty will be done, but let us buy you dinner. We get food here half price, and it's good."

"I'm really not hungry, but thank you." I wondered what Smith could be meeting Ziggy about. Something suddenly felt "off." Dave seemed fed up, but with whom?

"Did the meeting have something to do with me being here?" I asked Dave, knowing I could because he was a very "say it like it is" kinda guy.

"It might be," he suggested, "but I think it has more to do with the fact that Smitty's ex doesn't want you two living in her apartment!"

"His ex?" The feeling of something being "off" grew stronger.

"Yeah, Charlie Brown," Dave groaned. "He's still living with her even though they broke up."

"Charlie Brown?" I questioned.

Geri piped up, "She's a hippie, druggie songwriter who won't let go of Smith. She's not allowed in this club."

"Oh my God!" I cried, "Why the heck has he never mentioned her to me?"

Dave sighed and gave me a look that said, "If you only knew." The guitar player came over and told him that Ziggy wanted to see everyone in the band. I sat there, stunned, not knowing what to think or say.

Geri was warm, maternal and kind, assuring me it would all be okay.

"Smith is just a little immature and has a hard time taking charge of his life, and Charlie Brown is very difficult," she shared.

I didn't know Smith at all. Aside from the two short weeks we had gotten together before he left, everything else between us had occurred long distance. I felt confused and hurt that he'd never mentioned Charlie Brown to me. Who names their daughter Charlie Brown, for God's sake?

Smith came to our table about this time and said he needed to talk to me. Geri went backstage to take the rest of Dave's dinner to him in the green room. Smith slipped into the booth close to me.

"What the hell is going on, and who is Charlie Brown?" I asked.

Smith averted his gaze and sighed deeply before responding, "She's just an ex-girlfriend who doesn't want you and me to stay in her place while she's away for some reason."

"Why are you still living with her, and why haven't you told me about her?" I asked.

"Because I wanted to find a place for us and haven't been able to and because I sort of haven't completely left her yet!" he cringed.

"But you knew I was coming and said you'd have a place for us!"

"I just wasn't sure it was going to work out with us, baby. I'm so sorry." He couldn't meet my eyes. No one ever knows if anything is going to work out, for fuck's sake. This was disturbing. Is this really who he was?

"So, are we going to work out, Smith?" I implored in earnest.

"I don't know. I just don't have a place for us to find out," he said apologetically. "Maybe I'll get you a hotel for a few nights, and you can stay there 'til I know."

"When will that be, Smitty?" I asked bluntly.

"I don't know, but Ziggy is mad at me for inviting you here before I had it together and said we couldn't afford another crazy girlfriend hanging out in the club."

"Oh, now I'm lumped with your crazy ex?" I exhaled, completely exasperated. "Great, just great!" I was fuming. I fought back tears. This was not the reunion I had been picturing.

"I'm so sorry, Di. I didn't mean it that way. They are all just upset, knowing how Charlie Brown is."

"But Ziggy said he was interested in signing me as a comic?"

"I've gotta get ready for the second show now, baby. I'll have Ziggy come out and talk to you, okay? I'll go check my bank account to see if I can afford a hotel nearby! But don't cry, please?"

He kissed me on the cheek, left the table, and left me sitting there, completely distressed. What a fool I'd been!

How could I be so stupid? So naïve? I felt like I knew nothing about men, and even less about boys pretending to be men. I sat there in a daze for what seemed like a year, trying hard to not cry. I couldn't do that. Not here.

The show started, and there I was, sitting alone, forlorn, teary-eyed and tense. How could I have let this happen to me?

Ziggy came to the table and hugged me. "You okay, kiddo?"

"Not really, but it's good to see you!" I gathered myself and smiled at him.

"Let's go talk somewhere. It's too loud in here. The lobby is empty right now. Let's go out there."

I followed him to the lobby area. No one was there but us. We sat on a couch, and he looked at me point-blank and said, "Did you come to D.C. thinking I was going to sign you right away?"

"I know you've offered me that opportunity," I reminded him.

"I just think that it's a little premature for that," he stuttered. "I've never heard you be funny in person, and I haven't seen your act yet, so it's a little too soon for that."

"You know I've been doing stand-up on Paradise Island, right? I sent you my headshot and résumé when you asked."

"Yes, you did, but you don't handwrite a résumé on pink paper. You're just not ready. You would require lots of grooming before anything could happen, and besides, I didn't even know you were coming to D.C. this soon. Did you write three or four comedy sets as I asked?"

"No, not yet. Wrapping up my life on the island took up all of my time. I was going to begin that here!"

"That still doesn't mean I'm signing you right now. Maybe one of my successful female comics, possibly Jean Carroll, could give you comedy lessons and help with writing if she's available. I hate to be the second one to disappoint you tonight, but those are just the facts."

"I see" was all I could muster. I felt like I was being dumped twice in one night. I fought back the tears.

"As far as Smith is concerned, I hate to be the one to tell you this, but he hasn't broken up with Charlie Brown yet, I'm afraid," he reported. "Let me know when you're doing stand-up at the clubs." He gave me a little hug and walked away.

That was it?

Wow, wow, wow! My mind was blown. How could I have misunderstood the situation so thoroughly? Had I misread everything that had transpired between Smitty, Ziggy and me because I was so stoned on Black Beauties? I was profoundly shaken by the denial I had been suspended in. Tears streamed softly from my eyes; I couldn't help it nor stop it. I felt hurt, confused, scared and broken.

I sat there for a while, the sound of Clint singing his hit song "Playground in My Mind" in the background. Finally, I headed back to the table. Geri wasn't there. She must have stayed in the green room.

I felt so stupid. The tears began to roll again. I wiped them away quickly. I'd never felt more alone or uncertain in my life. I tried hard to stop crying. I was caught up in my thoughts, diving deep into myself, trying to figure out what the hell had just happened.

The show ended and there I was, alone. Forlorn, forgotten and swept aside. What was I going to do? Where was Smith? Why wasn't he here for me? The showroom began to clear out completely. Patrons evacuated the room, and only the servers remained, cleaning up. Where was I supposed to go? I started going through options, and there didn't seem to be much in the way of a solution.

Eventually, Dave and Geri arrived with my luggage in hand, ready to settle their bill with the club.

Geri, the quintessential Jewish mother, sat down, put her arm around me and said, "Smith has left and asked that we bring you your luggage. He's in serious debt and can't afford a hotel, I'm afraid."

Dave sat down on the other side of me and patted my shoulder. "Sorry, Diane. You certainly don't deserve this. Smitty's just a kid, an irresponsible kid who does stupid shit like this."

I was shocked that Smith didn't even come out to say goodbye to me!

"He wanted me here. He said he would have a place for us when I arrived," I choked.

"It's okay. You can stay with us," Geri offered brightly. "We have a two-bedroom apartment in Woodbridge, and we'd love to have you!"

"Really?" I responded hesitantly.

"We'd be more than happy to have you while you decide what to do next!" added Dave.

"Please say yes," pleaded Geri. "We'll have fun!"

"Oh, thank you so much, you guys," I cried in relief. "I'm so grateful. I don't know what else I'd do!"

"Well, then, it's settled. Let's go home," Dave said as he gathered my luggage.

As we drove to Woodbridge, Virginia, Geri started telling me all the

14. Birds with Broken Wings Can Fly, 1971

things we would do in D.C. Although she worked three or four nights a week, she had a list of things we could do when Dave was on the road. She offered to help fix up the guest room if I'd like. They were so sweet. I was beyond blessed. I must've been doing something right to have these beautiful people come to my aid.

As I tried to process all that occurred that evening, I vividly remembered my vision of my guardian angel's appearance a few days earlier. I heard that gentle, motherly voice once again say, "I will be with you." She was indeed. I knew without a doubt in that moment, that we do have guardian angels. The Divine had sent me Geri and Dave in my hour of need. They were two of the sweetest souls I have ever known. They provided nothing but unconditional love, patience, generosity, fun and kindness the whole six months I lived with them.

15

Elvis, Carolee and Me, 1971

None of my dreams worked out during my six-month stay in D.C. I did professional auditions for Broadway shows like *Hair*. I got a part-time job cocktail-waitressing at D.C.'s best dance club. Geri worked there and helped me get the job even though I was still only 19. We told them I was 21. I made lots of money there.

I had fun staying with Geri and Dave. They made sure I saw the Smithsonian and the presidential memorials and had scores of exciting adventures in D.C. and the majestic Blue Ridge Mountains.

I'd stayed in close correspondence with my former roommate Carolee McSwain since our early days in Montreal. She worked for the Rudas Dancers at the Tropicana Hotel in the "Folies Bergere" show. She encouraged me to join her in Las Vegas. She said a new show would be opening there shortly, and all I had to do was call Mr. Rudas and he'd make sure I got an audition with the choreographer, Jerry Jackson.

Vegas' Tropicana Hotel was called the Tiffany of the Strip. It had multiple, marvelous, graceful, glittering aqua fountains out front and a gorgeous showroom. Once I saw the magnificent show with its stunning and elegant showgirls, it became my dream to work there with Carolee.

Incredible Jerry Jackson was the choreographer, Tibor Rudas the producer and Ron Walker the assistant choreographer. I immediately began taking classes at The Barn with Nick Navarro and Ron Lewis, hot Vegas choreographers. Their classes were bursting at the seams with wannabe pros. When I saw how skilled the out-of-work dancers in those classes were, I realized how fortunate I was to have had the jobs I had.

Carolee was generous enough to let me stay in her new one-bedroom apartment behind the Tropicana. We could walk to the hotel from there. She was an excellent dancer and acrobat, tall (5'10"), cute and young. Few tall dancers could do back flips, but she could. She had been working professionally as an acrobat-dancer for over two years now.

Las Vegas perfectly suited me at this juncture in my life. We would go over to the new Union Plaza downtown on the "old" Strip off Fremont

15. Elvis, Carolee and Me, 1971

Street and dance in the club at the top of the hotel well into the early morning hours to the fabulous house band, Kenny Rogers and the First Edition. All the dancers on the Strip would head over there after work around one a.m. when Kenny was just warming up. Who knew then who he'd become? We gypsies knew this was the best live band we could find in town to go out dancing to after a show, to unwind and decompress.

Elvis was headlining at the International Hotel, and Carolee was dating his piano player Jerry. Oh, the stories she brought home about Elvis' suite at the International! My oh my!

Little 18-year-old Carolee from Perth, Australia, was much more infatuated with Elvis than with Jerry. Which was to be expected, I suppose. Elvis entertained many people in his suite after his shows.

A dancer or showgirl was the ultimate playmate or girlfriend in Vegas in those days. This was a time when a showgirl was treated like a celebrity. Of course, to play the part, we had to wear evening gowns to enter through the front entrance of any casino. If we showed up in groups of two or more, with gowns and eyelashes on, we'd automatically receive star treatment. It was standard knowledge then that if showgirls arrived to see any show in any casino on the strip, they were automatically escorted to the front center booth if available, and it was always complimentary, including our drinks, and we were never asked our age.

It was a charming era. Vegas was a small town run by the mob, and they looked out for us. This all appealed to Carolee very much. During the days I stayed with her, she would come home when I was waking up around noon with stories of Elvis and his posse and the shenanigans in his suite. He would hold court with the guys, their girls and whoever they were partying with each night. He would serve peanut butter and banana sandwiches with cocktails, and everyone would watch movies in his screening room.

Carolee eventually grew tired of sleeping with Jerry just to be near Elvis. She wanted the King for herself, but in due course, she also grew tired of him. It was the same scenario every night: everyone stoned, drunk, or both.

Carolee would invite me to the International suite, but I wasn't interested in the Elvis scene. I was a Beatles fan. If John, George, Paul or Ringo had been there, I would have bolted to Elvis Presley's suite! Carolee said that celebrities dropped by frequently. I begged her to run to the phone and call me if any of the Beatles ever showed up!

Shortly after arriving, I went to work with Carolee at the Tropicana. Meeting the line captain during my visit backstage, I inquired about becoming a showgirl in the new show they were casting. The line captain liked me and knew I had already worked with Tibor Rudas in Montreal and the Bahamas. She told me to call Mr. Rudas tomorrow.

The next day, I rang him in Aspen, and he asked why I was in Las Vegas after leaving Paradise Island for Washington to become a stand-up comedian. I explained briefly what happened with Ziggy. He asked if I'd return to the Bahamas and take a job in the show there again. I asked if my featured spot was still open as Jean Harlow and he said, "No, but I can make you one of the four featured dancing nudes."

I thanked him and politely declined and then implored him to cast me in his new "Folies Bergere" show at the Tropicana. I told him that I really liked Las Vegas, loved the show, and that since my arrival I had been in class weekly at The Barn with various choreographers. He said I would have to audition for Jerry.

I was getting better, and I was committed. These were exciting times for choreographers and dancers. I assured Mr. Rudas I was prepared.

I called Jerry Jackson the next day. Rehearsals were to begin in two weeks, and while he had already cast the show, he wasn't sure about one girl, so he arranged an audition with me the following week. I was excited. Carolee and I went to class every other day, and out to dance at night. We smoked our share of pot and snorted a tiny bit of free cocaine. It *was* 1971, after all, and I fancied myself a weekend hippie. Vegas was enchanting then. You could easily walk the Strip, from the Tropicana Hotel to Caesars Palace. Very few people drove. There were no crowded streets. Vegas was growing, but it was still a charming small town in a desert environment.

We knew people at all the shows. The Dunes would have been my next stop if I did not land the Tropicana gig. But in my opinion, the Tropicana was the class act back then. I remember how gorgeous and distinct their showgirls were. They wore lots of natural-styled wigs in blonde, black, platinum and red with three to four pairs of jet-black eyelashes. They had big eyes and bright pink, peachy lips. Tropicana showgirls were curvy and tanned.

I worked on my tan every day at the Tropicana pool, which we loved. We had to scope out places like the hotel roofs to sunbathe, as swimsuit lines were not permitted onstage. Tan lines would practically glow under the lights. It was common, professional practice to find ways to sunbathe in tiny little G-strings, topless. We managed; it meant our jobs! The Tropicana rooftop was our go-to secret. Tanning was very popular. We knew nothing of the dangers of sunbathing. We used our little combo bottles of baby oil and iodine for our rich, sexy tans.

Before I knew it, the day of my "Folies Bergere" audition arrived. I was nervous; it was my first Vegas audition. I had heard stories about Jerry's tough ballet auditions. Ballet was not my strong suit. I was a tapper and studied jazz fervently. But my real talent was selling dance numbers. My performance abilities surpassed my technical skills.

15. Elvis, Carolee and Me, 1971

I put on a leotard, fishnets and eyelashes. I took jazz boots and ballet slippers with me. Jerry had me do a ballet audition, which included pirouettes, arabesques, jetés and a 32-count jazz combination. He had me do the showgirl walk and asked how much ballet I'd done.

"As little as possible," I admitted.

He chuckled and said he could tell, but he liked me, and so did Mr. Rudas. I was too tall to be a covered dancer, but he could hire me as a swing girl for the nudes. A swing person learns all the parts, in order to replace anyone taking time off. In my case, it would be the dancing nude roles. Swing dancers generally covered people taking holidays. It kept things interesting.

"You're a real showgirl," he said. "There aren't many left."

There was that term again. I embraced it. I was grinning, even though I thought maybe I kind of sucked in the ballet portion of the audition. Jerry asked me to continue to take his classes and to study ballet at Backstage Dance Studio. I agreed wholeheartedly to do both. I would start rehearsals for the new show in two weeks. I was thrilled.

While in the dressing room, changing to leave, I ran into Shelly, a dancer who visited Carolee often. She told me she and her boyfriend Danny were both in the "Folies" show. Danny was one of the few straight boys in the "Folies." They were thinking of moving into our apartment complex. I invited them over the next day as she said they were seeking a one-bedroom, just like ours.

The complex was full of dancers. Every complex in town was packed with dancers, musicians, dealers and entertainers. It was not a family town. In those days, the Rat Pack ran Las Vegas.

Upon leaving the Tropicana that day, I felt like I had really arrived. Jerry Jackson had just hired me for my dream show! I had a brand-new life unfolding and would turn 20 that summer! What a year! I was on Cloud 9!

I felt good and decided to treat myself to a cab ride home. It was hot for May and one of those days where sands swirled in the wind. Dust storms were frequent and an issue in Las Vegas. Even the tap water was sandy when this happened. We had large Sparkletts dispensers at home; everyone did. Vegas water was the worst. We kept aluminum foil covers on our bedroom windows, mainly behind the curtains, to keep out the intense morning sun. The sand blew incessantly and often made it through the screens and windows. There were no skyscrapers to block the clouds of sandstorms from billowing wildly.

Once home, Carolee and I decided to celebrate. We were both thrilled about my new job! We wanted to go to a lounge show. Carolee had this night off. We decided to go see the hottest lounge act in town, Ike and Tina Turner, at The Sands at 4 p.m. All we had to do was call, make a reservation and tell them we were dancers from The Tropicana. And of course we were comped.

We invited Shelly and Danny to go with us. Shelly was in the show, and Danny was there for the new show, like me. He was one of the few straight boys in the company at the time. Danny was having a field day with a smorgasbord of gorgeous, talented dancers. He was a 6'2" cutie with dirty blonde hair, sparkling pale blue eyes, and a beautiful body, like most dancers.

We met at the Sands for Ike and Tina's show. None of us paid the $5 cover charge; we were all comped. We did spring for drinks. After all, we were in jeans, and it was a lounge show. Lounge shows were a big thing back then. You can't find many in Vegas these days. What fun that show was! This had to be one of the hottest acts we had ever seen!

Everyone was buzzing about Ike and Tina Turner, and now I saw why. We had a blast watching Miss Tina and her Ikettes shake and move to the upbeat songs that they performed loudly and with such skill. They were all wildly talented. We could barely contain ourselves in our seats. We wanted to get up and dance! We knew we were in the presence of greatness that afternoon, a couple on their way to fame and fortune.

Around 5:45, Shelly announced she had to get to work. Danny turned to Carolee and me and asked, "Can you give me a ride home?"

"We don't drive, we walk," I said.

"That's cool, I'll pay for a cab for all of us," he offered. What a gentleman.

Shelly said her goodbyes, we all hugged, and she took her car to the Tropicana. Danny had the night off. He hadn't had many since he was hired because they desperately needed a swing boy to give each boy dancer a night off. The three of us stayed for another round of drinks. The drinking age must have been 18 in Las Vegas because drinking was never an issue; we were never carded. The three of us had a great evening, laughing, chatting and getting to know Danny better. He was very cool and we really clicked.

We were asked to leave by the manager, as seating for the 7:00 show was about to begin. We gathered our things and left the Sands, heading down the Strip on foot.

Danny pulled out a joint. "Why don't we go to your place, smoke this, and go for a swim?"

"That sounds great. I'm hungry," said Carolee. "We can eat at the apartment."

"Our heated pool should feel pretty good about now," I suggested. "Plus, I could dig some Mary Jane."

It was agreed. We grabbed a cab and headed over to our apartment.

Once stoned and fed, we decided to go for a swim. It was a warm, beautiful spring night.

Danny hesitated, "Oh, wait, I don't have anything to swim in."

I offered him black dance trunks: "This should work."

We laughed, changed and headed to the pool.

As Carolee was locking the door, her phone rang inside. She answered, and we heard it was her best friend from Perth calling long distance.

"I'll be down in a bit," she called out to us, excited to hear from her childhood friend.

I wrapped a towel around my bikini-clad body and handed Danny a towel.

The pool was lovely, and we had it to ourselves that evening. The air was warm and sumptuous, and the pot relaxed us for a perfect evening swim.

Danny and I loved to talk. He was very open, easygoing, laid-back. I found myself attracted to his infectious spirit. We talked about his relationship with Shelly.

"I really like Shelly," I told him.

"She's my best friend," he added.

"How long have you been lovers?" I questioned.

"We've always been very physical with each other, very free. I feel very close to her, and we have a very open relationship. We both see other people."

"But you are becoming roommates now, aren't you?"

"Yeah, we just placed a deposit on a place here in this complex. There is one available in a month."

"That's cool. We might be neighbors if I stay here." I was excited.

"That would be awesome. We can all ride to work together and party," he flashed his sexy smile at me. I'm sure this worked well for him onstage and with the ladies.

I said, "If I stay in the complex, I plan on finding my own place once I start in the show. I like having my own place. Carolee does, too. We were roommates in Montreal and get along great, but we both like to have our own home."

"Is that so you can get freaky?" he laughed.

"You are so fresh, no!" I laughed with him.

"Too bad," he said flirtatiously, "'cause I'd like to get freaky with you."

"Oh, really? Define freaky." I was curious now.

He swam over and kissed me long and passionately. I liked it.

When the kiss finally ended, I looked him in the eye and asked, "Would Shelly be cool with this?"

"She would, actually." There was that smile again. "She would join us if you were into it."

"Whoa, hang on there, cowboy. I'm not into *ménage à trois*."

I'd actually never tried one, but I knew what they were. This was the sexual revolution. I couldn't imagine myself with two lovers at once. I was still learning to navigate one.

He laughed, "You're the coolest chick I've met since I got here, even hipper than Shelly." He put his arms around my waist. "I dig you." He pulled me closer, and I could feel how much he liked me, even in the water. We kissed again. I liked Danny a lot. He was incredibly bold and seductive. He persisted, but I resisted.

I had to check this out with Shelly. I didn't need drama backstage before I even started in the show.

A few days later, Shelly came by, upset, asking if we could talk. She and Danny were having second thoughts about moving in together. He needed to save money to buy a car. "I am in love with him, but he just wants to be free and feels like he's too young to be tied down," Shelly explained.

I could understand that. We were all about 19 or 20. So young.

Here was my chance to find out more. "Are you guys in a committed relationship?"

"Not really, I tell him I am open to anything because I just want to be with him."

"Open to what?" Now I had to know.

"Oh, you know, sexual things," she admitted.

"You mean he's freaky?" I asked.

"No, but he does like threesomes."

"With guys?" I inquired.

"No, he likes them with other girls."

"Are you into that, too?"

Shelly sighed. "Kinda. We have been with a few of the girls in the show, and it was fun."

Wow, Danny was obviously taking advantage of his straight-boy status in a primarily gay-boy scenario backstage. I understood that, but Shelly didn't seem happy. She sniffled, "We had a huge fight about him sleeping with so many girls in the show last night. I don't think I can keep doing this."

"What are you gonna do?" I held my breath, awaiting her answer.

"I think I'm going to go live with my dancer friend Jenny for a while or go to Europe and find work there and see if I miss him." She started to cry.

I hugged her. "I couldn't do it. I'm a one-man girl. I need all the attention."

We chuckled.

Shelly and Danny parted ways when she took a two-week vacation to Europe. She was distraught and unsure.

Danny was free to do whatever he wanted, and he wanted me. I felt closer to him than I did Shelly. I was incredibly attracted to him and simply ready to explore my newfound sexuality. Danny and I became passionate lovers. He was so sexy. We made love whenever Carolee was at Jerry's overnight or at work. We engaged in my first real physical affair. We were like bunnies. There was something about him that was just fun. I wasn't interested in a relationship with this gorgeous young dancer because I knew he was making the rounds everywhere. Backstage, several girls were into him, and they were all sleeping with him. Carolee brought home news of his backstage conquests. It didn't bother me at all. I was enjoying all the sexy things I was learning from this stud.

That is, until he came down sick. I took him soup one day and he asked me if I was okay. "Sure, I'm great. We start rehearsals next week for the new show. I can't wait," I said enthusiastically.

Well, as it turned out, I would have to wait.

He had something called mono.

"What the hell is mono?" I asked, worried now.

"Mononucleosis is a really contagious kissing disease," he explained.

"What?" I was horrified, "A disease from kissing?"

"That's what it's called." He said that I might get it too.

Sure enough, I got it. Danny was too sick to start rehearsals for the new show, and so was I. I called the line captain and told her that I had come down with mono. I had never been so sick. She told me that I was not the only one; it was going around backstage; several people had it. What was the other thing I was learning about? This thing called karma. Was this instant karma?

Carolee took care of me; I was really sick, and I was so worried she would get it. She gave me her room while she slept on the couch. She was such a good friend. All I did was sleep, in a feverish blur, for weeks. Eventually I needed to find a place to wait this out as I learned that mono could last for months. When I was strong enough to travel, my parents sent me a plane ticket to Illinois, and I made my way home.

I relaxed there for three months, restored myself and gradually got back into shape with daily walking, yoga and then running until I'd finally built some stamina. I enjoyed the time with my four younger brothers the most. I read a lot during those three months. I read more about karma and the law of *what goes around comes around*. I ruminated long and hard over ethical and spiritual issues. I guess free love wasn't all it was cracked up to be.

Living in Illinois again proved to be downright boring. I was grateful to have a home, a family, best friends and little brothers to bond with, but this place just wasn't me anymore. Nothing about me belonged there. Also, it wasn't easy for me to live around my dad's alcoholism and my mom's co-dependency.

Eventually I was well, healed of all signs of mono and becoming antsy to get back onstage. I had to find work. I knew I needed to fly again.

I didn't want to go back to Paradise Island; it was such a small island with very little to do but work and sunbathe. Yet I knew that just a few months prior, when I had called Mr. Rudas from Vegas about the Tropicana, he had wanted me to return there. I wanted to work and I was afraid of being stuck in Illinois. So I bit the bullet and called Mr. Rudas to ask for a job. Again.

"I don't usually take a girl back a third time," he claimed. "But since you were sick in Las Vegas, I will check to see if we have anything in Paradise Island. Call me back in one week."

"I will, and thank you, Mr. Rudas, I really appreciate it." I hung up and prayed for a whole week to get the hell out of Illinois.

One week later, I was on a plane to Paradise Island. I had a job. The girl I had trained, Johnette, was leaving the show when her one-year contract ended. Barbara wrote that Johnette was bored on the island. Mr. Rudas told me that Teri had my original solo as Jean Harlow. So I wasn't featured, but I was one of the four dancing nudes again. It felt good to be headed back, I was very thin and healthy again and a helluva lot wiser.

16

Making the Most of Island Life, 1971

Paradise Island felt like home. When I landed at the tiny windswept Nassau airport, I felt welcomed by its customary balmy breezes and sultry vibe. I was born to live in this incredibly appealing and divinely humid climate. It seduced me, and I felt welcomed by the warm, smiling faces of the sweet Bahamian people. I was determined to make this contract the best one yet. I wouldn't become restless and bored this time. I'd do something fresh. There had to be something new to study or pursue. No matter what, I couldn't make my job my whole life. Not this time. I would find balance.

I strove to become a better dancer and committed to learning everything I could from our company captain and choreographer, Ron Walker, whenever he came for clean-up rehearsals. This would be a productive period for me on this exclusive, quiet little island. Health and balance were becoming the ultimate goal for me. Good Lord! Was I growing up?

I did just that. I visited the local library and hotel bookstores and found numerous books on Zen; Alan Watts became my new favorite author. I knew I was on a one-way path to some enlightenment because there's no turning back once you commit. You can't and won't want to go back to any kind of unconscious life.

I had created a delightful little regimen that I made time for every day before work. I would put on a bikini and sunglasses and walk across the road to the beach. Once on the sand, I would walk to a private little stretch of beach we liked to call "The Cove" at around five each afternoon. It seemed like the most peaceful time of day to me. I would lie back on the shore on my elbows.

This stretch of beach was always secluded. With the tide washing over my feet and the pure aqua water of the Caribbean cleansing me in the sun, I was renewed. I'd researched where and what time to do this on my many walks to the yoga camp. I'd begun taking more and more pleasure in the simple things in life.

I relished everything the Caribbean had to offer. I would lean back, sunbathe in the warm sun, and drink in the nutrition of the island and the sea. I would unreservedly consume the end-of-day sun, taking its nourishment. The only sound I would hear, other than the ultra-soothing sea, was seagulls occasionally announcing themselves. It was the most Zen thing I could do. It relaxed and invigorated me beyond measure. It prepared me for any backstage bullshit I might encounter that evening. This kept me from becoming "hooked" by things that had once driven me mad. My first go-round here, I got into that *Valley of the Dolls* crap, and I vowed it would never happen to me again!

I had healthy routines in place to discourage that negative way of life. I may have been blindsided and manipulated by people the first time, but not now. I had some experience under my belt to guide me to a more disciplined existence. I knew who the smart and reliable people were. I knew who to listen to and who not to. Most importantly, I was learning to rely on myself.

Much of that year launched me into a newfound headspace and a need to connect more and more, collaborating with like-minded artists from all over the world. I was attracted to the musicians, actors and creatives I met on the island.

Aside from a few celebrities peppering our excitement backstage and occasionally enhancing our performances, life on the island was predictably slow. A highlight was when one of my favorite actresses from childhood appeared and was introduced to our audience one night before the 11:00 production. Susan Hayward was in our audience! That lifted my spirits so much.

We were also pretty pumped the night Bert Parks was there. He was the popular, charismatic host of the Miss America pageants. I grew up loving pageants and watching them with my mom. We ate that up when I was little!

I liked change, diversity and learning more about various cultures. I fell in love with Eastern Spirituality and yoga in 1971 and learned to meditate while doing yoga classes. If it was good enough for the Beatles, it was good enough for me. The more I grew from the disciplines I had undertaken, the more like-minded individuals I resonated with.

A miracle occurred during that period of elevated consciousness. Line captain Gina's contract was up and she was leaving. She, George and the kids were moving on to a more active place to live and work than in the crawl of island life. Hallelujah!

One of the most capable and talented Aussie acrobats in the show, Jeri, was appointed line captain! She was an impeccable line captain and a humble person. Jeri gave skilled classes with new combinations to

16. Making the Most of Island Life, 1971

ensure we kept it fresh and sharp. When Ron Walker came for a clean-up rehearsal, he watched one of our classes. He complimented me afterward, saying, "You're really getting it!"

Wow, I was surprised! It was true. I was becoming a better dancer. All of us loved Jeri's leadership and genuine helpful nature. I had to hand it to Mr. Rudas for hiring Jeri. She had been a dancer and acrobat in Perth. Backstage life became more fun, animated, happy and relatable than it was before Jeri.

I dated here and there, mostly visiting musician types. I dated my hairdresser in the Britannia Beach Hotel Salon for a bit. He was American, adorable, 24 or 25, straight, and really liked me. I don't know why I didn't go for him. He was sweet. Maybe he was too nice? Why were bad boys so appealing and comfortable for me? Oh, wait. Yeah, my dad was one.

That could be why!

Just when I felt I was achieving some personal enlightenment, elevated decision-making, and recognizing the errors in judgment I had made the year prior, the the Universe threw me a curveball. As it often does when we begin to think we're all that. A little test, perhaps?

Several dancers were celebrating Sandy's birthday backstage one night between shows. Sandy was one of the more mature Aussie acrobats. She was funny and kept to herself. When she did party, she was simply the greatest person to be around. We all loved Sandy. She invited us to take her birthday party to the casino bar after the second show, and there she offered to buy a round of drinks. We settled into a table at the bar and toasted Sandy's birthday while indulging in many laughs.

One of the British pit bosses, John Duckworth, insisted on buying everyone a round. No one let Sandy spend a dime on her special day. There were about six dancers and several croupiers who joined us. Many nights after work, we did that. I rarely stayed there long because I didn't really drink much, but tonight I had a few Dubonnets.

The waitress brought me the wrong drink during the second round. Once I realized no one had my cocktail, I approached the bar to exchange it. Katie, the gracious and gorgeous white Bahamian cocktail waitress, took my drink behind the bar to replace it.

Suddenly, someone wrapped their arms around my waist from behind and nestled their warm lips onto the back of my neck. Then whispered, in a deep, sultry baritone voice, "I thought you were gone forever."

I turned slowly and found myself face to face with none other than drop-dead gorgeous Calvin Lockhart. again.

"Calvin, how are you?" I grinned.

"I'm great now that you're here," he answered. "When did you get back?"

"About eight months ago," I replied, scanning his beautiful face with new eyes. This time, there was no speed in my system or substances infusing my brain. Nothing extra was befogging my perception of him. He was still incredibly sexy and arrogant.

He held me and spoke softly, surveying my eyes when he announced, "I am so happy to see you again. Are you here with someone tonight?"

"Just friends," I remarked. "You aren't mad at me for what happened the last time I saw you?" I asked, remembering me slamming the door on him.

He searched his memory bank quickly. "I just remember you leaving the island. When I asked about you, everyone said you went to D.C. to become a comedienne. I can't even remember the last time I saw you."

He must have been drunker than I realized at that last rendezvous. I wondered if he was drunk tonight.

"Are you intoxicated now, Calvin?" I asked forthrightly.

"Not tonight. I'm on a high seeing you, though." He smiled that wickedly sexy smile. "How about you come over to my place. I've just remodeled my home on Cable Beach. I'd love for you to see it."

This time, I couldn't resist his amorous advances. I was finally ready. Incredibly ready, and I had no reason to say no to him now. He wasn't as scary to me as he had been at our last two encounters. I felt like our time had come. I could feel it in every fiber of my being. This was an itch begging to be scratched.

"Let's go!" I slipped my hand into his lean fingers and smiled into his dreamy eyes. I gathered my things, said my goodbyes to the posse, and took my replenished icy cocktail in a casino highball glass with me as we made our way to his car. Calvin was driving his convertible sports car that night, and I savored the subtle scent of his expensive cologne in its leather interior.

We left Paradise Island and crossed the bridge and drove to Cable Beach in Nassau. It was dark, and I couldn't see much, but driving along the beach was balmy and sultry. The sea was bespeckled with reflecting stars. It added to the already steamy vibe we were ensconced in. We arrived at his gated home at two. It was dark. I inhaled the heavy air and felt the moist breezes whisper an inviting "welcome." It was a heady and torrid night full of endless promises of pleasure.

We went into his beautiful, modern estate surrounded by the sound of waves crashing against the shore. It was more like a romantic movie set than a home. He led me in the moonlight to his semi-enclosed patio and pulled me to him seductively in the dark, toward an overstuffed couch. He never turned the lights on. We enjoyed a lively conversation in the moonlight. Topics ranged from our love of classical theater to all things New York.

16. Making the Most of Island Life, 1971

Calvin was otherworldly. He just wasn't like anyone I'd ever known. This man was undoubtedly the most sensual man I'd ever encountered. Then he kissed me deeply, with all of himself. That was it. I was all in. I kissed him back with more desire than I knew I possessed. His beautiful hands slowly removed my red mini-dress while he kissed every quivering inch of me. I removed his shirt. He was alluring and perfectly toned. Our carnal appetite was unleashed, and I learned secret things about myself from him that I would never have known had I said "no" to him.

I swooned with pleasure unknown to me as he guided me gently to what he liked and where he liked it. I complied and found myself sexually awakened with every touch, every stroke. I was brought to my first explosive orgasm with his electrifying touch! It was literally the first full orgasm I'd experienced, and it was beyond delicious. This man knew how to extend himself in every way, lighting the way for our complete satisfaction. I will never forget the titillation that was forged in me that night. My sexual goddess had been awakened.

I lay on the enclosed patio, listening to the sound of the sea in his muscular arms, completely spent. He eventually led me to his modern, masculine bedroom and enfolded me in his entire body as we drifted off. We slumbered like babes.

17

When You Least Expect It, 1971

Pleasure is only temporary happiness.

Calvin gave me his number the following morning. I never called him. As stimulating as our union had been, I knew nothing else was there for me. As gorgeous and sexy, chiseled and velvety as that beautiful man was, I knew who he was, and he was not for me. He was a player and possibly an alcoholic. I didn't want those things in a relationship. Not that kind of drama. Sex with Calvin was like dopamine, and the last thing I wanted in my life was any kind of addiction.

I never saw him again. I will never forget him. Just writing about our experience brought back so much of my youth and the evolutionary year of my sexual odyssey. That entire year was one of experimentation, and I'm glad that I learned what I did and did not want in romance. In a sense, I passed the test. I caught that curve ball the Universe had tossed my way. I'm not saying I made the best choices in romance for the rest of my days, but I learned to recognize a player when I met one. I heard Calvin wound up having three wives before he passed at age 72.

I kept my focus on my spiritual quest. I was a seeker. I had been dissatisfied with organized religion since the age of 13. Yoga and meditation were the closest things I had found to fulfill my inner calling. Buddhism appealed to me.

One overcast day, months after my encounter with Calvin, I decided to take my new book, Alan Watts' *The Way of Zen*, to the beach. On a hotel lounge chair near the shore, I sat down to read.

With the cloudy weather, there weren't any tourists seaside, and I relished having the beach to myself. It was still warm and humid. A storm was brewing. Perhaps it was just an afternoon storm, which was not uncommon.

After about 20 minutes, a few raindrops interrupted my blissed-out Zen state of mind. I didn't want to ruin my new book, so I decided to walk home before larger doses of drizzle fell. As I got up and headed to the sandy path that led to my place, I noticed a fellow coming my way,

17. When You Least Expect It, 1971

obviously enjoying a walk on the rain-spattered beach. He, too, had a book in his hand. He looked familiar!

As I passed him, he nodded and said, "Hello."

I returned the nod. I saw the book in his hand and said, "Good day for some reading on the beach."

"Every day must be a good day on this beach," he replied.

"What are you reading?"

He held up his book, and guess what it was? *The Way of Zen* by Alan Watts! I pulled my book from my bag and held it up. He seemed surprised, and we both laughed.

"How do you like it?" he asked.

That moment was kismet. I gazed into his soulful, ancient eyes, and we connected on a profound level.

Our conversation began under sprinkles of raindrops. I learned he was also a devotee of Watts' work. We discussed Buddhism, Zen and how Eastern religion was invading Western culture. His name was Arnold Robinson, and he was attractive and American.

"Are you here on vacation?" I inquired.

"No, I'm here for the next two months. I am in a group playing the lounge in the Britannia Beach Hotel."

I told him I worked as a dancer in the casino's main showroom. We chatted for a while about the group he was with, Sonny Turner and Sound Limited; Arnold sang bass for them. Sonny had been the lead singer with the Platters before starting his own group. I asked if they did "The Great Pretender" or "Only You" or "Smoke Gets in Your Eyes." They did all the Platters' greatest hits.

"My mom loves the Platters' songs," I mentioned.

"Everyone's mom loved those tunes," he grinned. We laughed. This man was wise beyond his 28 years. He had a warm smile, and I could tell he had an elevated, exciting mind. I liked him.

The rainfall began in earnest, steadily interrupting our chat. I told Arnold I needed to make it to my place before it started pouring.

"Come see the show sometime," he suggested.

"I will," I called out as I quickly headed through the palms. "Nice meeting you!"

A few nights later, I ran into Arnold backstage in the dressing room hallway. We chatted briefly and shared more of our newly forged Zen wisdom. Our chat was not flirty, it was spiritual. He was dressed for his second show, and I was on my way home. Before we parted, he invited me to dinner on Paradise Island beach at the Hotel Gazebo the next night. He always had dinner before his first show, so we would dine early, around six. Both of our first shows started between eight and nine. I accepted.

A few months later, I left Paradise Island with Arnold Robinson said goodbye to the Rudas dancers for good. We had dated every single day after my first visit to his show. He courted me like a gentleman, and we fell in love. I was incredibly happy with Arnold. Enough to want to leave the island with him. I looked forward to leaving with him. I was glad we'd fallen in love on a romantic tropical island.

He didn't drink much, but he did like a little pot, which we enjoyed after work on our day off. We didn't play like Smitty and I played on Paradise Island. We dated like grownups. I needed that. We dressed nicely for dinner and had deep, existential conversations that connected us on multiple levels. I craved that. He was a leader, and I followed his lead. He had more worldly wisdom than I did, being eight years older, and I felt safe with him.

He took me on tour with him and Sonny Turner and Sound Limited for a year. He proposed to me during that year on the road. We were planning to marry once we settled down somewhere. We just weren't quite sure yet where that would be.

18

We Were Pioneers, 1972

I married Arnold at the ripe old age of 22. He was my guru. Kind of. I learned so much from him. He was a talented Native American-African American entertainer.

Arnold, originally from North Carolina, sang bass. He was everyone's guru. He was wise, funny, smart and talented. I seemed to fall for men with talent more than any other redeeming quality. I was attracted to Arnold for his talent, wisdom, vast life experiences and love of sharing them with others.

I wasn't incredibly physically attracted to him, and for the first time, it didn't matter. The connection I felt with him, his endless font of worldly knowledge, and his wise soul drew me in. The sex didn't create fireworks, but he was as deep as the ocean, and that was perfect for me. Besides, the fire starters hadn't worked out, had they?

One of the things I loved most about Arnold was his ability to help people be honest with themselves. Everyone loved Arnold. I learned more from him about life than anyone else I'd ever met. We really didn't experience much backlash being an interracial couple. None on the island, in fact. Possibly because it was a black country. It wasn't until I left with him and went on tour that I learned much more about life.

Arnold requested that we not show any public displays of affection, which was disappointing. I understood we would be in the spotlight much of our time on tour, but affection is a huge part of who I am. It was not part of his stoic Capricorn nature. I missed holding hands and having his arm around me as we'd done while dating in the Bahamas. Since this was my first adult relationship, I let it go. I'd later realize that letting go of my own needs in romantic relationships was something I did entirely too much.

Of course, those lessons could have been much harder had we not been in the entertainment industry, especially considering how famous Sonny Turner was. Americans put entertainers on a pedestal. They still do. We traveled first class all over the country and were treated like royalty wherever we went. Nevertheless, the lessons I learned were many. I learned the most about racism with him, clearly seeing how prejudiced people were before they knew I had a black husband.

We were married two years after we met. I was only able to tour with Arnold for one year. I thought I'd lose my mind if my creativity didn't have an outlet. Being a kept woman just wasn't for me. I launched into accelerated growth, learning more about myself than at any other time. That's what our 20s are for.

Before we got married, we actually broke up after that year on the road. They went on tour to Hawaii without me. I found out that he had cheated on me in Hawaii with a Japanese girl. Everything in our life went downhill after that. I left him and stayed in Atlanta. First, I stayed with my friend Reba, who was another guardian angel. I later moved in with my friend Patty, who had been on tour with the keyboard player in Sonny's band. We became close, and Patty said that I was welcome to stay until I found work and beyond. She needed a roommate, and so did I.

I began auditioning for theater and dance jobs in Atlanta, but there wasn't much happening. The only offer I had as a dancer was from a downtown go-go club, which held no appeal for me. My journey to the go-go joint had me pass by the very prestigious Playboy club. Having never been in one, I decided to have a peek inside. It was beautiful, upscale, modern, and perfectly Playboy-branded.

Once inside the lobby, I was greeted by a Hostess Bunny perched on a stool behind a long glass counter featuring Playboy merchandise. For some reason, I asked if they were hiring Bunnies. Talk about spontaneous!

In a charming Southern accent, she said, "The Bunny Mother always interviews new girls, but she isn't in just now. Y'all

Above and opposite: **Bunny Diane at the Playboy Atlanta club, 1972.**

18. We Were Pioneers, 1972

should call her because you are just what she's always looking for. Would you like her number?"

I wasn't convinced. Me? A Playboy Bunny? Even though I did look pretty good that day. I had just lost 15 pounds after going through the extremely emotional breakup with Arnold.

"Great," I answered, "When should I call her?"

The raven-haired, blue-eyed Southern belle gave me the Bunny Mother's card and recommended I call her between nine and five tomorrow.

"Tell her Crystal sent you," she added with a twinkle in her eye. "The money here is great, and the girls are dolls to work with. You'll love it!"

Wow, I wondered. Will I? I thanked her and looked around the hutch.

Every inch of the club was tasteful and classy. The low-lit ambiance was sexy. The sound system was purring, and music filled every corner. On the walls there were framed photos of Hef and the Bunnies with major celebrities who visited Playboy clubs nationwide.

Just beyond the sleek lobby was the bar where I could see the enlarged, lighted Playmate centerfold photos in gilded gallery-quality frames gracing all of the walls. In the center of the room was a bumper pool table and a gorgeous Bunny playing pool with club members. That looked fun. The Bunnies were all beautiful.

The club's key holders were primarily well-dressed, high-end men of all ages. They were seated at the bar and around the modern tables in the "living room," a sunken, dimly lit area in a large, open, club-like atmosphere in gunmetal grays and rich, deep purples. I noticed the Playboy logo on the royal purple carpet. Today the clubs are all gone but that logo lives on!

I was excited, knowing it would be a glorified waitress job, but it sure was a step up from the go-go joint down the street! I left somewhat uplifted. It wasn't show biz, but it was the burgeoning Playboy Club. On my way out, I turned and looked around before exiting. Nice place, I thought, taking in the posh 1970s feel of the club. Crystal gave me a li'l ol' wave, "Bye-bye."

"Ya'll come back now!" seemed to emanate from her pores. I like Southerners. They make me feel welcome, positive.

The next day, I called Dawn, the Bunny Mother, and she asked me to come in for an interview right away. We met in her office at a lower club level, near the Bunny dressing rooms. Dawn and I really hit it off. I liked this warm, affectionate woman. I was hired and began my 30-day training period immediately.

Once my training was complete, I began working as a Playboy Bunny. I even managed to become the bumper pool Bunny in the bar. I really had a lot of fun doing that. We earned a decent salary, and I easily cleared $250 in tips each shift. I worked five days a week, some days and some nights. I was asked to be a hostess upstairs at the very exclusive club on weekends. I could wear my own clothes for that, and I really dressed up for the upstairs club. That part of the club was amazingly full every weekend. Top-name headliners played there; I listened to their acts from the reception area, loving every second of it. The curtains on the small stage were shimmery gold. Everything in that room was tastefully designed in warm tones and rich mahogany. It had the feel of a grand library or den in a chateau.

I wondered if this replicated Hef's mansion. It cost about half a million dollars to join that level of the Playboy Club.

I never met Hef while working as a Bunny, but I did visit the Playboy Mansion in Los Angeles many years later. I was also asked to do test shots by the Atlanta club's photographer; the idea was that I could be a Playmate. Playmates are *Playboy* magazine's "girl next door" centerfolds. I declined, even though half the world had seen my breasts in the huge shows I had danced in. Posing nude for the extremely popular *Playboy* magazine just wasn't for me. I couldn't appear naked in my dad's favorite magazine, which he'd poorly hidden in our house since I was eight years old. I was honored and flattered to have been invited, though.

While I was working as a Bunny, Barbara wrote from Paris and told me that Miss Bluebell at the Lido de Paris was hiring dancers for the show where Barbara was now employed as the principal dancer. It sounded like just what I needed. I had not been doing well emotionally since breaking up with Arnold. I was profoundly lonely and hurt. I needed to perform again! Upon Barbara's request, I sent Miss Bluebell my photos, résumé and Barb's recommendation. She hired me long distance. I gave my notice, easily said goodbye to Playboy, and off I went to Gay Paree! Just like that.

19

Lido de Paris, France, 1972

At the start of my freshman year of high school, we chose our electives. My dad convinced me to take Spanish when choosing a language, because it was the most practical one to know since we would most likely use it often. Being 14, I did what I was told, like a good girl.

When I entered my sophomore year and saw the French textbook at a friend's home, that all changed! Suddenly, I knew I had to learn French. The photo on the front of the book was the Eiffel Tower, and it drew me in. It looked and felt remarkably familiar. I felt I needed to learn French. "I'm going there someday, I just know it," were my thoughts in the moment. I knew it the same way I knew I was destined for acting. A premonition indeed!

After studying French for two years in high school and then encountering a lot of bilingual slang in Montreal, I was now finally going to Paris! I always knew this day would come.

Before joining Barbara in Paris at the Lido de Paris, I had been mailing her marijuana joints in my letters because she said it was impossible to find or buy pot in the City of Lights, and she was longing for some. When I mailed them, I didn't add a return address. Easy peasy! They arrived just fine with no issues. She was over the moon with excitement and gratitude!

I felt compelled to take some marijuana with me to Paris. I knew the cost would be significant if I was caught since I was carrying a work visa and a letter from Miss Bluebell. I'd have to be very clever transporting even a single joint through French customs. I put a lot of thought into this and came up with a brilliant idea!

I carefully unwrapped one of the tampons from the box I was packing with my other toiletries and splayed the cotton tampon portion wide open. I lodged the joint vertically into the middle of the tampon, then closed it back up, replacing it in the tube. I glued the wrapper shut, resealing it perfectly. In fact, it looked untouched!

American customs were a breeze. Even though the luggage was inspected by hand, I looked around the airport to ensure that no dogs were

19. Lido de Paris, France, 1972

sniffing bags. Thank God I didn't see any! I made it, and I figured if I could camouflage it that well and make it through U.S. customs, I should be okay in Paris. Besides, who's going to rifle through a girl's tampons?

I smoked weed in airplane bathrooms several times while jet-setting in the '70s. It was fun doing things you weren't supposed to do from time to time, like getting stoned on a plane when you're 21! It happened with a French hairdresser that I sat next to on that flight to Gay Paree. He was my age, sporting a huge thrift store raccoon coat. He had gorgeous, long, curly hair that he wore like a freak flag. He was hot! We lounged on an entire row across six seats by lowering the armrests and kissed under his raccoon coat! The French loved passion.

A Barbara Beverly modeling shot, Paris, 1972.

When I went through customs in France, I was very nervous. I decided to make flirty small talk with the French customs officer who spoke English. When he inspected my contract, he grinned at me and mentioned that Bluebells were celebrities in Paris.

It worked! I made it through with one joint intact! Whew! Though it was just one joint, it meant a lot to Barbara to enjoy it once I arrived. We could not get away with that now with today's state-of-the-art airport security. That all changed after 9/11.

I made my way by taxi to Barbara's walk-up apartment in the Rue Pergoles, near the Arc de Triomphe. She and her roommates Neil and Eric, boy dancers in the show, had invited me to room with them. It was quite a large apartment, circa 17th century, and we saved money on rent, having four of us there. That taxi ride was much scarier than going through customs! The French seemed to drive around in circles quickly with no lanes throughout the city. I was dizzy trying to take in this magical, historical, ancient, snow-covered metropolis on that day in January 1972. Paris was beckoning me outside the glistening, frosted windows of the taxi! It felt like it was welcoming me back! What an eerie feeling to get from a city I'd never been to! Mon dieu!

I arrived in one piece at Barb's apartment. It was on a beautiful street near several major French landmarks at the city's heart, the Arc de Triomphe and Place Charles de Gaulle. We trudged up to the sixth-floor apartment with my luggage. I realized you had to be in good shape to live here, or at least *get* into shape for those stairs. We loaded my bags into our vintage dining room-girls' bedroom. The room had high ceilings and lovely tall windows that were heavily draped.

After I freshened up, Barbara insisted we go to dinner at her favorite café, L'Etoile Verde, before heading to the Lido to see the show and meet Miss Bluebell. Barbara Beverly was the only girl I knew who could consume several courses before a show. We made it a foursome, and I had the pleasure of dining with my new roomies Eric and Neil. To this day, I still adore them both. It was love at first bite. Or is it sight? Both! The food was incredible French fare, and the conversation was everything! We bonded immediately over crispy steak frites and raspberries avec creme fraiche. I couldn't wait to get onstage with the three of them!

Barbara and I decided to walk to the Lido on the Champs-Élysées after dinner. We walked arm in arm, French style, and caught up a bit even though we'd corresponded regularly. We wrote from wherever we were and never lost track of one another. That's how you kept your gypsy friends for years before cell phones and computers! When both individuals stay the course, that becomes one of life's greatest treasures: true friendship.

I had many questions for Barb on that chilly winter walk regarding the Lido and meeting Miss Bluebell for the first time.

"Don't worry about anything, Di! She'll love you, and she's very sweet. You'll see!" Barbara declared.

"Miss Bluebell," also known as Margaret Kelly, was an Irish dancer. She founded the Bluebell Girls dance troupe in 1932 while performing as a dancer at the Folies Bergère in Paris. In collaboration with Donn Arden, the American choreographer and producer, she began to produce extravaganzas at the Paris Lido. The Bluebell Girls quickly became the stars of the Lido shows and gained notoriety. Their shows became internationally known when they added troupes in Las Vegas, Europe, Africa and Eastern Asia.

When Margaret's husband and business partner was killed in an automobile accident in 1961 (he fell asleep at the wheel), she became wholly responsible for their four children. Despite this, she kept the Bluebell program in steady operation, even increasing troupes and adding

19. Lido de Paris, France, 1972

new elements and artists. One of her most noteworthy innovations was the introduction of the "topless" dancer in 1970— aka the nudes! Or the showgirls! (Although dancing nudes are not completely nude. Simply topless.)

Margaret was decorated Officer of the Order of the British Empire and Chevalier of the Legion of Honor for 72 years of professional activity as maîtresse de ballet. In 1986, the BBC drama series *Bluebell* depicted her authorized biography. Carolyn Pickles was cast as Miss Bluebell.

Needless to say, I was nervous about meeting this legend.

This glamorous city drew me in with every step. I felt alive here. Not only was I drawn to its beauty and antiquity, but I also sensed my other lifetimes here so clearly. Everything I encountered felt familiar. As we approached the Lido, we had to walk through a long entryway with built-in lighted kiosks primarily displaying pastries, sweets, jewelry and designer watches! I was mesmerized by the presentation of pastries and the beauty of these treats. I've never seen food look more beautiful. My French great-grandmother, Pearl Bennett, had been a professional chef, and so was my grandmother, Lois Pirmann. I wished I could present to them this grandeur in cuisine. I've never been especially drawn to sweets, but these had to be tasted! Ohhhh. Careful, Di!

I tried all the pastries calling my name within the first month there. I gained 15 pounds in 30 days! My God, it was tremendous! I am indeed a foodie, as is Barbara. I certainly couldn't eat the amounts she could and stay thin. My metabolism wasn't like hers, but we still both enjoyed what Paris had to offer in every delectable way.

The backstage door was unmarked, which was perfect. No one saw us beforehand as patrons entered through the showroom's grand front entrance. The Lido in 1972 offered an early (eight p.m.) dinner show and another production at 11, serving champagne and other drinks nightly. Two different productions per night. The producers lapsed their investments this way: they made more money if they extended one of the shows as opposed to creating two new ones. They also were better able to keep the first audience there, paying for two in one night if it was different from the early show. It was always packed, and so incredibly top-of-the-line in many ways! Set in the very heart of Paris, the Lido was by far the most famous cabaret in the world.

From the website cometoparis.com's article "A History of the Lido":

> The Lido opened its doors in 1933 and became one of the symbols of Parisian nightlife. A majestic, elegant, and sophisticated extravaganza. The venue attracted the creme de la creme of international audiences more than any other spectacle worldwide. In France, the Bluebell girls were indeed celebrities!

Margaret Kelly brought the sparkling Bluebell girls to the Lido in 1948. Over the years, the Lido has played host to and presented numerous legendary talents—from Shirley MacLaine, Elton John, Edith Piaf and Eartha Kitt to Marlene Dietrich and Josephine Baker. The Bluebells were handpicked by Madame Bluebell, and for over 40 years, she chose dancers who were classically trained but too tall for ballet.

The key to this Cabaret's historic success was the troupe of Bluebells, who were stunning, statuesque dancers. On the Lido stage they towered over the world of Cabaret. Bluebell girls and Lido boys. Any danseuse who ever donned the Bluebell feathers is an exemplary part of showgirl history.

We made our way to Barbara's dressing room upstairs, past the nude dressing room. Barb said, "Once you start rehearsals, I'll introduce you to the nudes."

We went up another flight of stairs to the dressing room Barbara shared with another principal dancer, who was presently on holiday. Miss Bluebell asked Barb if she would like to have me in her dressing room while the other principal was away for a month! Barbara and I were thrilled! We have always manifested magical experiences when rooming or traveling together. Sharing a dressing room with Barbara made my transition so smooth. She settled in to do her makeup, and like so many times in the Bahamas, we chatted in the lighted mirror.

My attention kept being averted to whatever this "thing" was that I smelled backstage. I inhaled deeply and realized it was the heady, musky, powdery and intense smell of pancake makeup. Within minutes of this realization, Barbara tossed and smashed a couple of loose pancakes into a bit of water in a big bucket and began churning it with a spatula.

"Di, can you paint my back for me, please?" She handed me a large sponge, explaining the body makeup the nudes and principal dancers wore. I watched closely to see the texture she wanted to achieve to know how much to put on her back. It was thick cosmetic paint—several coats, in fact! They did this twice a night and three times on Saturdays! Body paint! The smell of pancake permeated the very walls of the dressing rooms. This was Cabaret! I was home again, and the Lido was superior to any other place I'd been fortunate to work in!

Barbara said, "We need to leave in ten minutes to go to Miss Bluebell's office before the opening so you can meet her and see where she wants you to watch the show from, so I'll hurry!"

"I am so grateful, Barb. I needed this so much!" I exclaimed.

"But you were at Playboy, being a Bunny. That had to be fun?"

"It was fun, and I made some incredible friends, but I missed performing, and when your letter came, I knew I was meant to come here!"

"I told Miss Bluebell what an amazing showgirl you are!" Barb added.

19. Lido de Paris, France, 1972

"I love you, Barb!" I declared. "I'm so glad we're back together again. and in Paris!"

The dancing nudes and the Bluebells had separate dressing rooms. Barbara and I didn't get to spend much time onstage together aside from brief moments of feathers flying like soft wind across our faces! The pace of our work was quick and high-energy. It was like flying. In fact, we did everything from riding motorcycles to swinging on poles in a Rio number.

We also shared the Lido stage with horses, actors, champion ice skaters and headliners.

Astoundingly beautiful body paint and stage makeup complete, Barb and I finally went to meet Miss Bluebell. I was a little enamored, I must say, with the great Madame Bluebell! I was also a little nervous. We all want to be "enough" in person when hired with a photo, a recommendation and a résumé.

Barb delivered me to Miss Bluebell's office on the other side of the stage, away from most of the dressing rooms. We knocked and she said, "Come in," with her Irish-British accent.

When we were introduced, I shone brightly: "I'm so grateful and so excited to be here!"

"Wonderful," she smiled.

The loudspeaker announced, "Places! Five minutes!"

Barb turned to me. "Do you remember how to get back to the dressing room?"

"Oh, maybe not!" I admitted.

"No problem," piped in Miss Bluebell as she rose from her desk. "I'll walk you to the booth to watch."

"I'll find you afterward, Barb. Thank you!" I said as I waved goodbye to her.

The gracious, no-nonsense Miss Bluebell led me to a little table in front of the sound booth. "Make sure you watch the nudes, dear," she said. She also asked me to come to her office the following night to discuss my role in the shows and sort out the details. She had a waiter sent over so I could order 7-Up. It was a good thing he spoke English!

I was forever changed from that moment on. The phenomenal Lido production "Grand Prix" left me breathless. The cast performed a different show after this one—"Bonjour la Nui," I believe. Many patrons would stay for both. My mind was utterly blown by the quality and the production values of the Lido. The extravaganza was quick-paced with incredible choreography and it had everything from horses and jousting to erupting volcanoes and waterfalls. Plus, an ice rink rose from under the stage via hydraulics. The body makeup looked extraordinary on the beautiful nudes and principal dancers.

Buddy Vest and Sterling Clark were hot and supremely talented young vocalists and dancers. Buddy Vest danced with Barbara and two of the female principals in a disco number. I really loved that choreography.

It was the most dynamic, explosive show I'd ever seen. The productions were well funded, and Miss Bluebell and Donn Arden were geniuses together in executing their vision. The cost of the feathers, jewels furs, and custom shoes for the cast had to have been outrageous.

My head was spinning with excitement, and I was thrilled to see the phenomenal costumes and choreography for the dancing nudes. Barbara was the show's centerpiece and adorned that stage with her unique grace, talent and beauty. A star, indeed!

I saw myself performing here. I couldn't wait to find out which part I would be doing. There were 10 showgirls and 20 Bluebells. There were probably a dozen boy dancers and another six singers. Then there were the principal boys, principal girls, the stunt equestrians, the ice skaters—and Vest and Clark.

Wow! This was original French cabaret, complete with a full Fred and Ginger tribute, an underwater Atlantis number, an Incan number, a "Rio" number and a bordello number that the nudes did with Barb. In the bordello number, the showgirls danced on cane chairs, just like in *Cabaret* the musical. It was amazing, and I couldn't wait to do that one. We had a Latin pole number and an exciting New York motorcycle

Barbara Beverly (left) and Diane at the Lido de Paris, 1973.

routine as our opening with a lot of moving parts. There were three costume changes in the opening where we wound up in bright pink feathers onstage, and it was exceptional.

I waited until the audience filtered out of the showroom and wandered backstage. I asked for directions until I found my way back to Barb's dressing room. It wasn't easy.

"Oh my God, Barb!" I squealed when I saw her. "This is the most outstanding production I've ever seen!"

"I know," she replied, "and we are sold out every single night with packed audiences for both shows. We do three on Saturdays."

"I am so excited about doing this with you!" I said excitedly, "I can't wait to see which part is mine."

"I don't think anyone's leaving, so my guess is Miss Bluebell will have you swing for the nudes," she said as her dresser helped her out of her finale costume, wig, headdress and feathers. "She promised to hire someone to swing so they can have vacations, which in Paris are for a month or more at a time," Barbara explained. "The nudes haven't had any nights off for a while and no holidays."

"That should keep me busy," I said. "I'll come in tomorrow night to meet with Miss Bluebell before the show, and she will let me know exactly what I'll be doing!" I was so jazzed.

I told Barb how much fun I knew we'd have doing the numbers together. "The body makeup looks so exquisite onstage," I swooned. "I've never seen anything like it!"

"I think they wear it in the Crazy Horse Saloon, too. We have to go see that someday," Barbara replied.

We lounged in the dressing room that night between shows to catch up, laugh and plan. Barbara told me lots of Parisian stories. She had been there for a few years and had spent most of those years in French school. She was perfectly bilingual; I honestly don't know how I would have managed without her. I knew I was in for a wild ride in this dazzling city and at the Lido, and I couldn't wait to get started.

I was exhausted and travel-weary after the day I'd had. Barbara and I taxied down the glittering Champs-Élysées back to our apartment. I knew, like Shirley MacLaine's character in *Sweet Charity*, I'd landed in a pot of jam.

20

La Vie Parisienne, 1973

I was indeed assigned the role of swing girl for the nudes, and for my first stint in the show, I would learn an English girl's part. Her name was Pinky, and we became great friends while she taught me how to play her role in the show. She was going on a one-month holiday.

We had daily rehearsals on stage for the next few weeks. Learning both shows from Pinky was easy because I loved the choreography. It was magical, sexy, quick, feminine and beautiful. Everything was going well until we began dress rehearsals, and I learned that I would not be getting my own costumes. I would have to wear the costumes crafted for each dancer I replaced, including their shoes and boots!

We were all between 5'8" and 5'11", which helped, but when you start wearing huge 25-pound seahorse headdresses designed for someone else's head, things can get a bit more difficult. Inevitably, I'd wind up with the inner flaps of the eyeholes in my eyes and couldn't get offstage. Stop laughing! It was not funny! There were a zillion hydraulics on that stage, and I could have been sucked into God knows where.

Those Atlantis costumes were gorgeous but deadly to work in if they didn't fit exactly right. More than once, I was stuck onstage, unable to see. Once, Eric dragged me off, and another time, Mandy pulled me into the wings when I shouted, "Help me!" onstage from underneath that thing. Miss Bluebell came backstage to see what the problem was. When she arrived in Barb's dressing room, I was scratched near my eyes, bleeding and crying.

Miss Bluebell had a little habit of pulling on her earlobe when she was displeased. I noticed she did just that when she asked, "What happened?"

I tried to show her how the Evil Seahorse headdress did not fit over the bridge of my nose the way it fit Pinky, and the inner eye flaps slipped right into my eyeballs, leaving me blinded and scratched. She brought the wardrobe mistress in to look and see what she could do, but it only got worse. It never did fit me. Even when I could see out of the eyeholes, I could barely see, let alone do the choreography properly. I finally gave up and held the headdress in place with one hand each show, barely able to see.

20. La Vie Parisienne, 1973

It felt like Pinky was on holiday forever. When she returned, I was thrilled to sit next to her in the nudes' dressing room, but I was apologetic to her regarding the Evil Seahorse headdress. She told me it had never worked well for her either. At least she and I were the same shoe size. The next girl I replaced wore a smaller size, and so I had to wear tight shoes for six weeks! The ongoing dilemmas of a swing dancer were innumerable.

I didn't feel like Miss Bluebell was thrilled with me. She gave me weird side glances and spoke very little to me when she came into the dressing room. I asked Barb a few months in how I could win her trust and approval.

Barbara answered, "You could go talk to her. She's very open."

"What should I say?"

"Just ask her how she feels you're doing and what you can do to improve, maybe?" she suggested.

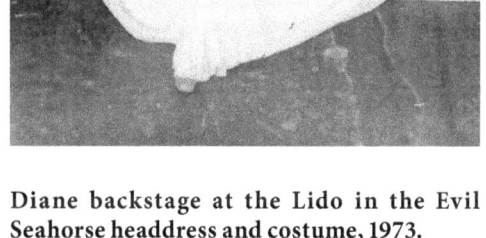

Diane backstage at the Lido in the Evil Seahorse headdress and costume, 1973.

I requested a meeting with Miss Bluebell to discuss my work and try to help her understand my point of view. I'd found that one must be very skilled to be a swing girl and tolerant of other dancers, wardrobe mistresses and their costumes.

I asked, "Is there anything that can be done with costumes, shoes and boots that don't fit when I swing for someone?"

"You can ask your dresser to adjust the costumes for you and ask her to put them back before the girl you are covering returns," Bluebell recommended. "As far as the shoes and boots go, you'll just have to tolerate a misfit."

"I will do that, thank you for the suggestion, Miss Bluebell," I replied.

"One more thing," she interjected. "I see you have gained some weight."

"Yes! Those beautiful pastries, bread and the cheese!" I tried to make light of it and prepared myself for the lecture.

"I don't mind a little bit of curve. I actually prefer it, just don't gain any more," she advised. "Many of the dancers gain their first month in Paris."

I thought maybe she grinned!

"I won't, I promise!" I smiled. I thanked her for her time and left. I was relieved, knowing I wasn't dealing with the unrealistic, misogynist views of Tibor Rudas regarding a showgirl's ideal weight. Perhaps she liked me after all?

I didn't gain any more weight, but it was hard because we went out every night and ate fabulous Parisian meals. We also danced in the underground discos into the wee hours of the morning. The discotheques were new in Paris in 1972, with lighted floors and special effects. It was so much fun! That is what kept me from gaining more weight. That and working seven nights a week.

I took Miss Bluebell's advice and spoke to the French dressers, who didn't speak any English and couldn't be bothered. The upkeep on the costumes was impeccable. They were extremely expensive costumes. Keep in mind, we did two different shows a night, and they had plenty to do and didn't want to continually make alterations. Somehow, between the girls who could translate and me, we got dressers to do the alterations. The problem was, I had to go back to the dressers before the girls who'd been on holiday returned and have them change them back. The dressers were not fond of me for that, and sometimes they didn't do them at all. For those that did, I gave them ten francs of my own money each week to thank them.

I had a hard time winning Miss Bluebell over. Then one night, one of the principal dancers, Christine, asked me if I could swing for her in a principal number. What? Really? Christine shared Barb's dressing room, and Barb suggested she ask me because I was the swing for the nudes, and I was best at disco, and it was a disco number! It was the routine three girls, including Barb, did with Buddy Vest. God, was Buddy gorgeous and talented. He had also danced in the movie *Sweet Charity* with Shirley MacLaine. He had to be the coolest male dancer I've ever worked with.

Christine cleared it with Miss Bluebell and taught me the disco number. The boots were a little tight, but I got to work with Barb in a featured number with Buddy Vest! It was the dance thrill of my lifetime! I lived for the nights Christine asked me to do it. This was my thing! It had high-energy disco choreography, and working with Buddy was so hot!

20. La Vie Parisienne, 1973

Christine had neck issues, and the number hurt her, so every now and then, she'd say, "Diane, can you do the disco number tonight?" There were so many head rolls, pops and snaps that she had difficulty coping.

Buddy and I always chatted as we left stage after the number, out of breath and spent.

We shared a love of disco. We became friendly. Between shows, he often spent time in Barb and Christine's dressing room, which I had also gotten into the habit of doing. Buddy was gay. Nevertheless, I had a huge crush on him. I believe Mandy had one, too. I think many girls in the show loved Buddy a little bit. He was incredibly charismatic, fun, sexy and adorably engaging with everyone.

The shocking thing that happened when I did the disco number was that Miss Bluebell came to my dressing room and said, "That number wasn't half bad."

I was so relieved that she saw where my talents were. That was her only version of a compliment to me. Ever. At least she came to my dressing room between shows and offered it. It was *something*. I needed *something*. I had worked hard for it.

After six months of being a swing girl, I got my own part in the show. One of the nudes was leaving, and I wouldn't have to swing anymore! I finally had shoes, boots and costumes custom-fitted for me. For the rest of my time at the Lido, there was no swing girl at all.

Diane backstage at the Lido in the disco number costume, 1973.

Which meant that none of us had nights off. I had one night off in the nine months I worked there. Fortunately, it coincided with a night Barbara had off, and we went out to a fantastic French restaurant that introduced me to escargot. Afterwards, we saw the Crazy Horse show. My one and only night off in Paris, and I chose to see cabaret over a visit to the Louvre! I never regretted it.

The Crazy Horse Saloon was a provocative French burlesque-style show with silhouette dancing. The titillating and sensual show proved that

Barbara Beverly and roommate Eric Brown at Lido de Paris, 1973.

20. La Vie Parisienne, 1973

striptease can be elevated to the theater. The Crazy Horse was the most avant-garde cabaret in Paris and has been for nearly 60 years. A temple to the female form, a place with its own mythology that celebrates nights when the City of Lights becomes the City of Delights!

Erotic paintings adorned the walls. The furnishings were lavish. They were at the heart of something entirely different from traditional cabaret. All the girls were the same height and shape. Modern, psychedelic projections lighted their nearly nude forms in each number, often in black silhouette. They all wore the same stage makeup and black pageboy wigs with bangs and bright red lips. The show was extraordinary and unlike anything else in the world. I was so glad I saw it with Barb. We loved it! The current director is Christian Louboutin, and it continues to creatively evolve.

Life in Paris unfolded. I had picked up a bit of French, but I was still scared to go out alone. I spoke more of it after a few glasses of Cote du Rhone, our wine of choice. It was about $1.50 a bottle and stupendous. I drank more wine than I had in the past. All of us did. It was so inexpensive and so good!

Occasionally, someone bought us expensive French champagne, which often happened at the fabulous new discotheques. Barbara and I had a favorite underground discotheque that we regularly haunted. It had incredible lighted floors and was *tres chic*. One night after the show, when we were dancing there, Barbara ran into some friends, three French gentlemen who had one of those expensive bottles of champagne sent to our table. We struck up a conversation with them. They were very interesting, but there was something about them. What was it? They were dressed in designer suits and possibly in their late 40s or 50s. When disappearing to the ladies' room with Barbara, she told me they were French Mafia.

Ahhh! That explains the vibe. She said her ex-boyfriend had been friends with one of them, Benoit, and they were nice. That night, after the disco closed, Benoit invited us to a nearby opium den for a late nightcap. Barb told me she had been before and that I had to see this!

"Well, of course, I'd never even heard of opium dens. Let's go!" I announced.

Off we went in Benoit's limo. Wow! Was it ever incredible. Benoit led us down a stunning hallway, laden with exquisite artwork and expensive wallpaper. He opened a door to a small, dimly lit room. In the middle sat a large, round indigo velvet lounging pouf. If you sat on the pouf cushion, you could look up at twinkling golden stars on the painted indigo ceiling. It was like a fantasy. He asked if we'd like a bit of opium. Barbara said, "Sure, we'd love to try some."

I asked nervously, "Can we try it on our own?"

"Of course," suggested Benoit. "You can enjoy some privacy for as long as you'd like. I'll leave you with this small bottle and I'll be in the foyer whenever you're ready to leave." He left us with a tiny spoon and a little cobalt blue bottle. He was most gracious and closed the door behind him.

"I'm glad you asked for our privacy. I wanted us to do this alone, too," Barbara added as she opened the bottle of soft white powdery substance.

"This is opium?" I questioned.

"Yes, and it's not like anything you've ever tried."

"What's it like?" I asked hesitantly.

"Kinda like a quaalude, but better."

"How long does it last?"

"Just a little while," Barb said. "I think you'll like it!"

"Okay. How do you use it?"

"Like cocaine," she said as she dipped the tiny spoon into the bottle, producing some of the powdery substance. "They only have the best stuff, so you only need a tiny bit. I think they bring it from Morocco and sell it."

I braced myself for the new experience. We sniffed a very small amount and waited for it to perform its magic. Our heads were swirling in a euphoric rush followed by relaxation and relief from all pain—which dancers always have a little, or a *lot*, of. We became slightly sleepy as the spectral visions began in our minds, eventually passing out on the velvet cushion and lying back to enjoy the ride and the twinkly ceiling.

So, this is what poppies produce? I always wondered. Could Dorothy have been having an opium trip in Oz? After all, she did doze off in the poppy fields. That all made sense now.

I later learned that opium is a highly addictive non-synthetic narcotic that is extracted from the poppy plant, *papaver somniferum*. The opium poppy is the source for morphine, codeine, heroin and more. According to Wikipedia, the poppy plant "was grown in the Mediterranean region as early as 5000 B.C. and has since been cultivated in several countries throughout the world. The milky fluid that seeps from its incisions in the unripe seedpod is scraped by hand and air-dried to produce what is known as opium."

After an hour or so, we rose and decided to get ourselves home. Unlike cocaine, which was all we had to compare it to, it was very soothing and relaxing.

Benoit had a car waiting for us and insisted we return sometime. We thanked him and stumbled to the limo that headed off toward our apartment. It was nearly dawn, and the smell of chocolate filled our senses as we reached our home. Every morning, the chocolatier on the ground level of our building began making the most divine chocolate in Paris. That scent

20. La Vie Parisienne, 1973

always takes me back to those late nights and early mornings in the Rue Pergoles.

We never returned to the opium den, and I've never been to one since that otherworldly experience in 1973.

Barbara and I attended classes during the day nearly every week: ballet with the legendary Peter Gosse at L'Opera, and jazz with Victor Upshaw. Peter's classes were full, with over 100 dancers! I didn't like ballet, and the large crowds didn't make it more enjoyable for me. But there was magic in ballet!

Victor's classes really challenged us. His classes were much smaller, 12 or 14 dancers. Victor made it feel good to be in class. He had been a choreographer for the Lido for years, and I loved his work. He had also choreographed shows in Spain, Hawaii and Lebanon. Victor was a genius. Going to his classes left us drained because they were a workout. He pushed his students, and we loved him. He was also great at giving everyone individual notes during classes. I learned so much from him. He was gone way too soon; he was only 50, when he passed in 1990. At the time of his death, he had a hit show at the Riviera Hotel in Las Vegas, "Crazy Girls"; he conceived and choreographed it, designed the costumes and wrote most of the music.

One Wednesday night, just before the Lido's 11 o'clock show, a waiter brought a note backstage to me from someone in our audience: "Hi, Diane. Carolee said you were here working in this production! We'll be at the second show tonight, can't wait to see you and the show! Let's get a bottle of wine after! Danny & Shelly xo."

I hadn't shared a single word with them since the Tropicana mono debacle. I sent back a quick note: "Meet me after the show. Just wait on the stage. I'll be out shortly after the finale! So great to know you're here! Diane xo."

We met for a drink and had a few late-night laughs, catching up over a good bottle of wine. They were adorable. They were traveling Europe, only working in shows when they needed money. They were vagabonds, gypsies in the most delightful sense.

Adventurers! Artists enjoying life, fellow jet-setters. We talked about the Lido and what it was like working in Paris. I was happy for them. I felt nothing at all for Danny. I can't say I ever did. He was a sexual teacher for me!

We kissed goodbye on both cheeks French-style, hugged like the Americans we were, and left feeling like old pals, reunited in this fabulous place. I was amazed at their zest for life, their *joie de vivre*. I told them about the shows to see. The Crazy Horse Saloon was at the top of that list and they did go see it.

It was so good to see them happily enjoying Paris. It felt like our reacquaintance had a purpose, but I wasn't sure what it was. I loved seeing happy couples at this juncture in my life, but it also added to my loneliness.

I didn't date much in Paris. Several waiters had asked me out, but they were too short for me. Many spoke pretty good English and tried hard, but I wasn't vibing with any of them. It was hard to meet men in Paris due to my work schedule and the language barrier.

I loved living with Barb, Neil and Eric. Home life was full of laughter, and working in the show was fun, but it was becoming my whole life once more. I was longing to be in love. Still pining away for Arnold deep down. I missed him. Sometimes, I wondered if I only missed him because I hadn't met anyone new.

On a rare sunny day in May, I received a surprisingly long letter from Arnold. Out of the blue! I'm not even sure how he found me. He was still touring the U.S. with Sonny Turner and Sound Limited. Apparently he was feeling the same way I was. He missed me, although he was with an Italian girl from Louisville, Kentucky—the daughter of some Mafioso. He was afraid of the family and discontent in the relationship. He longed for us to reunite.

That did it for me. It sent me into a spiral!

I responded to Arnold's letter, expressing my similar feelings. After a little correspondence, and a single phone call, it would seem we were reuniting. He asked me to come back to him. He begged me to meet him in Atlanta. He was booked in New York for a few months and was planning to leave the Italian girl and the band after his gig was over. He wanted to settle down with me in Atlanta and get married. Wow! This was all a shock. I still felt in love with him.

There was still a month to go before I left. Patrick, Miss Bluebell's son, was

Diane (left) and Barbara in a Paris park, 1973.

running everything at the Lido while she was out of the country. I asked for a meeting to give Patrick my notice. He barked at me, "You can't do that!"

I replied, teary-eyed, "I've given you a month's notice both in person and in this letter. I'm leaving Paris to get married!"

"When she's back, you can give Blue your notice." That was the end of the conversation.

I was pissed! I had done the right thing and given a one-month notice. Two weeks later, Miss Bluebell wasn't back yet. I went to Patrick again to remind him I'd be leaving in two weeks if he needed me to teach someone my part. After all, my initial six-month contract was complete, and I was working month-to-month.

He refused to acknowledge what I was saying and avoided the situation altogether.

I left when I said I would, without his acknowledgment. It made me feel like a thief in the night, disappearing from Paris that way.

I mailed my dated resignation letter to Miss Bluebell and thanked her, apologized and provided my forwarding address in Atlanta.

I contacted my friend Patty in Atlanta. She still had her two-bedroom apartment we had once shared. She needed a roommate and said she'd be happy to have me. I told her my story, and she said, "Whatever happens is cool. I may be gone for a while. While you're here, I'll pay my half of the rent when I'm away." I wondered what she would be doing. Patty said, "Just come. I'm sure you can find a job after being at Playboy. I'd love for us to be roomies, plus I know everyone in the restaurant, club and bar scene here!"

"I agree," I said, smiling, "but I don't know exactly when Arnold would arrive."

Patty knew Arnold well. We had all been on tour around the world together.

"You're both welcome to move in any time!" she offered. She was so sweet. I was so fortunate!

I had friends there, and I liked Atlanta a lot. It was a very happening city in the '70s and a big music mecca. Arnold would easily find work in one of its many recording studios. He had friends who were studio musicians in the Atlanta circuit.

"Call me when you get your itinerary, and I'll pick you up at the airport," Patty suggested.

"Oh, Patty, you're such a good friend! I love you. Thank you for understanding and for your offer." Once again, there was someone there to comfort and support me through a transition. I knew I had good guardian angels.

We enjoyed the moment of reconnection, and I was looking forward to living with Patty again. Our lives had been entangled with talented men we loved but whose lifestyle on tour challenged our relationships. Always back and forth. I suspected that would be the "going away sometimes" she mentioned.

I did two shows at the Lido on a Thursday, went home to collect my luggage and had a taxi deliver me to the Charles De Gaulle Airport at two a.m. It was a teary departure between me and Barb. We were very sad to part ways. I'd loved "La Vie Parisienne" immensely. I boarded the red-eye that would take me back to America.

Au revoir, Paris!

Diane in the NY number at the Lido de Paris, 1973.

21

Recovery and Romance, 1973

A lyric from the Platters song "Twilight Time" played on and on in my head on that twinkly spring red-eye from Paris to Atlanta. I wondered if I could listen to the Platters' tunes that Sonny, Arnold, and the group sang for another year on the road. No, I couldn't do it, and I'd told Arnold that. I would not live on tour again. It was not good for me at all. I was driven to do things in the world, and my creativity needed outlets.

This time, it was different. Arnold had proposed marriage and settling down together in a city we liked very much. The tunes he sang continued to haunt and soothe my weary soul like a salve, like some mystical siren beckoning me from afar. This must be love. I truly missed him and wanted a life with him. A creative, thriving life filled with love in one place. I was once again sacrificing my own career to be with him. Exchanging my loneliness for love.

I needed to recover from my job at the Lido. I loved it, but it had drained me. I was physically exhausted from working nine months with only one day off. The rigorous regimen of being the Lido swing girl had been a lot. As grateful as I was to have worked there, it was out of balance for me to work that much. I needed to recover and decompress while preparing for Arnold to arrive. I wanted time to settle into a routine, a life, so that when he came to Atlanta, this life appealed to him more than being on tour. Although it seemed he was already there! He, too, was burned out with touring and longed for change. We were on the same page at the same time. But isn't that what love is about?

Except that Arnold was still in a relationship with Sofia, the Italian girl in Kentucky. I knew Arnold Robinson, and he sounded broken and done! I was sure we would reunite. Deep down, I felt we still had a destiny. We were not finished. We were very incomplete.

The endless questions began gnawing on my mind on that flight until I finally succumbed to the Platters' tune whirling through my brain and got some much-needed sleep.

* * *

As promised, my dear friend Patty was there for me in every possible way. She drove to her apartment from the Atlanta airport and deposited me into my new room. Once we caught up a bit, I passed out in the soft sheets. I was travel-weary, world-weary, Lido-weary, and primed for sleep to enfold me into its soothing embrace. I slept deeply, dreamt of Arnold, our life together in Atlanta and all it could be. I slept most of the next day.

Patty was working in underground Atlanta at Scarlett O'Hara's, the very popular club where Arnold and her keyboard-playing boyfriend Joe had played with Sonny Turner and Sound Limited. (She had originally met Joe there when he played with Sonny and Arnold.) When Patty wasn't with Joe on tour, she served cocktails there.

One of Scarlett O'Hara's managers, Brian, was planning to open his own lunch restaurant in Atlanta: the Red Baron, with an aviation theme. Patty had offered to be the head waitress and train new staff for him. When the Red Baron was about to open, Patty was deeply involved with Joe and went off to Vegas with him for a few months.

I hadn't bought a car just yet as I was still new in town. But, poof!, just like that, Patty was gone! She'd highly recommended I replace her at the Red Baron. Brian was a great guy I'd known from Scarlett O'Hara's and he even offered to drive me to and from work if I accepted his job offer. He generously planned to help me find a car. How could I say no? Brian needed help getting started, and I needed money, friends and a ride. So I went to work five days a week. I helped open the place, saved money and bought a red VW Bug.

With a regular, constant lunch crowd, the Red Baron started off doing reasonably well. We had difficulty finding waitresses who wanted to work lunch shifts. While searching, I served all the lunches.

I'd saved money while in Paris. Enough money to buy the car, but I didn't intend to be at the Red Baron more than the first few months.

I regularly spoke with my friend and former fellow Playboy Bunny, Mariah. She told me the dinner restaurant manager at the exclusive Hyatt Regency Atlanta was looking for a female bartender. He knew that Bunnies were trained to know what was in every cocktail, and he asked if she would like to tend bar. But Mariah had decided to go back to school to get her degree for a career in medicine. "Would you like to interview for the bartending job at the Hyatt?" Mariah asked.

"Is it a full-time job?" I inquired.

"Yes, five nights a week. The manager is a really nice gentleman from Brazil whom you'll likely enjoy working with."

"Is there health insurance?" I questioned.

"Oh yes, it's Hyatt!"

21. Recovery and Romance, 1973

I did the interview, and I was hired. I now had good insurance through the hotel! That was a plus.

I told the Hyatt I'd have to give a two-week notice at the Red Baron and could start training afterward. It was processed through HR and confirmed: I would start in two weeks. Finally, I could make some real money in one of the classiest restaurants and lounges in town, where jazz singers performed nightly.

While all this was happening, Arnold and I had been going back and forth by phone, trying to work out his departure and return to Atlanta. This was not an easy process. I was stressed and distraught. The long-distance aspect of our relationship carried so much uncertainty. He was losing a lot, parting ways with Sonny (Arnold had been with Sonny for over eight years) and Sofia.

On my 22nd birthday, while getting ready to take over the bar for the night, Patty surprised me and popped in with a cake and a wonderful gift, my first *I Ching*. The lounge singer sang to me while my co-workers joined in, and we all had time for a little cake. It was very sweet and surprising because I didn't know Patty was back from Vegas. Arnold flew back to New York to break up with Sofia.

This was a challenging time for me. Arnold was calling every few days, and it wasn't pretty. We argued about his delayed arrival and the promises he continued to make with no follow-up. He was scared. Sofia was unstable, according to Arnold. He was having a difficult time breaking it off.

Arnold had promised so many times that he was on his way back—and then wasn't. I couldn't do this anymore. I was fed up with waiting, waiting, waiting. I needed my life back. I felt imprisoned waiting for Arnold, and although I was in love with him, I stressed trying to figure out how to get us back together. I talked to a psychic at work, did little spells, tossed the *I Ching*, you name it, I tried it.

I told Arnold I had met someone new and was planning a little trip to Vegas for a week. Of course it wasn't true. It was hard to lie to Arnold, but I did it to establish some boundaries, a concept I was just beginning to acquire. I forced myself to ignore his calls all week as if I was away. Patty even told him I was in Vegas one day when he called.

Exactly one week later, Arnold walked into the restaurant at the Hyatt. I was stunned! He'd finally completed all of the difficult deeds he'd intended to do and made his way back to me. I welcomed him with open arms. We loved one another, and finally, we were back together. I hadn't seen him for a year!

We settled into our apartment and Patty went back on tour with Joe every few weeks, even though they were on and off again. Relationships with people on tour were so hard.

Life unfolded beautifully for me and Arnold. He got a part-time gig doing vocals on "soundalikes" at Melody Recording. Soundalikes were records with tunes that sounded like the original artists. Arnold could sing like Barry White, Al Jarreau and many others who were popular then. Melody Studio hired a house band and various vocalists to record soundalikes. They made good money selling those records. Their ads stated, "Sounds like the original artist."

We started making lots of plans. Patty and Joe eventually broke up. She couldn't do it anymore. The long-distance relationship was hard on them, too. She started dating a musician. Everyone was happy and in one place again!

One breezy day, November 1, 1973, to be exact, Arnold and I dressed up and went downtown to the justice of the peace and got married. Just like that! Patty had champagne and cake for us when we got home. We began planning our new life together and started looking for an apartment of our own.

My former Bunny friend Mariah and her fiancé Danny had just moved into a gorgeous, brand-new apartment complex in Decatur, Georgia, in the Atlanta suburbs. After a lively visit with them at their new place, Arnold and I asked the leasing agent for a showing. The only apartment available was right across the hall from them. How ideal! Shortly after we moved in, Mariah and Danny asked us to be maid of honor and best man at their wedding. We became close and had fun being neighbors.

We decorated that apartment to our heart's content. Arnold's part-time singing gig became a full-time job at Melody Recording. He worked from midnight to eight a.m. Things were looking up for us. We couldn't have been happier. I didn't miss dancing at all. Still, I wished I could have both. I wondered if maybe Arnold felt the same way. All I knew was that we had a great big life in Atlanta and lots of new friends.

While living in this new complex, we had our only real run-in with overt racism and prejudice. While moving in, we came home and found that someone had written "MOVE NIGGER" on our front door in heavy black marker. We were horrified. We couldn't reach the managing rental office because it was after hours. Arnold photographed it and we called the rental office the following morning. They came over immediately and had their maintenance crew remove it post haste! They investigated and found it was one of our neighbors down the hall, people with whom they had already had some trouble. They were evicted immediately! It was reassuring to know that the complex was inclusive and expeditious.

* * *

Mimi was the name of the girlfriend of the Melody Recording sound engineer. She and I began sharing our handiwork while hanging out at the studio. We shared a love of all things creative and began to discuss creating a business selling our handmade clothing items.

In fact, my line of stage wear for musicians was born out of that idea. I became "Gypsy Peacock" and embroidered gorgeous custom-made stage wear for entertainers. Arnold and I and one of Arnold's wealthy musician friends, Lenny, began discussing opening a retail store.

I got a tiny little retail shop on Peachtree Street in Buckhead to start. Mimi, Nancy and I sold handmade items. We made everything ourselves: embroidered pillows, shirts, lots of denim, bags, candles, jewelry and assorted home items.

As the business grew, Arnold and Lenny decided to open a much larger Peachtree Street store, with antiques being the primary focus, with the custom clothing merging into that establishment as well. Buckhead was the Beverly Hills of Atlanta, a mecca of upscale boutiques, restaurants and music venues in ivy-covered brownstone buildings. Lenny's mom and sister bought antiques for our new store. They found incredible pieces, and Arnold and I secured a business loan through our bank to get our portion of the retail store underway.

Bleu Cheese, a very popular, trendy retail store, was adjacent to the spot we had leased. Once we decorated our store and began discussing advertising, we knew we needed a name for it. We debated dozens of ideas until we settled on House Dressing. Of course, everyone thought we were a division of the booming Bleu Cheese, but we were just clever in naming it. It grew steadily, and Gypsy Peacock really took off. I was creating stage wear for rock stars.

I also took a new job serving cocktails four short evenings a week because the Hyatt had become too much. It was at the Wits' End, a brand-new dinner theater at the Sheraton Biltmore Hotel. The place was extraordinarily successful. The owner had been in a comedic song and dance duo with Dick Van Dyke in Danville, Illinois, before Dick became Dick.

A former Playboy club manager ran the Wits' End, and we made incredible money. The dinner was Southern buffet–style, and cocktail waitresses only served drinks. The cocktail waitresses dressed in darling, sexy outfits that showed a lot of leg. It was a wonderful place to work. The patrons I met during my stint there included our exceptional governor, Jimmy Carter, and Rosalynn Carter. One evening I served Ted Turner and his party of four (this was pre–Jane Fonda). The writers and stage manager of the show was a young married couple, Bonnie and Terry Turner. Years later, they became the writers of numerous Emmy-winning TV shows, including *3rd Rock from the Sun*, *Saturday Night Live* (they created the Coneheads), *That '70s Show*, *That '80s Show* and *Normal, Ohio*.

The Wits' End show was brilliant! I worked four nights a week and

Diane outside the House Dressing store, 1974.

still managed to help Arnold with our retail store and custom clothing business.

Arnold and I decided to move to Buckhead to get out of the suburbs and be closer to our work. We found a gorgeous extra-large 1950s apartment on Peachtree Street that we loved. It was in a beautiful area with magnolia trees surrounding it, spilling fragrant magnolia blossoms into our windows when in bloom. It was one of the happiest times in my life.

Arnold and I had a large circle of artistic friends and a fun life together. While we owned the store, Arnold's gig at the recording studio ended. Soundalikes were seasonal and didn't employ musicians year-round. We certainly didn't foresee that. The soundalike recordings took about six months to record. Once mixed and packaged, their TV commercials sold most of the records. They didn't record more until they needed another album, so it wasn't consistent.

This put a dent in our family income, to say the least. Fortunately, I made great money at the Wits' End. But our retail store took up huge amounts of my time because Gypsy Peacock was more in demand than the antiques. Though Arnold ran the store in person every day, I had to be there to design, measure and work with tailors and seamstresses to do customer fittings. I did a lot of hand-embroidered designs on most of the clothing, which kept me working day and night, in addition to the dinner

21. Recovery and Romance, 1973

theater job. I loved all of it, but I was the primary breadwinner now, and I was slowly burning out. I was too tired to have fun, go out, or live!

Even though I was still in my 20s, this took a toll on me. I wanted to let go of the dinner theater gig, but the money was so good and I needed to support our household. I begged Arnold to find more work. Most of what he was offered required him to go on tour, and we agreed that didn't work for us. But something had to give! I was wearing too many hats and was way too tired for a 24-year-old.

22

Recapturing Lost Youth, 1974

Arnold was pretty frustrated not finding work in town. The fact that our retail store was still costing us money didn't help. We plugged away, Arnold working on building up our business and me being weighed down by the demands of two jobs. It was taking a toll on our relationship without us even realizing it.

One of the recording studio musicians phoned to ask Arnold to come hear a band that was recording at Melody. The band was called Passion, and the husband and wife who fronted the dynamic Southern rock group were from New Orleans. They were a huge success in Louisiana and were now recording their new album in Atlanta. They were seeking a manager with experience who could guide them both musically and professionally, someone who knew the Southern circuit and could help with connections and bookings to promote their new album and create their touring schedule. The studio musicians thought Arnold would be a great candidate. He thought so, too.

Arnold met with the couple and they hit it off. A six-month contract was forged, and Arnold became their new manager. He certainly knew the music industry and the Southern circuit and had endless ideas for them. The money was minimal but regular until he actually booked them. He would be required to do a bit of traveling to New Orleans, as well as some of the markets where they would be touring. His presence would establish the band professionally and solidify them in the eyes of those he connected them to. There was really no way around him having to do some traveling.

Arnold's first assignment required him to be in New Orleans for a month to plan local performances and schedule tour dates while their new album was being mixed in Atlanta. We agreed that would be fine. After all, it wouldn't be forever. And off he went to New Orleans.

At about that same time, I was asked to become a fashion coordinator for Mimi's, a restaurant that had recently opened at the Omni International in downtown Atlanta. How would I add more to my plate? I was hired to advise each new employee on how to dress for the exclusive French

22. Recapturing Lost Youth, 1974

Riviera–themed restaurant. It was only feasible for me to work part-time for its Austrian owner, Maximilian Schnallinger. This was a way for me to further establish our retail store and my label, Gypsy Peacock.

I scheduled meetings with the new employees twice a week and visited Mimi's once a week for dinner to ensure they were following the fashion protocol. The exquisite establishment overlooked the ice skating rink inside the Omni International, Atlanta's hotbed of cultural activity. It was an international tourist attraction with an adjacent indoor theme park called the World of Sid and Marty Krofft. With Mimi's culinary perfection, the restaurant quickly became an Atlanta landmark for tourists and visiting celebrities. My well-paid, part-time position was established. I was given a monthly dining budget and a generous paycheck.

All the beautiful local young actors, models and beauties wanted to work at Mimi's. The fashion statements I created for the employees enhanced that desire. The waiters, waitresses, bartenders and busboys were modeling Mimi's brand while working.

Before creating my vision for Mimi's employees, I met with their former fashion coordinator, David, and he guided me through what he had established at the restaurant, passing on the portfolio he had created for the staff to emulate. Of course, I added my own flair to it. He was incredibly helpful, and we became fast friends. In fact, he became my favorite party partner with Arnold away. He was a beautiful bisexual man, and he led me to party after party and club after club to have fun! Needless to say, I became even more exhausted. But I was doing something Arnold and I had not been doing, and that was acting my age. I'm not sure if that was because Arnold was eight years older or because he just wasn't much of a party person. He was a serious Capricorn most of the time.

I loved having fun again. I had missed this part of myself, and being only 25 years old, I certainly still had some oats to sow.

David and I were the same age and quite the fashionistas. He also sent me customers for Gypsy Peacock. We were together constantly, often falling asleep on one another's couches after late nights at the clubs. We saw delightful drag shows, frequented the gay bars to dance the night away, and attended local fashion shows.

Before I knew it, I was only home to care for my dog. Spending that much time with David made me realize that this was a type of relationship I had never had. Without even realizing what was happening, we became lovers. Yes, I cheated on my husband for the first time. Interestingly, though, I didn't feel any guilt. I simply woke up to the fact that Arnold and I had never been very sexual or fun-loving in our marriage. I needed to know what having an exciting, sexy lover was like. I was too young to deny this natural instinct.

Something sensual was awakened that I hadn't felt since my Calvin Lockhart encounters. My closest friends began to clue me in to the fact that I might not be happily married. Ya think? Obviously, the mere fact that I cheated showed me I wasn't happy with Arnold.

I didn't miss Arnold. That was my first clue. We spoke on the phone daily, and when he did return from New Orleans, I wasn't excited.

Arnold went back on the road with Passion for another month. He was making a minimal amount of money. It helped, but he was doing more for the band than they could afford to pay him. At least he was experiencing some creative fulfillment.

I didn't miss Arnold at all. In fact, I was having so much fun I barely thought of him. My good friends and I began to take a deeper look at my feelings and examined my new lifestyle.

What had I given up to be a wife at such a young age? I became increasingly aware of who I really was as opposed to who I was when I got married three years earlier. Things were not looking hopeful for me and Arnold.

Arnold finally came home. Passion was launched, and touring was underway. The initial six-month contract was complete. And Arnold was once again out of work. My lost feelings for him must have been obvious. He became controlling and anxious. The store was doing okay, but his friend Lenny pulled out of the partnership. We were now on our own with the store. The most successful thing about House Dressing was Gypsy Peacock, which was taking on more influence in the world of rock star fashion in the South.

Between that and my work at Mimi's, I was able to leave the Wits' End dinner theater. I was delighted to end my cocktail waitress phase once and for all. Plus, Maximilian at Mimi's was planning to open a second restaurant at the Omni, called, Max. It was to be an upscale, chic, Western-themed steak house and club designed by the internationally known Angelo Donghia. Max and his lovely wife asked me to create the look for the staff at this new establishment. It was so exciting to work alongside this group of European designers. My success as a fashion designer was soaring, and I was taken away from home more and more.

Arnold kept looking for work in Atlanta as a musician. to no avail. He branched out and began contacting his friends in Los Angeles to see if that could be a good direction in his search for steady employment. A dear college friend of Arnold's asked him to come out and help with his very successful contracting business in L.A. Once there, Ben offered him a full-time job. Arnold stayed in L.A., learning a new business, as I continued working and partying in Atlanta.

After about six weeks, Arnold suggested I close the store as our current lease was about to end. He advised me to sell everything in the store

22. Recapturing Lost Youth, 1974

and our home and bring the money to Los Angeles to start a new life. "We can have a fresh start here in L.A. and renew our marriage," he insisted.

"Will your job with Ben be solid?" I asked. "After all, he hasn't paid you yet."

"He has put me up in his home while training me, and he promises to pay me soon," Arnold said.

"I know. I just want to be sure we can get started there."

"The money from the store and everything we sell will do that!" he insisted.

"Okay," I said. "I'd love to start over in L.A."

I meant it. I didn't want to be that unhappy woman, having an affair with someone because I was overworked and under-supported by my husband. I really believed that if Arnold was thriving again, we would be happy once more. I wanted us to work. I take commitments seriously. Part of me remembered when Arnold and I were happy when he was successful. I wanted that back. How naïve I was.

David helped me close our store and sell everything in it and in my home. I wound up with $12,000 to take to L.A. to get us started, believing Arnold's job with Ben would be paying off by the time I arrived. It took me about a month to do this on my own and arrange to drive across the country. I was going with two dear friends, a couple, Dixie and Michael, who worked with me at Max's restaurant. They were also anxious to relocate to the Land of Milk and Honey.

I couldn't have done it without David's help. He even bought a lot of our furniture for himself. One thing I didn't expect was for David to say as my departure time was near, "I'm falling in love with you."

"Wait, what?" I was shocked. "I thought we were simply friends with benefits?"

"We are. But this last month made me realize how much I'm going to miss you and how I have come to need you."

I was dumbfounded because I had never allowed myself to feel the same until this moment.

"I care so much for you, David," I explained. "Are you suggesting I leave my husband without giving us another chance?"

"No, no, I'm not, and I want you to be happy," he stammered. "Just forget it. I'll put those feelings away. Let's just be happy for all we've enjoyed together." He rallied. I rallied. I gazed into his beautiful, soulful puppy dog eyes at length. We hugged a long embrace one last time and finally said goodbye.

The next morning, I drove my jam-packed yellow Saab sedan to pick up Dixie and Michael and we headed to L.A., saying farewell to our lives in Hotlanta.

23

The Land of Milk and Honey, 1976

Dixie and Michael and I were determined to make our trip fun without feeling rushed. It was a beautiful spring, and we planned to stop at several places we all wanted to visit.

Our first stop was New Orleans. We only planned a few days there and were utterly enchanted with the French Quarter, the Cajun dishes and the outstanding coffee. The people we met were fun-loving and interesting. The city had a vibe I'd never experienced anywhere else. There was more to NOLA than we had time to explore, but it was romantic, historical and mysterious. The architecture was fascinating. I wanted to stay much longer and explore this beguiling city.

Headed southwest, we decided to visit the Rio Grande. It was a picturesque valley along the southern Texas border representing Americana at its finest. We took the time to tour and hike the most beautiful vistas on our first day there and had memorable Tex-Mex meals.

My car broke down while we were there and we had to spend an extra night in our small motel waiting for repairs. It was a costly servicing. Then off we sped to Nevada. I hadn't been to Las Vegas since I had acquired mono there years earlier.

I dropped my friends off at their stop and was invited to have dinner with Barb and her husband, Piero. Afterward, I went with Barb to the Stardust to see the show and spend the night. When I arrived, Barb brought me backstage and I met several of the dancers. Dixie and Michael had friends in Vegas to visit as well, so at showtime, they met me, and we saw the show compliments of Barb. The Allez Lido show was off-the-charts magnificent. It was quick-paced and dynamic with modern music, choreography by Rich Rizzo and a huge cast. It was electrifying to see!

Barb met me in the casino lounge between shows to have a drink with her and Frank Rosenthal, manager of the Stardust. Rosenthal was later played by Robert De Niro in *Casino,* a film about Rosenthal's life.

23. The Land of Milk and Honey, 1976

"Lefty" Rosenthal was one of the last remaining mobsters running things in Vegas and liked having the principal dancers congregate outside the showroom near the sportsbook with him. They were his trophies. This was one of those nights. Barb and I had a lively conversation with him about our long friendship, and the slightly scary Frank Rosenthal asked me when I'd like to start in the Stardust's Lido show. I laughed and told him I hadn't danced in five years.

He seemed unbothered. "That's okay. You can have your comeback here!"

While the offer was sweet of "Lefty," just the thought of dancing again freaked me out. I felt out of shape, even if I didn't look out of shape. I was slim and only 25 years old. I was at my peak, actually. Dancing again hadn't occurred to me until this moment.

"Noooo!" I thought. I was on a mission to save my marriage. I had recommitted to my new hopes with Arnold. I didn't dwell on the dancing notion. I was flattered that "Lefty" had asked, though, and I thanked him.

Kathy Shriner (left) and Barbara Beverly on a postcard for the Allez Lido show, 1976.

Shortly after that rendezvous, he and the rest of the Mafia left Vegas.

Most of the film *Casino* was spot on, according to Barbara. Herb Tobman and Al Sachs took over as hotel managers shortly after I visited. Las Vegas became corporate-owned and no longer run by the Mafia.

For a few days we did a lot of catching up at Barb and Piero's home. It was good to see them happy and settled, even though I had always found Sicilian-born Piero much too serious. He was working as a craps dealer in Caesars Palace while Barb performed as principal dancer at the Lido. Barb was so stunning in it! As always, her performance was unique and legendary. We had a tearful goodbye, and I headed west to Los Angeles.

Arnold was uneasy and didn't want me staying at Ben's house. Apparently Ben and his family didn't want me for some reason. I found that weird. They were lovely people and had prepared a fabulous gumbo dinner for us. Still, after that initial night at their beautiful home in Baldwin Hills, Arnold arranged for us to stay with a darling Canoga Park couple he had befriended. They were a blessing. And they had a pool!

Dixie and Michael stayed with friends in West Hollywood for a while. Once we all found our footing and secured jobs, we agreed to share an apartment. Again, I found it odd that Ben and his family did not welcome me into their home. Had Arnold gotten involved with someone they knew? Had Arnold and Ben had a falling-out he didn't tell me about? It could have been any number of things.

I was incredibly intrigued with Los Angeles. My first visit to the Pacific Ocean was like a religious experience. The city felt immense and overwhelming. It made me wonder which way to turn and what to do. I didn't know people in L.A. and relied on Arnold to guide me. Most of his connections there were with people outside the music industry.

Arnold was angry because Ben had still not paid him for the work he was doing. I asked why he hadn't told me that before I arrived. "Because we have the $12,000 you brought with you," he said.

"Well, it's not quite that much now. With traveling, lodging, and the car repair, it's more like $10,000."

"You should have gotten much more for everything," he said.

"It was all antiques and used furniture," I said.

"It just seems like there should be more."

"Maybe I should've let you hold a month of estate sales all by yourself and see if you could've gotten more!" I exclaimed sarcastically.

I was furious that he expected so much of me when he didn't even tell me he hadn't been paid by Ben for months! They were at odds and it didn't seem like they would be able to work it out.

Sheesh! Ten Gs goes quickly in a city like Los Angeles. I knew we'd have to start job-hunting ASAP. Shortly after my arrival, Arnold parted ways with Ben. It just didn't work out. They had a disagreement, and

23. The Land of Milk and Honey, 1976

Arnold was fuming. It seems like their long friendship had been hampered by business and money. Arnold had insisted that he had a solid thing happening with Ben, but it turns out he didn't. I was frustrated and felt deceived.

Arnold contacted several of his music connections. He also arranged to meet with Earth, Wind and Fire in West Hollywood for lunch one hot afternoon. They were so cool and I loved them—such a spiritually minded family and group. We resonated with them. They offered to be on the lookout for studio work for Arnold.

We met Monte White, lead singer Maurice's brother and Earth, Wind and Fire's road manager. We really hit it off. Arnold exchanged numbers with several band members, including the bass player and vocalist, Philip Bailey. They said they'd meet with us again after they returned to L.A. from their upcoming tour. They were huge at the time.

We began apartment-hunting in Sherman Oaks with Dixie and Michael. We all thought living in Sherman Oaks would be affordable and convenient for everyone. We found a lovely two-story apartment with a double garage. It fit our budget, so we placed a deposit and paid the first and last month's rent. We purchased beds for our rooms and nothing else. Michael and Dixie rented a car to get around. We didn't want to go through our funds, which were dwindling rapidly. We all had bills to pay.

I waited to see what Arnold had planned for us, wondering if he would seek any kind of work to get us going here in LaLa Land. Nothing seemed to be going right for him, and I was determined to avoid the same scenario we wound up with in Atlanta (specifically, me being the primary breadwinner). The fact that he'd beckoned me to move to the Wild West without a secure position with Ben infuriated me. I felt misled, and I wasn't feeling the love and respect I once had. I was depressed and miserable. He didn't find work at all. He seemed to think he had to land some incredible music gig to even consider going to work. That was bullshit!

I begrudgingly began job-hunting and was hired in a retail position at a high-end boutique on Sunset that Cher frequented. The owners liked me.

I had no interest in working retail, but someone had to do something. Car payments, insurance, credit cards, utilities, food, phone and gas ate away at our nest egg.

We began saving every penny I earned. My paycheck barely paid rent and covered basics. I remember eating tuna out of cans and stealing toilet paper. It was awful, and I realized that I wasn't in love with Arnold at all. I didn't trust him or feel cared for by him. I respected and admired him once upon a time, but things weren't working out. I often cried myself to sleep, hungry, during those times. Arnold picked up a few painting jobs with his Canoga Park friend, a painting contractor, but we needed more than that.

Michael had quit his waiter job; the restaurant he worked in was horrible for him. Dixie took a job in a restaurant she hated. They, too, were miserable and poor. None of us were thriving in L.A. We simply didn't know enough people here or how to navigate this massive city. All of us were struggling and anxious.

As we all scrambled to pay the next month's rent after only two months in our apartment, Arnold received a phone call from Lenny, our former business partner in Atlanta. He was now living in Puerto Rico, working as a keyboard player for a band there. He needed a front man for an upcoming gig as a house band at the Sheraton in San Juan. Could Arnold come and fill that position ASAP?

Arnold let Lenny know that we had no money for airfare to Puerto Rico, or money to establish ourselves there. Lenny, an independently wealthy individual thanks to his family, offered to pay for our airfare. He proposed we stay in his one-bedroom condo on the beach in Isla Verde with him and his girlfriend, who had come from Atlanta while they rehearsed. We had no choice, so we took him up on his offer.

Off we ventured to Puerto Rico. Los Angeles was not Dixie and Michael's cup of tea, so they returned to Atlanta. We broke our lease and left our car with Arnold's friends in Canoga Park, who offered to turn it in now that we were about to have it repossessed for non-payment. I had never been in a situation like this, and it certainly wasn't what I wanted for my life!

In L.A. less than six months, penniless and destitute. Not to mention in a loveless state in our relationship. I didn't feel like things would ever work out for us. Not even as we headed to Puerto Rico with his alleged steady gig lined up. I found myself depressed at the prospect of another disappointment. One too many of my hopes had been shattered, and the fear regarding this relocation left me feeling totally discouraged.

I was miserable. I wasn't in love with Arnold anymore and wasn't sure I ever had been.

24

Island of Tropical Breezes, 1976

As our aircraft taxied down the runway in Puerto Rico, our captain announced, "Flight attendants, prepare for landing" in both English and Spanish.

I realized I would be able to speak Spanish here.

We collected our luggage, hailed a cab and made our way to Lenny's condo on the beach. We were greeted with as much warmth as Lenny could muster, he being a very solemn young man, and with lots of hugs from his 19-year-old girlfriend Valerie. She was especially happy to see us, and very sweet. Not smart, but very kind.

We smoked some great weed and had some wine. Valerie showed us around their one-bedroom condo in a high-rise overlooking the Northeastern Caribbean shore of Isla Verde, with its northern side facing the Atlantic Ocean. They had a great view of the sea from the 11th floor. Arnold and I would be sleeping on the queen sofa bed. It would be temporary until we got on our feet.

Puerto Rico was much different from the Bahamas. Beautiful, obviously, it was a resort destination, but the sea was not as aqua, more greenish, turbulent and tempestuous. This island felt boisterous, fiery and passionate like its inhabitants. I liked the Puerto Rican culture, and I loved the Spanglish everyone spoke.

We settled into a routine, with Arnold and Lenny rehearsing five days a week at a friend's house. That friend's name was Lizbeth Lopez, and she had worked in a band with Lenny for a short time when he'd first arrived on the island. I suspected they briefly dated before he brought Valerie from Atlanta to Puerto Rico. They rehearsed at Lizbeth's home, which she shared with her mother and brother. Lizbeth and I hit it off. She was always taking me somewhere to meet people and introduce me to the island she was so proud of.

She was a font of information for all things Puerto Rican, as she had grown up there. She looked like Gloria Estefan and even sang like her. Lizbeth was currently doing large concert gigs at an arena, opening for a few acts, including a new up-and-coming young boy band called Menudo. The band was made up of 12-year-old Ricky Martin and his four cousins. I had the privilege of being comped to a concert where Lizbeth performed and I saw Menudo. They were an explosive, cute flurry of talent and energy!

While Arnold and Lenny rehearsed for their upcoming gig at the Sheraton, I learned everything I could about the island from Lizbeth and began exploring my options.

The first thing I did was go to a café on the beach to search the community bulletin board for employment opportunities. I found that a little daytime bar and lunch place, the Office Lounge, was seeking a bartender and decided to give them a call. An interview was scheduled, and when I went, I was hired on the spot to be a part-time day barkeep.

It was a small but hectic little place. The owner, an American, seemed drunk most of the time. He was somewhat rough around the edges, but that didn't bother me. I wanted to make money and leave Lenny's. It would be another six weeks before the band began their engagement at the Sheraton.

In addition to contributing to our household, I saved some money because I made a salary and excellent tips. I was the best thing they had going for them, without a doubt. Lots of businessmen frequented the Office Lounge, and I was its centerpiece. I tended bar three or four days a week and saved, saved, saved!

While there, I heard lots of talk about the gambling many bar patrons did in the casino, night after night. The El San Juan Hotel was adjacent to where we lived and home to the largest casino on the island. I decided to walk down the beach to the El San Juan and check it out.

It was a gorgeous hotel, and the casino was grand. This is where all the international tourists gathered for entertainment, gambling and dining. I peeked into the elegant 700-seat showroom after I saw the marquee that announced its current production, "C'est Magnifique," a tits-and-feathers production in the main showroom, produced by Miller-Reich. I'd heard of them. They were well-known producers and, much like the Rudas Dancers, they had numerous shows in Miami, Japan and Las Vegas. After perusing the show photos in lighted boxes outside the venue, I could see that this well-produced spectacle was installed there permanently.

This gave me an idea. I could have a comeback here in Puerto Rico! After all, I was only 26. Young enough to still dance, certainly. Yet somehow, I felt old, over the hill, and much too out-of-shape to work. Of course, I wasn't old at all!

The next time I saw Lizbeth, I questioned her: "Is there anyone really good here teaching dance?"

"Oh, yes! We have several well-known choreographers here who work

24. Island of Tropical Breezes, 1976

with a number of artists who perform in many different avenues of entertainment," claimed Lizbeth. "I've studied with the best of them!"

"Really?" I asked. "Who would that be?"

"Jose Bettencourt," she replied. "He's done choreography for many great dancers and pop stars. Why do you ask?"

"I am a dancer and was thinking of taking classes."

"I'll take you over to his studio and introduce you to him. We call him Junito," Lizbeth offered excitedly. Once again, an angel was nearby.

Lizbeth drove me to Jose Bettencourt's studio and introduced us. He was a dramatic character, very fit, and handsome. Bald in a Yul Brynner way, including the earring. Jose seemed to adore Lizbeth and fawned over her. He asked about my dance history.

"Where have you worked?" Jose inquired in Spanish. Lizbeth translated our conversation, although some of what he spoke was Spanglish.

"Everywhere," I answered. "Paris, New York, Las Vegas, Paradise Island and Montreal."

We chatted about several dance companies, and then he asked us to watch him teach his next class, handing me a studio brochure listing his classes. Lizbeth and I found a viewing window.

Jose had a conga drummer playing for his class. His jazz class began, and I saw how challenging it was. Many talented young dancers filled the studio. Once the combination began, the conga player added a spicy beat to the music. I found it inspiring and challenging! Afterward, I spoke with the studio manager about joining classes. I found I could come to any of them at any time. There was a flat monthly fee, and I could take up to three classes a week. Jose's classes were three hours long! Whew! A good workout, for sure.

A few days later, during Arnold's rehearsals, I walked over to the hotel showroom and made some inquiries regarding "C'est Magnifique." The maître d' was extremely accommodating and took me backstage to meet the company captain, Denise, a lovely 40-something American and former dancer who couldn't have been nicer. We talked a bit about the show and my background. She said they were always looking for new people and asked when I would be interested in auditioning.

"Soon. And I'd love to audition to be a showgirl," I suggested. (Boy, had my tune changed!)

"We can always use another dancing nude," Denise said. "Can you audition in a few days?"

"I can come next week since I have a daytime bartending job at the moment."

"You are welcome to come by any evening before the show starts, if that's better for you," she offered.

"Would you like me to prepare anything?" I asked.

"No, no. We'll do some of the choreography from the show."

"Perfect, let's make it a week from today at this same time, six-ish?" I suggested.

"That's great!" Denise said.

I left feeling excited and wondered what Arnold would think about this. I'd decided to audition for a show without discussing it with him. I wanted to explore the notion on my own before I shared it with him, with no rebuttal. But what I was really worried about was my 142-pound body that wasn't in any shape for dancing at all!

I called to register for Jose Bettencourt's classes and found I couldn't begin for two weeks because Jose was out of the country choreographing in Spain. I'd have to figure out how to get back in shape on my own. I really wanted to work with him. I liked his vibe and his studio.

The "C'est Magnifique" program, 1976.

I started jogging on the beach every day. As I glided down the sandy shore on my tippy toes outside our condo, I began to connect spiritually with how much I really wanted to dance again. With the desire to dance

24. Island of Tropical Breezes, 1976

returning, I knew I'd have to tell Arnold what I was up to. There was no way around it. Why was I hesitating?

So, I decided to tell him, listening to my inner voice, my highest self, and the importance of truth and integrity. That's who I am now, no more lies.

When I got home, I told Arnold I had been jogging on the beach and had decided to do so every day. I told him about discovering the dance studio with Lizbeth and visiting the casino's showroom. I told him I wanted to audition for the show, and to my surprise, he seemed fine with that.

"What do they pay?" he inquired right away.

"I haven't asked but would imagine much the same as most shows do. It's pretty standard everywhere."

"Will it pay more than the Office Lounge?"

"It certainly will, and I won't be slinging drinks in a dive bar. Plus, I'm really excited to work again."

"Good, because we won't get paychecks at the Sheraton for at least a month," he told me, "They will be paying the band every two weeks."

"What will you be making there?"

"Around $200 a week."

He seemed distracted with a song list he was creating for their upcoming rehearsal ... or maybe he was embarrassed at such a pittance compared to his last gig with Sonny Turner. The conversation sort of just ended there. I didn't hear anything from him like, "Are you happy?" Never. Nada. This compounded my discouragement with our relationship. I didn't feel heard, seen or cared for by him beyond what I could earn. He didn't even really seem to be listening to me. Another nail in the coffin of our marriage.

So that was that. I began dieting, stretching and jogging daily on the sand. It was at this time that I decided to give up red meat and pork.

One week into this routine, I felt a bit stronger. I was not totally ready for my audition, but dancing is like getting on a bike. It all comes back. I had more discipline than I had five years ago. I was still weighing in at about 138 pounds at 5'9", though, and that was not my dancing weight.

On Tuesday night, Denise greeted me backstage, took me to the dressing room and introduced me to a young Puerto Rican wardrobe mistress, Yolanda, who was there early to set and prep costumes for the show. While I changed into my leotard, fishnets and dance boots, I easily got to know her, and I loved this girl. She was so special. Yolanda became my first friend backstage.

Yolanda was extremely psychic, and something about our connection seemed incredibly familiar. You know when you meet someone remarkable and feel connected right away? She was very encouraging. She told me that one of the showgirls who had just gotten married wanted to leave to have a baby, but they had no replacement for her.

"You're going to do great, I just know it!"

Obviously, this was another fantastic human crossing my professional path! She was so in touch with creative people. I cannot begin to stress how fortunate I am, with living and *unseen* guardian angels always showing up on cue!

I believed Yolanda. I felt empowered and nailed the audition. It was really very easy, and I felt like I had returned home. I felt great doing the audition. Everything Denise asked me to do was much like something I had done in a previous show. After my last job in Paris, swinging for ten nudes with much more complex choreography, I breezed through this audition. I realized I was far from old.

Denise was very impressed with my résumé and said she would let me know in the next few days if I got it. She told me the contracts were only for six months because the new show would be starting, and then new contracts would be issued for a one-year commitment. I would be making $225 a week as one of four dancing nudes. Rates had increased a bit since I'd been in Paris, where I'd made $175 a week.

It all felt very positive, and I left sensing that I had a great shot at this job. I wanted it badly! There was more than just a gig at stake. I was hoping to earn freedom from my increasingly unhappy marriage and to be able to again support myself doing something I loved.

25

My Comeback, 1976

I went to work at the bar the next day and found myself consumed with imagining myself dancing in the "C'est Magnifique" show. Hoping for a call, I gave the company captain my home number. I went home late that afternoon, anxious to hear back. Arnold and Lenny were getting ready to go to Lizbeth's to rehearse. I asked where Valerie was.

Arnold took me aside and quietly said, "Don't ask." Huh? What the heck did that mean?

Why couldn't I ask?

I noticed she had not been going to rehearsals with Lenny recently and instead went out more and more often on her own. I wondered what was going on. I couldn't tell if they were splitting up or what.

I told Arnold I wouldn't be going to Lizbeth's that night because I was waiting to hear from the El San Juan. He chuckled, and that surprised me. What the hell was that about? They gathered their things, piled into Lenny's van and left.

After a shower and a little dinner, I settled in on this tropical night to write a few letters. Ten p.m. was fast approaching, and since I didn't need to get up to go to work the next day, I stayed up late waiting for that call. Around 10:15, Valerie came in, all decked out in her disco best.

"Hey, how are you?" I asked.

"Pretty good," she answered. "You're not at rehearsal?"

"No, I'm waiting for a phone call." I explained the audition to her.

"That's great," she said. "How cool!"

"Yeah, I'd like to go back to work dancing! Do you ever miss working?"

"Oh, I work," she said. "I was working tonight!"

"I didn't know you had a job!"

"Yeah, it's not a real job, but when we need a little extra money, I work at the hotel," she explained vaguely.

I was dumbfounded. I didn't know she could do anything!

"I'm gonna take a shower," she said. "Tonight was busy!"

I had no idea what she meant by that and I was afraid to inquire further, remembering Arnold's "Don't ask!" What the heck did she do? Why shouldn't I ask?

Once out of the shower, Valerie sat down with me to towel-dry her hair. We watched a movie, and she began to tell me that she missed Atlanta and was thinking about going home for a month for Christmas. She missed her family, and wasn't getting along with Lenny.

"Is it because Arnold and I are here?" I had to know.

"No, no, not at all," she insisted. "Lenny's still addicted to heroin, and he always wants me to sell it for him."

"Is that your job?" I asked.

"Part of it," she stammered. "The other part. I can't talk about. Lenny would get mad at me if I told you." She looked away, not meeting my eyes.

"That's okay, you don't have to tell me if you don't want to," I assured her. Whatever it was, she seemed ashamed. I could only imagine. I felt bad for her.

Lenny and Arnold returned. I looked at the clock. It was nearly midnight. We all smoked a joint and decided to turn in. I saw Valerie reach into her bag and hand Lenny a fistful of cash as they went to their room. He grinned wickedly at her. Ewww.

Nothing about any of this felt right to me, and I asked Arnold to tell me what was going on with them.

"You know Lenny," he groaned. "He hasn't changed."

"Are you saying he's still doing drugs?"

"He's just who he is, and that's never going to change," Arnold said. "His parents are cutting him off, and he needs bread."

"So what is Valerie doing working for him?" I wondered aloud.

"She might be selling some dope for him," he added. "I don't really ask. I told you not to ask."

"But we live here, and if she's selling drugs, we could be in danger!" I exclaimed.

"No, we aren't. Just don't ask. It's better if you don't know!"

"Do you know?" I asked, feeling like he was hiding the truth from me.

"I think she might turn tricks sometimes, but please never say anything!"

"That is horrible!" I blurted. "How can he do that to her? She's a child!"

"Shhh," he hushed me. "It's none of our business, and Lenny has really helped us out. It's better just to stay out of it."

"Oh my God, Arnold," I whispered. "How can you let us live here with all of that going on?" I was truly horrified.

Lenny was pimping out his girlfriend, who was 19.

"We'll be out of here in a month, so just drop it!"

25. My Comeback, 1976

I couldn't sleep that night. I was so uneasy with all of this. My heart was breaking even further for Valerie and for me! How did I wind up in this situation? This was not my doing.

I was struggling to find logic in this scenario, and I was panicking. I finally fell asleep, and as I drifted off, I realized I hadn't gotten a call from the company captain.

The following day, Arnold and I walked over to the café on the beach for lunch. I was very reserved. I was struggling with this latest news and wasn't sure how to process it. I was in a fog, tired, restless and anxious to hear from the show. More reticent than usual and unable to discuss Lenny and Valerie's situation further, Arnold and I were utterly estranged.

We returned to the condo and I changed to go jogging. I needed to clear my head. It always helped to connect with nature and the sea. My head was spinning, and I forced myself to breathe deeply, pushing myself further than I had before on this stretch of beach. I needed to tire myself out and stay out there for a while to figure out what to do, reduce some damn stress!

When I returned, it was late afternoon, nearly five. The guys usually left for rehearsal at six or seven. After I showered and helped Valerie with dinner, the phone rang.

It was Denise calling to let me know that I had been hired to replace a Miller-Reich showgirl who was leaving the show! Hallelujah! I was so excited. I got the job! She asked if I could start rehearsing with her in three weeks.

"Of course I can, that's perfect! I will have time to give a two-week notice at the bar and take some classes. Thank you!" I gushed.

I was on Cloud 9. The company captain said that she would draw up a contract for me and asked if I could come by tonight to sign it. "Sure, I can. I would be delighted to."

"Great! How about between shows, around eight or nine? That way, you can meet some of the girls."

"Perfect," I said, "I'll be there!" I hung up the phone.

"What's that about?" Arnold snarked at me.

"I got the job. I am going over to the hotel to sign my contract!"

"When?"

"Tonight!" I exclaimed.

"How are you going to get there?" he asked me, continuing his interrogation.

"I can walk over to the hotel and be there in ten minutes."

"I don't want you walking alone at night!" He commanded.

"Oh my God, Arnold!" I cried. "That's ridiculous!"

"I said not tonight!" he growled.

"I'm going!" I shouted. "What the hell is your problem? I got a good job!"

"You're not going to dance in some show!" He screamed in my face.

I'd never have expected this reaction from him.

"So, you're going to tell me what to do when you can't even support yourself?" I shouted back as I stormed into the kitchen, trying not to cry. Fuck him. I would go anyway.

I was planning to get to the theater to sign my contract around eight. In the tropics, it's still light at that hour. I could walk there down a path from our condo to the El San Juan.

Arnold and Lenny seemed out of sorts. Something felt "off" with them. Ugh. I couldn't worry about that right now! I was about to make a comeback, and that was important to me.

Arnold and I ate some dinner together, even though tensions were high. He seemed disgruntled about something he wasn't mentioning, so it had to be Lenny. Lenny was in his room. Valerie was already headed out somewhere. I said I was about to go over to the El San Juan to sign my contract.

"What contract?" he questioned, as if I hadn't already told him!

"My six-month dancing nude Miller-Reich contract for the show!" I repeated.

He snapped, "You can't sign a contract. What if things don't work out for me here?"

"Well, I'm going," I snapped back as I grabbed my bag. "I want to dance again, in case you wondered!"

"No, you're not! And you aren't ever working as a showgirl again!" He actually shouted at me.

I headed for the door. Arnold came around me and blocked the door with his body. Very roughly.

"What are you doing?" I asked, trying to remain as calm as possible.

"You're not going to dance in a show, and that's that!" he growled at me. Growled!

"You can't tell me what to do. I'm not Valerie," I retorted.

"Shut the fuck up!" he shouted even louder, stretching his arms across the door.

"Who the hell are you, Arnold?" I cried.

"Your husband, and you're not dancing!" he snarled.

He was scary. I'd never seen this side of him.

Something snapped inside me then; a whirlwind began swirling around me, drawing me up and away. A mini-, emotionally charged inner tornado. The winds of change, perhaps? I hoped it was there to guide me back to a life I loved.

I retreated to the living room while he and Lenny gathered their gear for rehearsals: mikes, keyboard, amps, etc. Arnold and I were silent. I was so pissed off and hurt and done! It was about 7:15 and the sun was still shining.

"Don't leave here tonight. I will know if you do!" my husband threatened before he left.

What the fuck? How dare he command me? I was acutely aware of how much I had grown up in that moment. Why was he digressing into this horrible, controlling and frightened man?

"Fine," I snarled. I called the company captain to tell her I'd have to come by tomorrow night to sign the contract.

"Let's make it two nights from now," she said. "I need to be off the island for the next two days."

Why couldn't I just dance and have a husband? There are lots of married showgirls. Why couldn't I have both? That's all I really wanted, to balance a marriage and a career.

Once Arnold and Lenny left, I began rummaging through the condo for my personal belongings. Once I determined where my suitcases were in the hall closet, I checked that off mentally. I did the same with my toiletries, clothes, shoes and miscellaneous belongings. I knew they would all fit into my luggage. No need to pack now. I would pack while Arnold was at daytime rehearsal tomorrow. I would leave. I would take my stuff and my little black terrier Sasha and leave. I knew I had to. This was it. It was time. My anger was driving me now.

I crashed before they returned, so the living room was dark when they came in. I played asleep. Then tried to sleep, but that wind tunnel around me continued. I didn't get much rest that night. I was mentally organizing my departure. My mind was working at light speed.

Despite Arnold's manipulations, I was still excited. In two days, I would sign my contract and give notice at my bartending job! That made me as happy as getting the new dancing gig. I desperately needed to be happy again. I've always been very in touch with what I wanted next and why. I needed to end my marriage peacefully.

I also knew what I didn't need. I didn't need drama!

I couldn't believe how much shit we had been through in the last few years. A downward spiral in every aspect of our relationship. I now knew that I wanted my single life back.

The next morning, I left to jog on the beach, like any other day. I returned at around 2:00 to find Arnold and Lenny preparing to leave for Lizbeth's

I took my time in the shower, waiting until they all left. When I came out, I was alone with my dog. I skillfully packed everything I owned. I had a suitcase, a footlocker and my dog.

I called Lizbeth. She was home and the guys were rehearsing in her garage. "I'm leaving," I announced when she answered, knowing my secret was safe with her.

"What? When?" She sounded stunned.

"Now! I don't know where I'm going, but I'm packed. I'm leaving Arnold, and I'm really done!" I began to cry. "I got the job in the show, and he won't let me go sign my contract!"

"I know, Diane. I know, and you are coming here!" she commanded.

Lizbeth had known about everything. She had been my primary friend on the island and knew me well. I'd shared my disillusionment in my marriage with her often.

"What do you mean?" I whimpered.

"You can't spend money on a hotel. You need to save and find a small place to live near the hotel. In the meantime, you come here!"

"I agree with you, but I have Sasha!" I lamented.

"I love Sasha. Just get in a cab and come over now!" Lizbeth insisted.

"But Arnold is rehearsing there now!"

"It doesn't matter. My room is at the front of the house, and they are out back in the garage! I will meet you out front and bring you in secretly when you get here!"

"Thank you so, so much, Lizbeth!" I sniveled. "I am so grateful!"

"I am your friend, and that's what friends do!" she declared.

I told her, "I feel so lucky to have you!"

We hung up. I called a cab. I gathered my two pieces of luggage, leashed my pup, left my key on the counter and evacuated. No note. I took the elevator down and felt that gusting zephyr sweeping me away. Away from unhappiness, Arnold's control, and Lenny and Valerie. I don't know what kind of life they were leading, but it was all just too much for me. I was trembling.

The taxi was there as I got off the elevator. Taxis lived near the El San Juan Hotel next door. I gave the driver Lizbeth's address as he kindly loaded my luggage into his trunk. We drove straight to the house my husband was in.

26

Transforming My Life, 1976

As the taxi rambled down the street, I was in an altered state, numb, yet aware enough to write down a phone number from a sign I saw in the yard of one of my neighbors: ROOM FOR RENT. At this very poignant moment, I somehow had the presence of mind to get those digits! I don't know how, considering the streaming tears I was producing. Possibly divine guidance?

As we drove across town to Lizbeth's house, 20 minutes away, tears continued rolling down my cheeks. I was leaving Arnold. I was relieved, hurt, scared, broken and angry all at the same time.

What was I doing? Had I gone insane? Proceeding to the house where the man I was leaving was rehearsing!

Complicated, yes, but Lizbeth was my good friend and I trusted her.

When we pulled up to Lizbeth's house, she came out immediately, as promised. I paid the driver as he unloaded my bags. Lizbeth directed him to her room. He deposited my rather heavy luggage into her bedroom very carefully. I tipped him well as Lizbeth walked him to the front door.

I took Sasha to pee out front, then returned to Lizbeth's room. I fell into a heap on her shoulder and cried for what felt like hours. She patted my shoulder and held me like a sister.

We whispered and talked, and she put on an album. The soothing bossa nova helped.

I was determined. Just aggrieved. Lizbeth understood. Her presence healed me; she had that kind of energy. I was so vulnerable and blessed that night. Lizbeth insisted on taking me to her psychic friend, Catalina, the next day. It was the Puerto Rican way. The culture was obsessed with clairvoyance, and something about this blustery island seemed to summon it.

Every now and then, Sasha would let out her little yip when she heard the drums in the garage. Lizbeth turned up her vinyl. I was afraid that Arnold and Lenny would hear Sasha. In fact, I was visibly distressed. Lizbeth decided to go see when they would finish up. It was nearing six o'clock. She made her way to the garage.

Shortly after, Sasha and I heard them leaving. I was terrified that Arnold would hear our dog. I continued to stifle my terrier from barking with little dog treats. I had no idea how this scenario would play out. It seemed insane. Lizbeth came back about ten minutes later and exhaled deeply, "They're gone."

I cried a little more. We somehow pulled it off. I could relax.

Lizbeth wanted to make me some food, but I couldn't eat. I told her I had a stress headache as I blew my nose and wiped my moist eyes with tissues. Lizbeth offered me Tylenol; I took one. She told me to relax and sleep in her room. She would sleep in the living room. Her mom and her brother were in their rooms.

I wondered how Arnold would feel. He would certainly know soon that I was gone. He would never in a million years guess that I would be tucked away at Lizbeth's. Perhaps she was a genius. I thought it was an amazing feat to pull off. I was enveloped with the deep, organic sense of the power of females united. With Sasha at my feet, I slept well that night. Better than I had in weeks, actually.

That gale was gradually withdrawing.

* * *

I was very fortunate to be able to stay with Lizbeth at her home for another week. She and her mom were wonderful to me in every way, driving me around and feeding me, despite the band rehearsing at her house several evenings a week. I began taking dance classes with Jose during the evenings while the band rehearsed there. The Universe once again supported this massive change in my life by providing living guardian angels. I couldn't have been more grateful.

I couldn't talk to Arnold directly. I knew how angry he would be, how controlling and manipulative. I couldn't go back. I was determined to dance again, and if he couldn't support that or me, I had to move on. I wanted my life back!

I signed my contract with Miller-Reich and began training with Jose Bettencourt three days a week. I would start rehearsals in a few weeks and had to be ready. I loved his classes. I worked hard, and he and I became good friends. He promised to come to the show once I finished rehearsals. I was also very attracted to him. I thought he was gay. I wasn't sure that I should get involved, but that's obviously never stopped me in the past. I left that open as a possibility for the future. I was in no rush and newly free.

Lizbeth took me to visit her psychic friend shortly. I found Catalina to be very interesting. When we met her at her house, which was small and somewhat darkened by the dense tropical area near a rain forest, the petite

26. Transforming My Life, 1976

Puerto Rican woman in her 70s took one look at me and spoke in perfect Spanglish, "There is negative spirit attached to you and I need to remove it, inmediatamente!"

The psychic lit her smudge stick, incense and a few candles and began praying over me. She began slowly, chanting in Spanish. The chanting intensified and became louder and louder as she smudged the smoky sage around me until she was shaking and nearly exploding emotionally. I was freaked out. I'd never experienced anything like this.

I looked at Lizbeth, who was sitting silently in a chair nearby with her eyes shut, holding the space for us. She was praying. Whoa! This was unusual for a psychic reading. At least compared to any I'd ever had. Once the psychic was finished, she sat and said another prayer in Spanish.

Then Catalina looked deeply into my eyes and said, "You have had negative spirit attached to you for a long time. That spirit was summoned by you!"

"What do you mean?" I asked.

"You summoned help from a dark force at some point, and it stayed with you. You must never do such a thing again."

My mind raced. When did I do that? Maybe in Atlanta when I was burning photos and summoning Arnold to return to me? I thought it was harmless. I had read it in a book of spells that I'd borrowed from the library when I wanted him to hurry back to Atlanta. But, according to this psychic, it wasn't harmless, and I had opened some sort of portal.

"You must leave your marriage and never look back and never speak of him again!" She repeated: "Never!"

I obviously did not heed her dire warning. After all, here I am writing about Arnold. I thanked her and asked how much she charged for the reading.

"No charge," she insisted. "You are clear now."

Lizbeth hugged the psychic and said something in Spanish before we left. I secretly placed a $20 bill on her table on our way out.

Maybe the "bad spirit" was why Arnold and I had so much bad luck during our marriage. I do know my life felt a lot better after that.

"C'est Magnifique" rehearsals would start soon, and I wanted to find a place to live before that. So I called the number with the ROOM FOR RENT sign. The owners had a casita for rent next to their main house. I went to see it. The older Puerto Rican couple I met couldn't be sweeter.

The casita was a separate, very clean, furnished studio apartment with appliances, bed, dresser, comfy chair and a little yard. Sasha would like that. It was only $75 a month, and it was a month-to-month lease. Perfect! I didn't need more than that, so I agreed to take it. It was walking distance to the El San Juan Hotel and perfect for my needs.

I asked if I could call a cab, and they kindly did so. I could tell I would be very happy here. We shook hands and I told them I'd be moving in immediately. They were excited to have a tenant employed at the casino, and they liked my little Sasha, the easiest dog of all.

As I left the house to walk my dog, I looked toward the high-rise condominiums where Arnold and I had stayed with Lenny. I noticed Arnold walking very slowly toward the beach. I froze. I did not want him to see me. I scooped Sasha up and turned away. Just about that time, my taxi pulled up. I was far enough away that Arnold did not see us. As I plunged into the cab and gave the driver Lizbeth's address, I looked out the cab's back window as Arnold headed toward the café, looking very dejected. I'm sure I had hurt him. I began to cry again. I didn't cry because I missed him, but because I was sad that our once promising relationship had ended this way.

Lizbeth helped me move into the casita the next day. I completed my work at the bar and continued dance classes until rehearsals began. I would be rehearsing between shows from 9:00 to 10:30 five nights a week with one of the showgirls. When I arrived, the company captain took one look at me and exclaimed, "You really lost a lot of weight! You look fantastic!"

I said, "I've been training with Jose Bettencourt" even though I knew most of the weight loss (down to 125 pounds) was due to stress.

"Excellent! He's the best on the island and choreographs for lots of local celebrities! But you really lost a lot of weight quickly."

I admitted the truth: "I've also just gone through a breakup with my husband."

"Oh, sweetheart, I'm so sorry," she sympathized. "If there is anything I can do, please know I am here for you. Do you need an advance in pay while you rehearse?"

"I think I'm okay, but that means a lot to me. Thank you!" I knew that I was in good company.

Everyone backstage was wonderful. Every single dancer in the show was exceptionally kind and I easily made friends with the entire cast and crew. I loved being back on the boards, and rehearsals flew by. The show was easy, and I had one featured spot. It was fun working again. In fact, I felt on top of the world. I felt the camaraderie that show people have when working as an ensemble. Two weeks flew by, and I was ready to open.

I was excited, my heart fluttering, on opening night. I hadn't performed in a big show since Paris, and nearly four years had passed since then. As soon as that spotlight warmed my face, I was all in! I performed like the professional that I was born to be. Happy to be back in the saddle.

A few weeks after opening, I was backstage just before the finale when

26. Transforming My Life, 1976

one of the stagehands brought me a note. It was from Arnold, who was in the audience. He asked me to have a drink with him in the casino lounge between shows. I hesitated as I wondered why he was here, watching a show he didn't want me to do.

As I dressed in my yellow finale costume and donned my feathers, I presumed he would have something important to say, so I sent a note back and told him I would meet him in the lounge in 15 minutes.

I later made my way to the lounge and saw Arnold at a small cocktail table, alone, nursing his Scotch on the rocks. He smiled at me. I didn't return his smile. I wasn't feeling it.

"Great show!" he offered. Small praise. "Would you like a drink?"

"Just a coffee. I have another show tonight at 11," I answered. He ordered, then turned to me and asked, "How are you?"

"Happy," I told him. "And you?"

"As well as can be expected," he said. "How's Sasha?"

"She's fine," I responded. "Have you opened at the Sheraton yet?"

"We did, just this week." He reported.

My coffee arrived. We sat in silence.

"So, what's up?" I wanted to know.

"I miss you," Arnold professed, "and Sasha."

"She misses you, too," I added.

"What about you, Diane? Do you miss me?"

"I don't miss having someone tell me what to do every minute of the day," I said honestly.

"When did I do that?" he asked, seeming offended. Was he that oblivious?

"Seriously, Arnold?" I winced. "You didn't want me to be in this show. You wouldn't even let me go sign my contract, or have you forgotten?"

He stiffened. "I still don't want my wife showing her body to the world."

"Well, I was doing that when you met me, remember?" I replied. "Performing is what I do and love."

"You don't have to be topless!"

"I like being a showgirl! It's a great job with an excellent company, and it's not like I'm turning tricks like Valerie is for Lenny!"

"She's gone back to Atlanta," Arnold muttered.

"Well, I wonder why?" I snapped back. "How could you let me live in a place where Lenny is doing heroin and having Valerie sell drugs and her body for money?"

"We had no choice," he added seriously.

"We always have choices, Arnold!" I exclaimed. "And I don't choose that kind of life, and I don't want to be with a husband who can't provide better for me!"

"That's cold, Diane. I've never seen you so cold!"

He was right. I felt cold. He could call me anything he wanted. I didn't want him back at all.

"Is there anything else you need from me right now?" I asked tightly.

"I want you to come back," Arnold said as he reached for my hand.

"I'm never coming back," I said as I retracted my hand. "I'm done with this marriage."

"Where are you living now?"

"Alone," I answered as I gathered my bag and stood up. "I'm happy again. Goodbye, Arnold, and good luck to you!" I fought back tears on my way backstage.

I left, and that was it. I was glad I'd met Arnold in a public place because I am confident he would have been insistent on having his way had we been alone. I had no feelings for him anymore and was certain he would not change any time soon. I exhaled and headed backstage to my new life.

Once in the dressing room, I started reapplying my makeup for the second show. As I did, Yolanda, our dresser, came over to me and asked, "Are you okay? You seem upset."

"I just saw my husband, who came to the show unannounced, and I had to leave him all over again."

Being psychic as she was, she got it. "You have so much going for you, and you are such a good performer. You won't be happy if you go back to him."

Yolanda was such a warm, comforting spirit. I knew her words were spot on.

"I have something for you," she said. "A special gift." She went into her purse, withdrew a tiny velvet bag and handed it to me. I opened the pouch and found a beautiful pair of small gold, marcasite and pearl earrings.

Yolanda said, "Something very special that belonged to my grandmother from turn-of-the-century Spain. Wear them when you really want something, they will bring you what you want."

"Yolanda, these are beautiful and so incredibly special! I am honored that you would give me your sacred family heirloom!"

"I have blessed them for you with holy water in the church, and you are going to be very fortunate now," she stated confidently.

I hugged her as tears began to well up again. I was so grateful for her. I was truly blessed, and my heart was opened wide.

"You are so kind and I feel so lucky to have met you. Thank you so much!" I cried.

"You are very, very special, and never forget it. You deserve only the best that life and love can offer you!" Yolanda declared.

26. Transforming My Life, 1976

"I feel incredibly blessed right now. I will wear them when I really want something!" I promised her.

I meant it and suddenly felt much better. Ready to do the next show and ready for my future. Ready to receive the beautiful life I had hoped for and finally knew I truly deserved.

27

Extra Spicy, 1976

With each storm, we grow a little more into the soul we are meant to become, like branches on a tree that have been struck by lightning. I could feel the accelerated growth inside me. I was growing up, finding who I was and what I was meant to be. They say that trees that have been struck by lightning are always the most interesting ones.

In addition to evolving, I simultaneously defined what it meant to be young. I was only 26, yet I had thought of myself as "old" before returning to the stage. I felt young again. I still needed to have some fun, and Puerto Rico naturally provided that, especially during the dynamic disco era. We were at the heart of disco, and on this turbulent and passionate island, I was part of the most wonderful group of dancers to enjoy that with!

We began to hit the discos after work nightly, dancing into the wee hours. While kicking up a little hijinks and folly, I bonded with several of the gay boys in the show who enjoyed the nightlife as much as I did: Jamie, the new 18-year-old pretty boy from New York City; Donny, the hunky bisexual Puerto Rican dancer from Florida; the older, very British, hilarious Peter, and the extremely creative South African Errol Manoff, creator-star of our headlining act, the Puppet People.

Tita, one of the new Puerto Rican showgirls, loved to boogie. Our disco nights replaced the dance classes I had been attending. I am certain I was making up for the lost party years from having been married so young.

Jose Bettencourt's assistant, Juan, called me backstage one night, to ask me if I would come to a surprise birthday bash they were throwing for Jose in a few weeks. It was being held at a club near the studio on a Sunday night. We were off on Sundays, so I could go! I asked if I could bring one of the showgirls with me.

"Sure. It's very upscale, so dress up!" Juan instructed.

I asked Tita that night if she'd like to go. "Oh, yes, girl!" she responded when I told her where we were going. "That is a fabulous club, with a DJ and everything! I know just what to wear. I have a new long dress."

27. Extra Spicy, 1976

"A gown?" I questioned. "Really?"

"It's a very ritzy place. We'll need to dress up!"

"But I don't have a gown or any nice long dresses."

"Don't worry, I'll bring you one tomorrow night to wear," Tita insisted. "We are gonna have so much fun there!"

"Why don't you come to a dance class one day with me at his studio this week?" I asked her.

"I will, yes. I need classes." Tita said.

And we did just that. Tita loaned me a slinky white floor-length halter dress that fit me perfectly, showing off my island tan very well, without being too much. I took her to a class the following Wednesday afternoon and she met Jose. She had not trained with him but knew of him. Of course, we kept his secret upcoming party on the down low.

It was so good to see Jose in class. He knew I had been in rehearsals and seemed equally enchanted to see me. I offered him two industry comps for our show and encouraged him to come. He promised he would be there very soon!

I was eager for him to see my work in the show and began to fantasize about him coming to see me. He had that effect on me. I hoped he would like my work and performance.

Two boys in the show, Jamie and Peter, had rented a three-bedroom cottage from an older American widow named Mrs. Johnson. It was on the beach next door to the hotel. They asked me if I'd like to share it with them.

"Yes! I'd love that. When can I move in?" I squealed.

"We are moving in next week," Peter replied. "You can move in whenever you're able."

I would be paying nearly the same rent I was on my casita. Only $25 more a month for an entire house.

I gave them part of the rent and submitted a one-month notice to my sweet landlords. The casita landlords said they had a cousin who needed a place, and I didn't have to wait a month if I wanted to move sooner. Perfecta!

Sasha and I moved into our little blue cottage with a white picket fence one week later, just after the boys had settled in. The house sat adjacent to the condos I had lived in with Arnold and Lenny. It was darling! It also had a large backyard with a papaya tree in full bloom. Yum! It was at this time I developed a taste for papaya shakes.

The kitchen was huge and primarily windows. We could enjoy sitting at the large kitchen table overlooking the garden and could be on the beach in a minute flat. I was thrilled. My room was bright and large, with windows that opened to the fragrant garden. Plus, the whole house was furnished, and a housekeeper came once a month, included in the rent. What a deal!

Sashita, as we had all started calling her, was very happy there and cozied up in my room when we were away. She loved the fenced backyard, thrived on my roommates' attentions and was never without snuggles and treats.

Peter, Jamie and I got along famously. Though we lived and worked together, we were not home much. None of us cooked, and mostly we hung out in our own rooms or in the kitchen, making tea or coffee.

The week after I gave Jose the complimentary show tickets, he came to see me in "C'est Magnifique" with Juan, who called me backstage before the show to tell me they were there. He claimed Jose had a gift for me after the show and asked if I would meet them afterward, outside the showroom. "Of course I will!" I gushed.

I gave my most dazzling performance that night! It was such a thrill to have them there. When we met afterward, Jose offered to buy us drinks in the lounge. Juan interpreted for us, and I took Tita along, who did the same. Jose spoke very little English for some reason. He brought me a little disco purse, a sneaker-like satin shoe shoulder bag. Very popular with the disco divas.

Juan translated when Jose gave me the gift: "A shoe for Cinderella from the prince."

Awwww, that was so sweet! I thanked Jose and hugged him. He didn't let go. This sexy, viral man was so hot for me! We sauntered to the lounge for cocktails, and Jose proceeded to buy us all drinks, thanking me for the comps. He whispered something to Juan that made him give me a raised eyebrow.

"What?" I asked.

"Nada!" replied Jose. He shook his finger at Juan as if he didn't want that secret translated.

Juan winked at me. Such intrigue. When Jose went to the restroom, Juan told me what Jose had whispered: "He said you were so good in the show, and your body was so gorgeous that he could make love to you!"

"But he's gay, right?" I inquired.

"Mostly, but not always!" Juan winked. "He likes jouuuuu!"

I didn't know what to say or do with that tidbit. Jose was my dance instructor, a fierce and fiery talent. Where were the boundaries there? I didn't know. The '70s were the decade of "anything goes." Everyone was trying everything, which led to the downfall of the sexual revolution by the early '80s. Plus, we now know I tended to crush on gay or bisexual men. Whatever it was, it turned me on.

When Jose returned, he sat very close to me. I batted my false eyelashes and he made me blush. We carried on until Tita and I needed to rush back to do our second show. We said adios and everyone hugged in a flurry of "thank yous" for a fabulous night!

A week later, Tita came over on Sunday afternoon. We fluffed, buffed, smoked a joint and got all dolled up, getting ready to go to the party together. Her white dress looked fabulous on me, and after adding a little disco glitter makeup and scrunched blonde beach hair, I decided to carry the little satin shoe disco bag that night. Tita looked stunning in her long tropical print dress. She plucked a single coral-colored hibiscus blossom from my garden and pinned it into her full dark hair on one side. She looked just like Rita Moreno in *West Side Story*. Gorgeous. We wore simple eyelashes and red glossy lips. Then we sped off in her car for Jose Bettencourt's surprise birthday bash!

After we valet-parked, we went into a modern club with lush red and white velvet decor. We were quickly escorted to the private party realm where everyone was very hush-hush while appetizers and drinks were being served. Most of the guests were dancers from Jose's studio. Several of them came in with pies, cupcakes and flan for the dessert table; the rest was catered food. I assumed it was a Puerto Rican thing, making dessert for the birthday person because so many desserts were arriving. Tita and I tried to find Juan but couldn't. He must have been on the lookout for the guest of honor in anticipation of the big surprise moment.

We sipped champagne and visited with several dancers, awaiting Jose's arrival. Tita seemed to know absolutely everyone wherever we went. She had grown up in Puerto Rico and was quite popular, talkative and funny.

Tita introduced me to a group of musicians she had danced in concert with. While we were talking, one of Jose's protégés, who was present in every class I had attended, approached us with what looked like a lemon meringue pie in her hand. She'd always given me the stink eye in class and never spoke to me. She walked over to us, glided directly up to me—and smashed that pie in my face!

"Bitch!" she shouted at me, and walked away.

"What the fuck?" cried Tita, immediately chasing after the girl. Tita went off on her, shouting in Spanish as she went.

I was stunned. Within seconds, numerous dancers from the studio surrounded me with tissues and paper towels and started cleaning me up. Tita was still raging at the girl in Spanish. Suddenly, Juan appeared. He was horrified when he learned what had happened and he ushered my attacker out the back door.

I couldn't help but laugh! I lost it laughing with the people from the studio, who started telling me how jealous this girl had been of me since day one. I had no idea why. I only knew this girl gave me the evil eye in class. I had no idea she hated me!

Juan returned shortly after banishing her from the party and rushed to me to see if I was okay. "Of course I am. I'm fine, just a little shocked."

"She is so jealous of you because she has always been in love with Jose, and she can tell he likes you. He's never liked any of the girls at the studio, and she can't handle it!" he explained.

Just then, one of the boy dancers came over to Juan to let him know Jose was arriving. Juan quickly hushed the crowd.

Jose entered the darkened private room and we all shouted, "Surprise!" The lights blasted on, and confetti fell from the ceiling. I could tell he was delighted. The DJ started playing disco music, and for some reason, I was the diva everyone wanted to dance with, even with pie in my hair.

One thing about this evening was clear: Puerto Ricans are spicy! The whole culture is like that. People were passionate and fiery. It was a simultaneously endearing and disturbing quality! I loved the culture for that very reason.

Eventually, Jose found his way to me. We all danced disco in a group, laughed and had a ball. He had heard through the grapevine what had happened and apologized for the girl that threw the pie in my face. He said in Spanish that I looked beautiful and insisted on paying for my dry cleaning if my dress needed it. Tita translated for us. Such a gentleman.

The night was enjoyable, yet after a few dances, a little food and a few glasses of champagne, Tita and I decided to call it a night. The evening had been both stressful and entertaining.

As weird as it all was, we laughed about it for weeks. I managed to get Tita's white dress dry-cleaned to perfection with a bit of help from dear Yolanda. For some reason, I no longer felt attracted to Jose, and I wasn't sure why. Maybe it was all a bit too peppery for my taste.

I'd had enough salty drama in my childhood, which seemed to have followed me into adulthood. I wanted to stop attracting more of it into my life. Perhaps that is why I decided to turn away from beautiful Jose.

28

Manifesting Love, 1976

Though I thought I was manifesting something extraordinary, like Arnold, I may have been attracting more evolved bad boys in the guise of good guys. I wondered if I myself wasn't very committed in relationships or if there was more to learn about what I was manifesting. Constant vigilance had become a way of life for me now. I had incorporated small, specific verbiage for what I wanted in my life, among other things. Not only did I declare it, but I also became hyper-focused on enjoying those things. This was my awakening to becoming a much more powerful manifester.

Then I met Vince, star of the "Holiday on Ice" world tour. A celebrity in the skating orbit. We met on a Sunday night when a bunch of the dancers (the Puppet People) and I went to see the show.

When Vince hit the ice and performed a frosty swerve right in front of me, I let out a Universe-shattering "Yeow!" It echoed through the venue, over the music and sounds of skaters, and landed right on cue! Vince let out a "Yeow" right back. We established our connection right then and there. Even the friends I was with could feel our chemistry! He hadn't even seen me yet. But of course, he did when our entourage progressed backstage to meet the cast and congratulate them on a fabulous show.

Our entourage must have made quite an impression backstage because we were surrounded by most of the skaters within minutes. As we chatted and took photos together, without warning, the gorgeous, tall, dark and extremely handsome Puerto Rican star of the show, Vince, appeared in all his scrumptious glory. He was nothing short of beautiful.

As he approached, I let out a mini "Yeow!"

He laughed a radiant, charismatic, sexy laugh and looked me over from head to toe, saying, "I hope that was you."

"You bet it was! What a performance!" I blushed through my own radiant smile. And there it began, an attraction so fierce, our connection was conceived from across the ice.

We engaged in introductions and spent some time visiting with the cast when finally someone said, "Are there any discos open?"

We all found taxis outside and agreed to meet at our favorite disco. Vince insisted he and I get our own cab. Oh, good, he is a man with good form. But first, he needed to use the ice arena pay phone to call his aunt and uncle. He said, "I don't want them to worry. I'm staying with them."

Oh! A thoughtful man, too. Movie star good looks, kind and talented, I was swooning inside. There was something magical about Vince. He was very "in the moment" and charismatic. He had star quality in the traditional sense. And yet he was a little bit of a smart ass. Cheeky.

Vince and I were like magnets at the club. Dancing was something we both loved, and disco was his thing, too! What fun I was having with this sexy star! I hadn't been this attracted to anyone since Calvin Lockhart, and I missed it. Our fireworks and chemistry were off the charts. I could relate more to Vince than Calvin, being only a few years apart in age, unlike the 18 years between Calvin and me.

Vince was staying with his aunt and uncle, even though the cast stayed mostly in hotels. His parents lived in Santa Paula, California, but were also originally from Puerto Rico. Vince was born a California boy.

Throughout the evening of disco-dancing, Vince and I drew closer and closer. We drank a little, partying with our crews, who began teaming up like we had. The boys in his show and the boys in our show got along famously, and we all had a blast. Then Vince asked if I'd like to go somewhere and smoke some weed.

"Sure I would," I replied, "We could go to my house."

"Are you sure?"

"Of course, let's go," I insisted.

We caught another cab to my house. Our lips found their way to one another's as soon as I gave the driver my address.

We talked a bit more. Vince was witty, sassy, fun, chatty, lighthearted, seemed sincere, and was just so damn hot!

I was breathless with this guy. Just swept away. I was so enamored with his essence. His very pores oozed sexuality and his skin was smooth and toned. He was in perfect shape from skating. There was an Olympian quality to him.

I soon discovered that he had indeed been a contender for the Olympics while still very young. He had the opportunity to skate professionally, and being a dancer himself, he leaned into working in ice shows after suffering an illness just before going to the Olympics. His life and mine had taken similar detours at a very young age. He was only 25. I was a few years older. Both of us had seen our share of the world as performers.

In the next month and a half, we spent as much time together as we could manage with our jobs. He came to see my show the week we met on his night off, which was Monday. We spent time with our castmates

28. Manifesting Love, 1976

and his aunt and uncle, who invited me to brunch on a Sunday with his extended family. We formed bonds with all the boys in both shows.

Vince was there when I began rehearsals for our new show at the El San Juan. We were falling in love, and had so much fun together. There were challenges because we knew his departing date for the European leg of his Holiday on Ice tour was looming.

During this time, the headlining act in our show, Errol Manoff's Puppet People, began to prepare to go to New York for their next run. We had a new headliner coming to do our show, a husband-and-wife acrobatic team.

Errol and Peter began planning to work in New York for the holiday season in a new disco show called "Le Clique." The producer had seen the Puppet People in Puerto Rico and booked them for a three-month run in New York. Stewart and Marlene Feinstein had created a theatrical disco troupe that performed primarily in discos for private parties and they felt the Puppet People, a larger-than-life dancing-singing puppet show lit entirely in blacklight, would be a dynamic addition to their disco show "Le Clique."

"Le Clique" was a group of about 20 varied performers called "fantasy players" who staged, choreographed and designed their own

The Puppet People with Errol Manoff, 1978.

costumes for unique events and private parties in discos in the city. A traveling road show of sorts, a portable party. Each party had a theme, such as "Spring Prom," "Valentine's Ball," "Send in the Clones," "Circus Magic," etc. Their catchphrase was, "We make fantasy into reality." The cast included the incoming Puppet People and dancers, magicians, singers, jugglers, fire eaters, acrobats, contortionists, mimes and several other novelty acts. Special guests included everybody from NFL players to porn stars.

The exclusive private disco parties were given by people like Grace Jones, Bianca Jagger, fashion designer Hardy Amies, and dozens of New York socialites at super-hot discos at the time, including the Emerald City, New York New York, Uncle Sam's, the Inferno, Roseland and the Funhouse. "Le Clique" apparently had given extended life to the disco scene in New York and they were in demand.

Errol and Peter wanted to add a third performer to the Puppet People. I had collaborated with them on so many creative ventures in Puerto Rico that they invited me to leave with them, go to New York City and join their act. They made me an attractive offer, and I'd be making more money than I was in the show in Puerto Rico. I accepted the offer. I would be donning giant costumes and performing as a larger-than-life Puppet Person. I felt it would be a smart career move to be in a specialty act.

Errol encouraged me to wait a few weeks to give notice so that Miller-Reich would only be mad at him just before we left. He didn't want the organization who had hired him to know they had "stolen" me from their production shortly after they had made me a featured dancing nude in the new show. I had not signed a new contract yet.

I practiced with the Puppet People in secret, and Errol began measuring me for new costumes. It was quite challenging to dance while wearing character suits. I had to create larger-than-life movements while wearing enormous heads that covered my face.

The time came for Vince to leave. He was off to London for their next stop and would be there for a month before going to Sweden. Holiday on Ice was a major tour. We said our tearful goodbyes and made passionate love in my room before he left. His aunt and uncle picked him up at my house to take him to the airport.

I was not doing well after Vince left. It took every ounce of my energy to rehearse with Errol and Peter and the new Miller-Reich show. Errol was annoyed with me, being so sad and forlorn. I felt like a zombie without Vince. I had really fallen hard. He was great about calling me backstage the week after he left. Since he had a few weeks off before touring Europe, he visited his parents in Santa Paula. He missed me, too. We were in love, and those phone calls helped. But, as his time to go to London approached,

28. Manifesting Love, 1976

it got much harder. He tried to cheer me up on our calls, but we were both very emotional.

The night came when I knew he'd be leaving for London, and when he called me backstage before the first show, I was full-out weeping. I missed him so much. He promised to write every day. I did, too. We left that conversation depressed, longing for one another. It was the most emotional call we'd had.

I somehow managed to get my stage makeup on and drag myself onstage for the opening number. Once I felt the lights warming my face, it helped. I went into automatic performance mode and did my thing.

Vince, star of Holiday on Ice, London, 1978.

Just about the time the music died down near the end of the opening, I heard a loud "Yeow" from the back of the showroom near the entrance doors.

Am I hearing things? Losing my mind? That shout sounded like Vince doing exactly what I had done when we met. I glanced over where the sound had come from, and there, under the entryway lights of the front door, stood the beautiful Vince in person! The light framed him like an angel, and I began shaking. How could he be here when I spoke to him in California a few minutes ago?

I finished the opening and ran backstage. I shouted, "I think Vince is here!"

I was trembling and shaking out of my skin! All the girls in the dressing room were nodding.

"Yes, it's Vince," said Tita. "He called backstage to tell me he was here to surprise you."

"Oh my God, I can't believe he'd do this. How sweet of him!" I squealed.

Everyone reveled in my joy and helped me into my next costume since I was shaking with joyful exhilaration. Surprising me like that was one of the most romantic gestures anyone could make. It was one of the best things that could have happened, making me love him even more. Just like my high school love Blase, he too was a Gemini, and Geminis can be so romantic. Vince and I enjoyed three blissful days together.

Somehow his leaving wasn't quite as bad this time. I felt loved beyond anything I'd known to date, and with his surprise gesture, I was sure our love would last a lifetime. He really was magical.

I saw Arnold again before I left for New York City. I gave him my parents' home phone number and address in case he ever needed to reach me. He said goodbye to Sasha, and I took her to Illinois with me to stay with my parents. I knew I would miss her terribly, but I would be lodged at a Sheraton in New York and was uncertain when I would be in one place long enough to keep her with me. Arnold was already dating one of the new dancers in the Miller-Reich Production. Weird. He didn't want me working in the show, but it was a fine place for him to meet someone new. We were divorced seven months later. Arnold wound up having four wives before he passed at age 70.

Going to New York didn't make missing Vince any easier. Even after the high of his surprise in Puerto Rico, I left the island feeling pitiful.

I wondered how I would go on without Vince. I was utterly depressed, knowing full well that again I was back in a long-distance relationship.

29

Start Spreading the News, 1977

My visit home was brief—only a few days to see the entire family and leave my precious little Sashita with my more than willing parents. They loved my little pup.

My dad said, "It's good to have her here. It feels like having a part of you around while you're living like a gypsy!"

"That's what dancers are called, Dad," I interjected. "Because our work takes us all over the world."

"I know, and I'm proud of you, Diane. We just miss you." I knew he meant it. I always knew my dad loved me.

On the other hand, my mom had told the extended family that I "ran away." I was informed of that year after year by my four brothers, sisters-in-law, cousins, aunts, uncles and others.

A life I loved was all I was ever after, and I found it in show business.

I couldn't blame her for not getting it. We were very different people. I knew she loved me. When I first left home, I saw her break down while I was taxi-ing down the runway on my flight. It broke my heart to see that and to leave her alone with Dad, who was always unpredictable.

After several days of bonding with my brothers and high school BFFs, I flew to New York City. I landed there shortly after Thanksgiving 1977. The holidays were upon us, and I somehow managed to muster a little excitement around becoming a "Puppet Person." The Puppet People, including Errol, Peter and I, arrived and were driven to a cozy Sheraton Hotel near our producer's home in New Rochelle. We would rehearse in the convention rooms and Errol could create his new puppets and work on our phenomenal costumes. One of our producer's associates owned the Sheraton.

I would eat, have dinner with the Puppet People, rehearse inside the giant Puppet suits, then retire to my room to write letters to Vince and wait for his calls from London. With him back on his Holiday on Ice tour and the time difference, our calls were much scarcer, and I felt lost. I missed him with all my heart.

We were to open in our first "Le Clique" performance in a few weeks.

I wasn't excited or happy. I think it was because I wasn't enjoying the puppets. The costumes were like theme park characters but bigger. The bodies of the puppets were big fuzzy costumes we climbed into, and then giant foam heads were placed over our heads. I found them slightly claustrophobic, huge and bulky. It was awkward and uncomfortable.

I wouldn't just be in the puppets. We were also creating a very magical routine with Peter as a wizard, Errol the sad French clown, and me the dazzling, sexy fairy queen. That was a fun number, and the costumes were unbelievably gorgeous. I think we raised the bar for the fantasy players of "Le Clique" with Errol's incredible creations.

One of the best things about working on "Le Clique" was that white limousines would pick us up, deliver us to every show, and then return us to our homes afterward. The paparazzi hounded us wherever we arrived, and our photos wound up in several newspapers each week, including the *New York Times*. "Le Clique" was big in New York, and we all had our 15 minutes of fame. We were recognized often. Disco was at its peak in 1977, and so were our careers.

Our first performance was unforgettable. The disco was New York, New York. We arrived in costume, in our limousines, and the paparazzi

Diane in a fantasy costume by Errol Manoff in "Le Clique" in New York City, 1977.

29. Start Spreading the News, 1977

photographed us. We also took publicity pics with our producers' photographers. Grace Jones opened the show by singing. Once she finished, we were delivered center stage. It was amazing, the way we appeared here and there throughout the magnificent club.

Although our entrances were theatrical, we sort of blended into the fabric of the discos we worked in. Confetti fell from the heavens when we arrived, and Stewart and Marlene always chose great disco songs like "Le Freak" by CHIC for our entrance, with booming music blasting through the most state-of-the-art sound systems money could buy.

We were the stars of the New York disco scene. Our dance routines included the latest disco moves. Everyone wanted to dance and interact with us, so we had to have very firm boundaries in place as a troupe. We knew exactly how to swoop in to save one another if some partygoer had a little too much of this or that and became overly aggressive. Plus, Stewart and Marlene were always with us, dressed for each theme party themselves, watching out for their "Le Clique" "children" on those crowded dance floors.

After just a few shows with "Le Clique," Errol and Stewart realized that the Puppet People were just too cumbersome for the disco scene. The act was more effective on a proscenium stage. I never performed more than once in those puppet suits. Errol dissolved my contract with him because it wasn't working.

"What about future Puppet People gigs?" I asked.

"You just aren't quite strong enough for these suits, and you're such a good disco dancer. You need to be in sexy costumes showing off your face and amazing body. So we're going to dissolve our verbal contract with you."

"And just abandon me in New York?" I was blindsided.

"I'm sure you can find work here." He seemed unconcerned.

"Errol, I left my job in Puerto Rico to work with you!" I whined.

"Well, I didn't know you'd be this miserable without Vince. Maybe you should go to London to see him!" Errol snapped back.

"Oh, so that's the problem?"

"You've lost your focus for the Puppet People, but your dancing is great!" he countered.

"That's fine, Errol. Thanks a lot," I cried. I was angry—and a little bit relieved.

I went to my hotel room that night and tried to sleep. I had in no way planned to be dropped my first few weeks with the Puppet People and "Le Clique." I felt abandoned.

We had a show the next night at the Emerald City Disco with a fantasy theme for the holidays. The entire troupe was able to repeat the presentation we had done at New York, New York. I did not perform in the puppets at all, I just did the fantasy number with Errol and Peter.

While working that night, I had a conversation with two performers in the show that I had really connected with, Sindra and Danger.

"I won't be able to stay after next week's performances because Errol is dissolving the Puppet People with 'Le Clique,' and my contract was with him," I moaned. "I should've insisted on a written contract! I have no idea where I'll even be living. I certainly won't be able to keep living free at the Sheraton."

"You can crash at my apartment anytime you'd like," offered Sindra, who had a phenomenal place on the 33rd floor of a high-rise at 56th and Broadway. "So don't even worry about that!"

"Really?" I asked tearfully.

"Absolutely!" she said. "I have a one-bedroom with a sofa bed in the living room, and you're welcome to use that! Besides, it's too expensive on my own, I need a roommate!"

"Wow, that's wonderful, Sindra." I hugged her. "I will let you know how this all plays out in the next few days. I'm so incredibly grateful."

"We call Sindra's place the Salvation Army House," chuckled Danger.

"It's true," laughed Sindra. "When anyone needs a place, I make sure they have one. But I'd rather have a roommate! Whatever you need, just let me know!" She was such a generous person.

Once again, guardian angels were sent to protect me. These were good girls. I was extremely lucky.

I felt blessed, grateful and not so freaked out. Knowing that a friend was offering me a home in the heart of New York City made me much less afraid of this change.

The next day, our producer, Stewart Feinstein, called me early in the morning to invite me to be a full-time fantasy player with "Le Clique!" Bam! Another angel was right there, offering me a job.

"Oh, Stewart, thank you so much! I was so worried when Errol gave me notice!" I exhaled.

"Are you kidding? We would be honored if you'd join the troupe. You are so gorgeous and so talented. You will be a centerpiece in the show. We really hope you'll say yes. You'd bring so much professionalism and pizzazz to the troupe."

"I'd love to, Stewart, and I thank you both so much! I have also been a costume designer, so this will be a creative outlet for that, too!"

Marlene came on the phone and told me they were excited to have me work with the troupe. They were never anything but wonderful to all of us. I adored them.

29. Start Spreading the News, 1977

The phenomenal thing is that "Le Clique" still exists today in the club scene. Disco may have died, but "Le Clique" did not!

I felt so protected and loved by the Universe. This was a good thing because New York City is a scary place to be out of work.

I called Sindra and told her the news. She squealed with delight. Her dad had been footing the bill for her luxury apartment until recently when he told her to start paying rent herself. She was making good money with "Le Clique" and certainly made enough to live in her stunning apartment with a roommate. So, we'd be helping each other. It worked out beautifully. She had rent relief, and I had a wonderful building to live in adjacent to Carnegie Hall, and just across Central Park sat the Dakota.

Danger, whose real name was Deborah Dangerfield, lived in the city, too. So did all of the other troupe members. We could rehearse and create together. Choreography, costuming, props, you name it, we created it all. It sounds expensive, but our producers paid us well and we had plenty of money to spend on costuming and designing every themed show. We could reuse many of our costume pieces from performance to performance. It wound up being one of the most creative times of my life. We were on fire.

Errol and Peter stayed through New Year's when their contract ended with "Le Clique." We did an incredible black light African number together at Scotland, the Yard Disco without puppet attire. Our photos were plastered all over the papers on New Year's Day, 1978. It was a safari theme, and I was the principal dancer in that vision of Errol's. I even had glow-in-the-dark makeup on with his elaborate designs with black light feathers and an African headdress with neon fabrics. We had our last hurrah together before the Puppet People departed for Japan to headline in a big production.

Errol, Peter and I parted friends to some degree.

I stayed another four months in New York City. It was an incredibly fun four months when I wasn't mooning over Vince. I missed him so much.

"Le Clique" was in demand at all the clubs in the spring, and New York was everything. I enjoyed the recognition, the troupe and discos very much. I vibed with the fantasy players, especially Sindra, Danger, Everett, Jimmy and Randy. All of that creativity healed my lonely heart most of the time. There was no shortage of good-looking guys asking me out, but I was committed to Vince.

Until the day Vince sent a British skater from the U.K. to deliver a message from him in person. Vince called me and alerted me that he had a messenger on the way who would bring a little of him to me.

"What do you mean?" I asked him.

"A dear friend of mine is coming to New York and will bring you a message from me sometime today or tomorrow!" he added mysteriously.

"Is that all you can tell me?"

"Her name is Patsy. Just keep your mind open," he said vaguely.

Patsy did just that. On my day off, there was a knock at my door in the afternoon. I knew Patsy was coming up because we had a doorman who would only allow guests up if we placed them on his list to be admitted. "Hi, Diane," chirped the redheaded punk chick he had sent. She looked a little like Cindy Lauper. "I'm Patsy!"

"Come in, Patsy," I said, opening the door. "Vince told me you'd be coming!"

"Oh, don't you just love Vince?" She said as she entered our living room and hugged me.

"He's such a doll, and he asked me to give you something when I got here!"

"Cool, what is it?" I curiously inquired.

"This," she whispered as she kissed me fully on the mouth.

"Oh," was all I could muster. I was confused and freaked out. "That's it?"

You can't make this stuff up. I mean, who does that?

Patsy laughed and added in her British accent, "There's more whenever you're ready!"

What the heck did that mean? I wondered but was afraid to ask.

"So, did you skate in Holiday on Ice with Vince?" I asked, changing the subject.

"Yes, I did, but when my contract was up, I decided to come to New York City because there's a guy here I'm into. He's really into the grunge scene and plays with a punk band in the East Village."

"Is he your boyfriend?"

"Not exactly. We were together in the U.K. but we broke up when he came here, so I'm going to surprise him. I'm still crazy about him."

"Wow," I said, remembering Flip and my surprise. "Good luck with that. When will you see him?" I asked.

"He has a show this weekend, and I thought maybe we could go if you'd like," she suggested.

"I'm a disco queen, not into punk. But I am curious, so, let's go!"

"Great! I'm at the Chelsea Hotel, and hopefully, soon, I will be back together with him," she said.

"Does he have a place here?"

"He does, and he has roommates, but he should be happy to see me and want to be together."

"I hope so, especially since you traveled all the way from the U.K.," I said.

29. Start Spreading the News, 1977

Patsy and I continued chatting and getting to know one another. We ordered food from the deli and had it delivered. We told one another stories about "Le Clique," Holiday on Ice and boys!

We made plans to get together on Friday since "Le Clique" wasn't doing a show that night. Everett, Jimmy and Randy wanted to go, too. We all tagged along with Patsy to the Mudd Club to surprise her ex-beau. We wanted Danger to come, but she said, "Fuck punk!"

When our taxi delivered us, we embarked en masse into the club. As the six of us entered the large, dark, dingy Mudd Club, someone shouted, "'Le Clique' is here!"

That's how it was in New York; people always recognized us. We were *the* disco entourage, and many people still went to discos. Shortly after we arrived, some dank punk dude came over to us at the bar and announced in dreary grunge fashion, "Disco is over, and you're not welcome here!"

"We aren't performing tonight, and we can go anywhere we like," announced Everett, one of our fearless lead boy performers. He was a regal lion and took charge. Everett and I were born on the same day, August 23. Leos. No one messed with us after that.

Patsy was about to surprise her ex after their set. The Mudd Club was a dump, but that was punk. Black walls were splashed with neon graffiti. It was early 1978, and disco was being replaced by the grunge movement. I couldn't understand how the bright pizzazz of disco could ever be outshone by the punk scene.

But it was packed. Times were changing, at least in parts of New York City.

Patsy surprised her ex, and he seemed genuinely happy to see her. It was obviously a significant risk on her part.

They reunited happily, but Patsy called me in tears a few days later. I insisted she come over and tell me everything. I wanted to hear what happened, and also wanted to hear more about Vince.

When she arrived, she was very upset. They had had a fight over something they always disagreed on.

"What is it you can't agree on?" I asked.

"I don't want to go into it right now," she claimed. "But I know we love one another."

Patsy didn't know if they could work through it, whatever "it" was. She was sad because she really loved this guy. We talked and talked and smoked a joint until she felt better.

Once she was a bit happier, I asked, "How long did you know Vince?"

"Oh, we worked together in London for the last month, and we really got on great! I had a bit of a crush on him, but after our initial get-together, he did tell me all about you!"

"Oh, really? What did he say?"

"That he loved you and that you were this incredibly talented, beautiful dancer in New York City." She smiled. "He told me you were a free spirit who wouldn't mind that we had been lovers. When he found out I was going to New York, he insisted that I come here and make love to you for him."

I only heard about every fourth or fifth word after "we had been lovers." The planet cracked, and I was glitching out internally.

"Are you okay with that?" Patsy asked after a long silence.

"Which part?" I returned a question.

"All of it?"

"I'm not that much of a free spirit, and Vince never mentioned any of this," I stuttered.

"Well, maybe we should make love and then call Vince," she suggested.

"But I'm not a lesbian," I told her.

"Oh, you don't need to be. We can just enjoy a little sensual experience and think about Vince," she said as she stroked my hair.

Soft tears spilled down my cheeks. Vince had cheated and sent Patsy to tell me all about it!

"Oh, luv, don't be sad. It's fine. It was just sex, and Vince thought imagining the two of us together would be a fantasy he could enjoy," Patsy added in her heavy British accent.

"But what about what you and I want?" I asked her.

"I'd love to make love to you," she proposed.

"I've never been with a woman, and I'm not really feeling it."

"It's okay," she murmured. "Maybe it would be good for both of us."

"What makes you think that?" I asked.

"I had a threesome in London with Vince, and it was great fun!"

That was it. I started sobbing. This was not who I thought Vince was. I knew he had a cocky, edgy side to him, but this was flat-out cheating. I thought we were exclusive. He had a threesome! What the fuck?

I couldn't stop crying. Patsy tried to comfort me, and she embraced me while I wept.

I think she realized she'd said too much and stopped talking. Once I began to pull myself together, she apologized. "I'm so sorry, luv. I thought from the way Vince spoke about you, that you were cool!"

"I am cool!" I blurted defensively. "I've just never been with a woman or had a threesome. This is not a part of Vince he ever shared with me. Is this a regular thing for him? Were you two with another girl in the ice show?"

"Yes, and it meant nothing. I don't know if it's something Vince does regularly, but I do know he loves you and wanted something for you, too!"

29. Start Spreading the News, 1977

"Meaning you and me?" I questioned.

"It seems so." Patsy said.

I was confused and emotional. I don't know what I expected in this moment at all. I was overwhelmed and in shock. All I could feel was how hurt and angry I was at Vince for sending this girl to me. I started to cry again.

Patsy said, "I'm so sorry, luv. There, there now. It'll be all right!"

I dried my eyes and went to make tea, and we drank a cup. She didn't know what to say. I liked Patsy. She was harmless and a vulnerable character at heart. I just wasn't vibe-ing with this plan.

After we had tea, Patsy decided to call her ex. They talked and he asked her to come over to his place, and she happily went, hoping to rectify their spat. I was happy to have her gone. I wrote in my journal, hurt over being cheated on, and then tried to organize my thoughts, wondering what I would say to Vince.

He generally called on Monday, his day off, and it was only Wednesday, so I had several days to sort through my feelings regarding all I had learned tonight. Damn it! Why couldn't I just have a career and a relationship work out at the same time? I couldn't understand what it was I was doing to manifest this hot mess.

30

An Eye for an Eye, 1977

Then something surprising happened: I ran into Robby, an old musician friend in my neighborhood one day. We chatted, and I asked what he was doing. He was playing drums with a band across the street at the Sheraton during Happy Hour. He had worked with another popular band at Max's in Atlanta when I was fashion coordinator. Robby was a doll. So cute. We had chemistry when we met in Atlanta, but I was married and not fooling around, so I didn't act on that attraction. But here he was, and here I was, right here in the heart of New York City, and both single as a one dollar bill.

Robby asked me out after Happy Hour, and we went to a nearby Irish pub and had a cocktail or two, and caught up. He'd only been in New York for a few weeks. I guess the Universe knew just what I needed at this moment and sent me sexy Robby.

The funny thing about him, in retrospect, and I knew it then, is that he was a sweet guy. Really good-hearted, no bullshit. Not a smart ass or a know-it-all or a controlling personality. Just a hot, talented drummer who comforted me, adored me. He expected nothing. He just loved being with me.

We became lovers, and I felt justified. I needed what we had. It was sweet, consistent, and it helped me. He listened to me. He didn't push. He was a fantastic, attentive lover. He came to my shows often and treated me like a queen. All my pals from "Le Clique" loved him. We hung out and had fun together. Aside from having a unique, creative and fulfilling job as a performer, the time I spent with Robby was my best experience in New York City. He helped heal me.

He knew all about Vince. After the Patsy debacle, I had let Vince know that I felt it best for us to see whomever we wanted, and he agreed. I was still in love with Vince, and Vince didn't want us to end either.

I know that Robby would have been a wonderful partner. He was good to me. Why didn't I say "yes" to the ones I knew were truly good guys? The drama that the bad boys created wasn't really what I wanted, but

30. An Eye for an Eye, 1977

there was that comfort I felt with them. It was because of my childhood. I learned that in therapy. Subconsciously, I chose my dad over and over, a womanizer, alcoholic, drowning in disappointment.

Robby and I parted after his two-month gig at the Sheraton. He was headed back to Atlanta to work with another band. I would miss him but I still loved Vince, who had begun writing more frequently, trying to make plans to reunite with me when his contract ended. It was now late June. He wanted to come to New York and look for work, possibly as a dancer, to get off the ice for a while. He also wanted to live with me.

Our relationship was not making me happy long-distance, and as much as I wished he could be trusted, I absolutely did not want to wait around for another man to get his act together. I told Vince that I'd be willing to give it a go after he found work and felt secure again. His letter-writing began increasing in its proclamation of love for me, more emotional than before, and he seemed desperate in his desire to reunite. He was pulling me back in strongly despite the cheating and the pain he had caused me. Ugh! Why did I love him so much?

Our "Le Clique" shows continued growing, and we grew stronger as a troupe. I was very close to everyone, and we created magic in our shows.

One of the things I missed most while living in New York City was nature. A true nature girl at heart, I thrive in a natural setting. Nature fills up my soul. New York was thrilling, but after six months, you just want to go to the beach, take a hike or ride a horse.

Don't get me wrong, Stewart and Marlene Feinstein invited the cast to their sprawling family home for barbecues and long Sundays in a natural setting. They had a lovely home in New Rochelle, with sloping lawns and catered food. They treated us well, and we all appreciated getting out of the city to enjoy a day in the suburbs. Despite these occasional getaways and a fantastic job, I longed for a more subdued, consistent lifestyle. Was I maturing?

* * *

Barbara and I talked on the phone regularly and wrote letters filled with pics of our shows, friends and lives. I missed her. She was now the legendary principal dancer at the Lido in Vegas. She and Piero had divorced, and she was inviting me to come to Vegas and be her roommate again. That sounded wonderful to me. She told me that the company captain, David Wright, was hiring girls for the "Allez Lido" show at the Stardust and that Siegfried & Roy were headlining to sold-out crowds nightly. That appealed to me on many levels.

Barbara told me she had spoken to David about me, and he was willing to hire me sight unseen, on her recommendation. "But I left the Lido in

Paris, Barb," I reminded her. "Miss Bluebell would never hire me back!"

"She won't even remember, and she's never here anyway. She's in Paris most of the time. Donn Arden comes to Vegas more often than she does, and that's only about once a year to see the show! You don't have to worry about that at all!"

"Really?" I wanted to make sure.

"She wouldn't care, anyway. You'd be great in this show. The ten nudes have great choreography and magnificent costumes and are really featured!"

At the same time, I had heard from a dance friend who was working at "Hallelujah Hollywood" at the MGM Reno. She wanted to know if I'd like to come work there, as they too were hiring. She told me about all the hikes and skiing they enjoyed in Lake Tahoe. That certainly spoke to my need for nature.

Siegfried & Roy starred in the Lido at the Stardust, 1979.

I really had to meditate on this, to figure out what I most wanted. I surrendered for a few days, turned it over, and asked for guidance. What I really wanted emerged crystal clear. I wanted to go to Vegas and work at the Lido. I wasn't getting any younger. I didn't love the desert, but at least there was Mt. Charleston and Lake Mead. Los Angeles and the Pacific Ocean would be four hours away. But most of all, I wanted to be with my closest friend again. We were great roommates, and always loved working together and enjoying life.

I was afraid I wouldn't have enough to do if I went to Reno, whereas Las Vegas was laden with numerous opportunities to model and act. Reno might be too small a town for me. My spirit needed a good balance of nature, activities and friendships. I somehow knew that I would have that in Vegas. I accepted Barbara Beverly's offer to come to the Lido and called David Wright to accept the job. I would be a dancing nude in "Allez Lido."

It felt right. I was happy with my decision. I gave "Le Clique" two weeks notice and arranged to arrive in Vegas to begin rehearsals in three weeks. I had just enough time to take a little trip home to Illinois, spend a bit of time there, collect my Sasha and then continue on to Vegas.

One of the best "Le Clique" bookings had to be when we did a mini-tour with the Village People to Boston and Miami. We took a train from New York to Boston, then a bus to Miami, and back to New York. We had two one-night performances, opening for the Village People. Those two shows were exciting for all of us. Only a handful of the "Le Clique" fantasy players went on that wild ride. I roomed with Danger and Sindra, and we hit it off with Felipe Rose, who was Native American. We partied all night. We went out to dance everywhere and had such fun. We became besties in a nanosecond. Everyone on that excursion came home exhausted and fulfilled. I always wondered how the Village People sustained that amount of party energy on bus tours, no less.

Or maybe it was like Felipe expressed while departing: "You're our people!"

One of the last, and certainly one of the most memorable performances was when "Le Clique" opened for Sylvester, the disco sensation from San Francisco. His acclaimed hits at the time were "You Make Me Feel (Mighty Real)" and "Dance (Disco Heat)." Not only did we adore this rare gem, who had gained the moniker "Queen of Disco" along with his backup singers Two Tons of Fun, we also couldn't believe that Roseland was the venue that featured him. From Wikipedia:

> The Roseland Ballroom was a multipurpose hall in a converted ice-skating rink with a colorful ballroom pedigree in New York City's theater district on West 52nd St. It opened in 1922 and closed in 2014. Over the years, it became known as a "cheek-to-cheek dance venue" for marathon dancing, until it was banned. Many big band performances were broadcast from Roseland on the radio in the 1920s and 1930s. Bands like Count Basie, Tommy Dorsey, Harry James, Vincent Lopez, Glenn Miller, and Sonny Burke. In 1940, young Ella Fitzgerald fronted the Chick Webb band there.

As the club grew older, it began regularly scheduled disco nights. When we opened for Sylvester to a sold-out 2500 standing-room-only audience, it felt historic and fabulous. The interior had purple and cerise tent-like decor that created a harem effect. The entire ballroom was a gigantic dance floor with strobe lights around a small stage. The primarily gay crowds went crazy for Sylvester, and we had so much fun cavorting with him. We stayed to dance once he came on, even though our work night was completed after opening for him. It was a colossal disco extravaganza. Lady Gaga completed a short residency as the last performer to work there before it closed in 2014.

31

The Wild West, 1979

The Feinsteins told me I would always have a home with "Le Clique" should I ever decide to return to New York City. I loved them. We agreed to stay in touch, and I would scope out any possibilities for them in Vegas at the discos in the big hotels.

My short visit home to Illinois proved fulfilling. I always needed to be with my colorful family, and I was able to do a local interview for the hometown newspaper while there. I visited my relatives and my high school BFFs, Corky, Patty and Louann. My parents promised to come to Vegas once I opened in the show. They had never seen one of my shows together, and this would be a great opportunity for them to enjoy an overdue vacation while seeing me perform in the best show on the Vegas Strip.

My mom once came on her own to Montreal while I was still a covered dancer. My dad had never seen me dance professionally. By now, they were aware that I was a showgirl, appearing topless. They seemed excited!

While in Illinois, Vince called me from London nearly every night. He claimed, "I've become forlorn without you, Di, and wanted to make sure you arrived home safely."

"Of course I did," I told him, unsure how to proceed.

"My contract will be ending around the same time as your new one starts in Vegas. I want to fly home to see my folks in Santa Paula and then go to Vegas to find work. Would you like to come meet my parents?"

I was so touched by this.

"I do want to meet your mom and dad," I told him.

"They want to meet you, too, baby," he cooed.

I arranged to spend four days with him at their home before heading into rehearsals at the Stardust. Vince offered to drive me to Vegas afterward. He wanted to make the rounds in Vegas to find work as a skater or dancer by connecting with his friends in the shows.

The daily phone conversations brought us closer, and I regained some trust in Vince, feeling he was fighting for me. He even asked to meet my parents on the phone! He was doing everything right, making me believe

Publicity photograph of "Le Clique" in New York City, 1978.

he truly loved me, and regretted assuming we were free to date whomever while we were apart. We had never discussed exclusivity before. We agreed to have a monogamous relationship from this day forward. I'm not sure what made me trust him, but I was still in love with him, and he was introducing me to his parents! That meant a lot to me.

Vince picked me up from LAX on a hot day just after the Fourth of July, which I had celebrated at home with fireworks on the Mississippi River. We ran to one another in the baggage claim area and had one of those movie kisses that never ended as he twirled me around in his arms.

"Baby doll, I've missed you so much!" he squealed. Vince really was magical. Some of the most romantic moments of my life were spent with Vince, as were some of the most painful. Geminis. The duality never ends with them!

We drove in his parents' well-preserved, cool 1967 green convertible Mustang to Santa Paula after collecting my luggage and my precious Sasha. We were greeted by his parents, who were in their late 60s. Quite a contrast to my mid–40s parents. They had had Vince much later in their lives. He was their baby. He had one older brother, who was married and had a family.

31. The Wild West, 1979

Vince's parents were a lovely Puerto Rican couple who embraced me with such warmth, just like his relatives in Puerto Rico had done. We spent an idyllic few days with them and enjoyed avocados from his dad's prized trees in their backyard.

While having coffee one morning alone with his mom, she asked me if I loved Vince. I told her that I loved him very much. She asked, "How will you stay together if he goes back on tour and you're in Las Vegas?"

"That is a question I ask myself all the time. I dream of having it all, the man I love and our careers all at once," I confessed.

"Do you think you will get married?" she pressed.

"It's too soon to know yet. We have just reunited after spending seven months apart. We really need to sort out our careers before we can even begin to discuss something like marriage."

She wanted Vince to settle down soon and seemed hopeful it would be with me. I liked her honesty and maternal nature. We got on very well.

That night at dinner, Vince's father brought up marriage again. "Do you two plan to get married?" he asked. I wasn't touching this subject twice in one day.

Vince grinned, "What do you think, Di? Are you ready for that?"

"Maybe?" I smiled back. He squeezed my hand with a look that said, "Just humor my parents." It was a sweet moment.

Marriage seemed like such an anomaly at this point in our relationship. Plus, I was technically still married to Arnold.

Vince and I didn't discuss it again while visiting his parents. He was exhausted and needed some rest. He didn't want to go back on tour and hoped he could find work in one of Vegas' casino shows. They had hydraulic ice rinks on every showroom stage. In fact, most of the major hotels on the Strip had an ice-skating act in 1979: the Dunes, the Stardust, the Flamingo, the Riviera, etc.

After our visit, Vince and I drove to Vegas in the Mustang with Sasha to deliver me to my new job and Barbara's house. Knowing Vince, she had insisted he stay with us as long as he'd like. Barbara was always such a generous and supportive friend.

It was so good to again reunite with my best friend. The last time I'd seen her in person had been right after she'd gone on a cruise to Puerto Rico with Piero and her parents. They came to see my show, and then Barbara came to my house alone the next day. She shared with me that she was pretty sure she would be leaving Piero. His machismo Italian personality had become controlling and aggressive physically. I reassured her that she would be okay if she did decide to leave, and I knew firsthand having left Arnold. She seemed extremely unhappy and left Piero shortly after that.

Now in Vegas, Barbara and I were thrilled to share a home again. Our doggies got along famously. Barb had a white Pugapoo named Mini and a gray cockapoo named Maggie. Sasha loved them and was so happy to be with me again.

Barbara was off the night we arrived, and Vince went to bed early. I tucked him into my charming, furnished room in Barbara's cute cottage. Barbara and I caught up while Vince slept. I made our favorite, frozen lime daiquiris, which we sipped by the pool. The arid, warm summer night in Vegas felt so refreshing to me.

She told me that company captain David Wright wanted me to come in the next night. I called him to reassure him I would be there "reporting for duty," ready to sign my contract and begin rehearsals.

Barbara's one-story house was adorable and had the cutest pool. It also had two bedrooms and a large office with a sofa bed for guests. Eventually, my dad named our place "The Beverly-Mann Hotel" because we always had guests. I had finally changed my stage name to "Diana Mann," an offshoot of "Pirmann."

Barbara and I loved throwing parties and having friends and relatives come to stay. We always had that in common.

Vince asked me to see if the Lido was hiring boys. I agreed I would, but I was not completely certain I wanted to be in the same show as him. I'm not sure why I felt that, but I did. Could it have something to do with trust? Perhaps I didn't want to work with him where there were so many beautiful girls. He hadn't exactly been a beacon of trust.

The night after our arrival, I went to the Stardust with Barbara and met David. We spent some time getting acquainted and discussing my contract. If I signed a year at a time, I would get full insurance coverage: health, dental and even cosmetic surgery! That's how extraordinary dancers' contracts were in Vegas at the major hotels on the Strip. How could I say no? I decided to sign for one year.

David also wanted to know if I had any interest in doing outside jobs for various companies that needed dancers to make disco appearances from time to time at events. I did! David was aware I had just starred in a disco show in New York City and assured me the pay for these appearances would be great. I learned that local events were always hiring dancers from the big casino shows to make appearances, as well as fashion shows, commercials and acting jobs. This was perfect. It seemed like I could work all the time here.

I asked David if he was hiring boy dancers. He said he wasn't because he had several full-time swing boys. Boys were not as in demand as girls in the huge productions. There were four times as many girls in the shows. So I wouldn't be working with Vince after all. That was okay with me.

David sent me up to the sound and lighting booth to watch the show.

31. The Wild West, 1979

Again, I was blown away by the exceptional Allez Lido production. The phenomenal Siegfried & Roy were astounding magicians.

I was excited about the numerous outside opportunities available to me in Vegas. I liked making money. I wound up working nonstop for the three years I was employed at the Stardust. I worked in feature films,

Siegfried & Roy in the Allez Lido show at the Stardust, 1978.

An "Allez Lido" publicity photograph taken at the Stardust, 1981. Diane is the nude showgirl center left in the rounded hat.

fashion shows, television and radio commercials, voiceover, print work and TV shows; it was never-ending. But the real treasures in Vegas weren't the outside jobs, the fantastic production I was in, or the acting opportunities. It was the alarmingly brilliant cast of the Lido de Paris.

I have never experienced a cast quite like the one in "Allez Lido." I'm not sure whether it was because we were all close in age, the fun disco mentality of the late '70s or that almost everyone had a major interest in something substantial besides dancing. Dancers usually came to Vegas to complete their careers because those were the cushy dance jobs: great pay, unlimited days off if needed, and everyone was preparing to do something else once they couldn't dance anymore. A dancer's career normally ends by the time they reach 35.

Barbara was going to school full-time at UNLV majoring in English.

31. The Wild West, 1979

All the other dancers in that show had something else going on too. There were lots of go-getters, and I can't think of one soul, including the dressers and crew, that I didn't love.

Barbara and I had a very close-knit group of friends who hung out every week. Barbara and Kim Cornell and her husband Kenny, the youngest maître d' in Vegas, would spend Thursdays with us before work.

Vince got along with everyone, and he was a huge part of the fun. Our posse also included Kathy Shriner and her Italian husband Nino, both singers. There was Cheryl Fraza, a beautiful principal dancer who was fun to cavort with. Kim Lonsdale and Sharon Tegano were absolute dolls. Then there was James Maxwell, one of the boy dancers from Southern California who had started his career at Disneyland. James and I became close. He exuded a sort of spiritual sexuality that was his superpower! He was incredibly charismatic and much loved by everyone.

There was the boys' line captain, Neil Letham, and his wife Karen, two of my all-time favorite people to play with. The darling Lynda Ferrell was a stunning Welsh girl who charmed all of us. Beautiful Jane Millett and I had everything in common: dancing, knitting, acting and musical comedy. We never stopped sharing our love of all those things. Michael Baker was our warm-hearted, gorgeous South African ballet dancer who looked much like Nureyev with a heart of gold.

Canadian Kenny Mazlow was an exceptional Lido singer who kept us constantly laughing backstage with his whip-smart humor. He, Neil Letham and the hysterical Britisher Neil McGee entertained us between shows like it was their job. Doug Woods, Jim Zarro and Bob Michaels were also very dear to me. Then there was hilarious Mindy Hall, a darling former Ice Capades skater and showgirl, who had once dated Vince when they were skaters. We became very close and shared hundreds of stories, laughing every night backstage.

Shirley Allen became another lifelong friend. Liz Hayden was our outstanding

Diane and James Maxwell backstage at the Stardust, 1980.

nudes' line captain. She was intelligent, gorgeous, and loved everyone. She was the most supportive person I knew in any show anywhere. Liz had a way of getting everyone to stay on top of their game without ever offending anyone. She loved you into being great.

The adorable Suzan Baucum later became *the* Las Vegas judge for 12 years straight. I loved her, too. Then there was Marian Palmer, a former competitive swimmer who never lost her exceptional athletic figure or edge and loved to have fun!

Joanna Pecitto, one of my dearest friends, eventually became the nudes line captain when Liz left. Joanna was Mama Bear to all the girls, and we loved her for that. Diane Duckworth was only there for a short time. We hit it off when I arrived and had tons of fun outside the Lido. When she left and became a top masseuse at the Bellagio, I knew her healing light would be in demand for a long time. After a ten-year stint as a masseuse, she became the #1 real estate agent in Las Vegas. A brilliant and beautiful Goddess.

Several of the boys I couldn't get enough of: Jeff Adair, Carter Poust and John Kendricks (Carter and John would later be one of my all-time favorite couples). Then there was John Klineline, Herbie Korn, Clem Zelewski and Doug Woods. Each held a special place in my heart.

The boy dancers I became closest to were James Maxwell and Vimmi Kruger, a gorgeous blonde South African who was also a top photographer in Vegas outside the Lido. He was in a relationship with Roy Vanoy, another dynamic boy in the show. I became a makeup artist for Vimmi's photoshoots, and we were also dance partners in the African number. We remained very close until his passing in 2022. For a time, I was secretly in love with Vimmi. He wanted to have a baby with me and asked me to live with him and his lover.

"Uh. I know we love each other, Vimmi, but I don't think so," I told him.

My other dearest friend was singer Michael Gallagher, who got me back into acting full-time with his incredible coach, Joseph Bernard. I'll never forget the first scene we did together from *Same Time, Next Year*. We moved to Los Angeles at the same time and became working actors while studying together at Strasberg's with Academy Award nominee Sally Kirkland.

Michael was the first person I lost to the AIDS epidemic in 1983. Of course, many of the brilliant, beloved talents I've mentioned here were lost to AIDS by the mid-1980s. The most heartbreaking time of my life. We lost so many of our nearest and dearest, and my heart still breaks for them and their families.

I mention these people by name because we had something so

31. The Wild West, 1979

Ms. Bluebell & Donn Arden, creators of the Lido de Paris, 1978.

special, unlike anything I'd ever known. There was a wonderful balance of male-female, Yin-Yang energies that made our time together a pure lovefest. No other time has ever compared to the camaraderie we shared in that production. Most of those I named here who are still with us are still some of my closest friends.

It felt like we were all magnetized to one another and were destined to be close friends forever. Not only did we work together, but we also partied hard together! We put the "wild" in the wild west! You can imagine the onstage presence we shared and the vivacious energy we generated in that show.

I believe that the "Allez Lido" show, which Donn Arden and Ms. Bluebell had produced in two locations (Las Vegas and Paris), was their longest-running production. I'm sure it had much to do with the outstanding energy imprinted on the very boards of that stage and in the fabric of the curtains by the loving, talented cast.

My initial two-week rehearsals were the start of it all. That's when I met Shirley Allen, a beautiful blonde, 30-something showgirl who was making her Lido comeback after a brief hiatus. I learned so much about Las Vegas from her. Boy, did Shirley have stories to tell! She's the only person I know who actually dated Elvis.

32

Let the Games Begin, 1979

Our first day of rehearsals with the nudes' line captain, Liz, included a brief lineup to present us to the Stardust's casino boss, Herb Tobman. A gentleman in his 50s, he had recently become co-owner of the Stardust with Al Sachs after Frank Rosenthal was banished for fixing NFL games in his sportsbook there!

Mr. Tobman seemed like a nice man. Liz had the three newly hired nudes line up in leotards, fishnets and dance heels onstage for our first afternoon rehearsal. That's always a nerve-racking thing to do. Just the fact that some man looks you over like a horse trader is such an objectifying thing to endure.

That is possibly part of why showgirls have become extinct. Women don't have to do that kind of thing anymore. We've come too far in our quest for equality to work topless and line up like mail-order brides on display. No one really liked this part of the job. The world has changed. Thank God.

As the three of us stood tall center stage, Herb Tobman walked down our short line, gazing at us. There was super-thin, blonde Shirley Allen, rising to a statuesque 5'10". The beautiful, young, thin-framed blonde, Debbie, maybe 5'7", had grown up in Vegas and was new to dance. And then me, the 5'9", curvy yet slim, honey-haired diva. He stopped dead in front of me to look me straight in the eye (as if he knew I had fled in the night from the Lido in Paris). I flashed him the biggest, warmest smile I possessed. It was my superpower. I'm not sure why that occurred, but it scared the bejesus out of me!

Mr. Tobman turned to Liz and said, "Great, thank you!"

I guess in Lido language, that meant we were all approved for delivery! The things we endured.

I loved the choreography for "Allez Lido." I trained with Liz and the girls. We all became quite close.

Shirley and I slipped into the lovely choreography like a new satin gown with no issues and delivered as appointed. On the other hand, pretty little Debbie was struggling. She was darling indeed, but didn't have much going on as a dancer.

"You're one of the last real showgirls," Shirley Allen proclaimed a few days in. "Just like me, you don't see many of us anymore."

I asked, "What does that mean, exactly? I keep hearing this from everyone, everywhere!"

"You know, a real showgirl. Like a good dancer, but a real presence!" She added, "That's what we really were back in the day."

"Oh, do you mean like not a great dancer?" I asked, insecure.

"You are a great dancer, but so many dancers are just that and don't have the personality to be a showgirl!" Shirley explained.

"You are certainly that, too!" I told her.

"Oh, God, don't I know!" She laughed. "I've known that since Elvis pointed straight at me onstage at the Desert Inn one night in the show 'Bedazzled' and said '*You!*'"

Wow. That's how Elvis and Shirley began dating. What an experience. Shirley was fun-loving, gorgeous, funny and warm. Maybe Elvis knew that just by looking at her when he selected her from the audience of her show.

I chuckled, "Once I was a covered dancer and hated the idea of being topless. It scared me to death!"

"I never wanted to work that hard!" Shirley laughed and rolled her baby blues.

Shirley and I became great friends backstage and beyond. I adore her to this day. We played dice games, sometimes for shots of tequila. I remember telling her it was time for me to divorce Jose Cuervo (tequila) because he was adding little lines to my eyes.

Liz thought we should try on the "Pink Hats" while rehearsing the opening, which included several quick changes in the wings. The 30-pound "Pink Hats" were feathered, pointed, hot pink hats that we wore with minimal rhinestoned costumes. We had cute and sexy choreography, mostly from the neck down, because balancing those hats was intense. That was when Debbie caved. She broke down after rehearsal, and when I went to comfort her, she asked if we could meet after rehearsal to talk.

"Of course. Let's go across the street to the Peppermill after rehearsal today and have a bite to eat," I offered. I could see she was really struggling.

We ordered iced tea and salads when we got to the glorified diner we often frequented. Debbie began to cry softly.

"I don't think I can do the show. I'm just not strong enough for the headdresses or in shape for this."

"Do you want to do it?" I asked.

"I don't think I do. I think I want to go to school instead at UNLV."

"Does Liz know this?"

"No, I haven't told her, but I just don't feel strong enough to do this," she confessed. "I don't know what to do!"

"Oh, Debbie, you're so young. How old are you?"

"I'm 19, and my parents are really bugging me to go to school, and I still live at home, so that's hard, too!"

"You have to decide what you want and then tell Liz soon because she will need to hire someone else. She's very compassionate, and she will understand," I assured her.

"I don't think I want to do it," she said. "The show is hard for me because I haven't had much dance training, and it's hard to pick up the choreography and those pink hats! I feel bad because I thought this would be good money for school. But now my parents have offered to pay for school," Debbie told me.

"There's nothing wrong with changing your mind. You're young, and even though you'd make a beautiful showgirl, it's also a good time in your life to pursue college," I advised her encouragingly.

"What should I do?"

"Just call Liz tonight backstage and tell her. I think Liz will be very understanding."

"I will. I knew you would know what to do," Debbie said, looking more confident in her decision.

"It's better to let Liz know now before you learn any more of the numbers in the show," I reminded her. "Plenty of girls want to be in this show."

So pretty, young Debbie left the show. We stayed friends and we went out to see a few shows, including the "Casino de Paris" extravaganza at the Dunes and a lounge show at the Sands. We did that before I started working evenings.

Vince was making the rounds and looking for work. He had a few complimentary tickets to shows he was considering auditioning for. There were so many huge productions in Las Vegas then. I got to know what was going on in town. I also started socializing during the day with many of my new friends who were close to Barbara. We went to day spas in the desert and horseback riding in Lee Canyon. Vince got along famously with everyone. We were very happy in Vegas, falling deeply in love.

I came home from rehearsal, and Vince was headed to the Dunes to see some skaters he knew who were now in the "Casino de Paris" show. Barb was headed to the Stardust for the first show.

That gave me some alone time to shower and settle in for the evening. I read the daily newspaper, the *Las Vegas Review-Journal*, and saw an advertisement for new shows at the local hotels. Appearing this week were—the Village People! It was their first performance in Sin City

32. Let the Games Begin, 1979

(Vegas), and I thought I would track down Felipe and see if we could have a drink while they were there. It would be fun to see them again.

That night, Vince came in quite late, sometime after midnight. I had been asleep already because I had rehearsal the following morning. He crawled into bed and said, "I have some good leads at the Dunes."

"That makes me happy," I told him through my sleepy haze. "We would be working in the same town, both dancing!"

"I may talk to them about skating as well," he interjected as he wrapped his arms around me.

I had taken a few classes with Vince in Puerto Rico. He was a decent dancer. We dozed off and I slept like a log. Deeply. Contentedly. Until nine a.m., when the bright summer light filtered into my room and roused me. I stretched like a contented cat when I realized Vince wasn't there!

Where could he be? I listened for a sign of him stirring in the house, but heard nothing. Barbara was already attending her morning classes at UNLV. I rolled out of bed and noticed a folded note on Vince's pillow. I unfolded it and read.

> Morning, baby doll.
> Sorry I didn't wake you. You looked so deeply asleep and happy I didn't want to disturb you. I need to take the Mustang back to Mom and Dad in Cali! See you in a few days, Love, Vince xo

"What the hell?" I asked myself aloud. He hadn't mentioned this to me. Why didn't he tell me when he came in last night? I was baffled. This wasn't sitting right with me.

With no cell phones back then, I assumed he was on the road. We spent more time being confused and stressed back then, not knowing things. (Cell phones have given us both greater peace of mind and much more complicated degrees of stress.) I wasn't happy about this. I felt it was a bit covert, especially after hearing the happy possibility of him having a job opportunity at the Dunes.

As I got myself together for rehearsal, my phone rang. It was Debbie, wanting to let me know she had called Liz the night before as I had suggested, and that Liz understood her decision to leave.

"Oh, good, Deb," I said, relieved. "I knew she would."

"Thank you, Diane. I feel so much better. I want to take you out for a drink tonight."

"Okay, cool, I'd love that!" I answered. "Why don't you come over to my house around seven. We can go anywhere you want. Vince is away for a few days in California, and I'm free."

Debbie agreed to do that, and I tucked away my frustration with Vince for the day. I had a show to learn!

Diane, Bob Michaels and White Gold backstage at the Stardust, 1980.

Rehearsals went well. Shirley and I learned the African number and we loved it. We danced to "Getaway" by Earth, Wind and Fire. Liz told us there would be real elephants onstage for this number, plus an erupting volcano! It was a massive production number, with lots of moving parts, including major hydraulics. We each danced with one of the boys in a sensuously choreographed routine. I danced center stage with Vimmi.

Liz had sensed that Debbie wasn't going to be able to cut it. She said one of the Bluebells had asked to swing for the nudes, so Liz had no pressure just yet to hire someone new. That all worked out. She asked Shirley and me to come in and watch the show again before we opened in another week.

Liz suggested, "Wait until you've learned all of the choreography before you watch so you can get a perspective of your placement in each number onstage." That was a good idea. It's always different once you are in costume, surrounded by a cast of nearly a hundred.

Debbie came over around seven, as planned. She seemed relieved. There were so many options in Vegas for a cocktail; we decided to drive down the Strip to see what caught our eye. We drove around chatting and laughing when we stopped at a stoplight in an intersection with a

32. Let the Games Begin, 1979

big apartment complex near the Dunes. Debbie was driving. As I gazed around with the window down on this warm summer night, I suddenly noticed Vince's green convertible Mustang in the apartment building parking lot.

"Wait!" I called to Debbie. "Pull into this parking lot. That looks like Vince's car!"

She asked, "Isn't he in California?"

"That's a good question!" I mumbled. "I swear that looks like his Mustang."

She turned into the lot and pulled up to the Mustang. I didn't even have to get out. I saw that it was definitely his car. I checked out the California plates and saw his personal articles inside.

"Why would his car be in this apartment's parking lot?" I asked aloud.

"It's weird," answered Debbie.

"Very," I added snidely as I got an idea. "Let's do some investigating. Can we go over to the Stardust and talk to Mindy Hall backstage? She should be between shows."

"Why Mindy?"

"Because she used to date Vince and knows all the dancers in town who used to be skaters. She might have some info!"

"I feel kind of strange going to the Lido, since I just quit."

"Oh, right, that's okay. I can talk to Mindy tomorrow. Let's go over to the Excalibur, where the Village People are playing this week. I worked with them on the East Coast and would love to say hi."

We did, but when we got there, we found that the Village People didn't open until the following night. We stayed and had a drink in the lounge anyway.

The next day at rehearsal, I asked Liz if it would be okay if I came backstage to talk to Mindy that night. Liz said, "Sure. I can give you her number if you'd rather call her."

"I'll do that. Thank you." Liz wrote down Mindy's number for me.

After rehearsal, Shirley dropped me off at home at around 4:30. I had time to call Mindy before she left for work.

"Mindy, it's Diana Mann, how are you?"

"Hi, Di. How are your rehearsals going?"

"Really well. I love the show and can't wait to start." I continued: "I have kind of a weird question for you. Do you know any skaters that work at the Dunes?"

"Definitely. I know one of the principal dancers, Carol," she answered quickly. "A gorgeous brunette. I worked with her in Ice Capades. Why do you ask?"

"Do you know where she lives?"

"Yeah, I've been to her apartment near the Dunes a few times," Mindy told me.

"Is it at that big complex near the Dunes intersection, just off the strip?" I asked.

"Yeah, it is. Why? Do you know her?"

"I thought I saw Vince's car there yesterday and wasn't sure why," I admitted.

"Vince used to date Carol," Mindy added, "when we worked in Ice Capades!"

"Really?" My heart sank.

"Yeah. Why? Did he go to visit her?" Mindy questioned.

"That's what I'm trying to figure out," I confessed.

"Do you want me to call Carol?" Mindy offered, "See what's up?"

I said, "I'll let you know."

"Sure, Di," she said, "Anytime. But are you okay?"

"I'm not sure yet, but something's fishy with Vince. He said he was in California for a few days, yet I saw his car at that apartment complex last night."

"Had he reconnected with her recently?" Mindy inquired.

"I do know he said he had a good lead at the Dunes. I need to figure some things out."

I felt comfortable with Mindy. She, too, became a lifelong friend. She is hilarious, gorgeous, witty, dry-humored and sharp. She made me laugh often and still does. Mindita!

I told Barbara what had happened, and she said, "Just go over to the Dunes tonight and see if he's there. You can take me to work and then take my car. I'll ride home with Rick."

Rick was a cute busboy in the Stardust showroom. Barb was having fun dating him; he was a doll.

33

Viva Las Vegas, 1979

I slipped into a cute outfit, set forth into the warm August night and headed for the Dunes in Barbara's baby blue Buick Regal. I pulled into the front parking lot to see if any parking was available and cruised slowly around. On the third row, I slowed down, looking for a parking space, when I spotted a familiar car.

Right out in the forefront of the hotel lot was Vince's Mustang, facing the Strip as if on display. I checked the plates. It was definitely his. I imagine he never expected me to be driving around Vegas since I didn't yet have a car.

My blood boiled and my heart began breaking in two. I was shaking when I realized that I'd chosen a liar. Why had I trusted him after the incident in New York City with Patsy? What the hell was wrong with me, going back to men who had done me wrong in the first place? I did it with Arnold, and here I was doing the same thing with Vince. Just because they pursued me, claimed to love me, saying they wanted to marry me shouldn't be enough to convince me to return to them.

What was it about me that attracted guys like this? So many questions flooded my consciousness, so much self-doubt. I didn't go into the hotel. I felt dumb. I drove back to the house and climbed into bed. I cried myself to sleep.

I awoke the next morning ready for rehearsal and somehow managed to get through the day. Work was the best distraction. Liz was kind enough to pick me up and drive me to rehearsal that morning and then home afterward. I later had time to share my discovery with Barbara.

"How weird that he didn't even leave Las Vegas, and you saw his car at two separate places in the last few days," Barbara commented.

"With no word from him at all," I added. "How could he flat-out lie to me about going to California? I am so pissed and so tired of liars and cheats!"

"But you don't know he cheated Di," Barb suggested, always the Libra considering both sides.

"What part of this is not a lie?" I asked her.

"You're right. Vince told you one thing and didn't do that and is hanging around where that girl lives and works."

"Yeah, it's pretty obvious he's doing something he can't tell me about!" I moaned.

"Why don't you call his parents' house and see if he's there?" Barb suggested.

"I don't have their number," I realized. "He has always called me."

We made a little dinner. I could barely stomach food. I decided to watch a movie and settled in around six to try and relax. I needed to call the Excalibur and see if Felipe Rose was backstage since the Village People were definitely in town by now. That would be a pleasant diversion from the angst and hurt I felt about Vince.

About an hour into the movie, the doorbell rang. It was nearly sunset, and I wasn't expecting anyone. I jumped up and peeked out of our blinds in the office. Oh my God! I saw Vince's car parked in front of the house. He was here!

The doorbell rang again. What was I going to say?

There was no time to think. I answered the door, opened it, stepped out onto the front porch wearing a loose kimono over a teddy, the door mostly closed behind me. There he was. Gorgeous as ever and smoking a cigarette.

"Hi, babydoll! I've missed you," Vince said as he hugged me.

"How was California?" I asked immediately.

"Oh, you know, same ol', same ol'," he threw out.

"How are your parents?" I asked directly.

"They're good. They say hi," he added.

"Really?" I asked, skeptical.

"Yeah, let's go in. I've missed you so much." The lie was written all over Vince's face.

"Um, yeah, well…" I stuttered. I gazed down at the sidewalk below us.

"What's wrong?" He inquired. "Are you okay?"

"I have someone here," Blurting out the first thing I thought of.

I have no idea where that came from. Vince stared at me. His face hardened, and he clenched his jaw.

"Who's here?" he asked tightly.

"Felipe," I lied. Vince heard all about our shenanigans with Felipe Rose but didn't know he was gay.

Vince flicked his cigarette hard into the driveway. He looked like he was about to say something but changed his mind and stormed toward his car, face emblazoned red.

I turned and closed the front door, shaking. I locked it with my back against the door, with my eyes closed until I heard Vince's car pull away.

33. Viva Las Vegas, 1979

There it was. My own lie. God knows where I got it from, but it was designed to hurt him. It happened instantly, without forethought. I was done. I didn't care what he thought or felt. In that moment, I did what I needed to do for me. He could derive anything he wanted from that. My instincts were to end this facade of a relationship he had created. He lied to my face about being in California. Consequently, my reaction was born.

Years later, one of my therapists told me that was an act of self-preservation.

I often wondered what his story would have been. I even spoke to him briefly once in the late '90s. When I called him intending to find closure, I found he had just fathered a new baby girl, which stopped me from bringing up the past. He did tell me that after I left the Stardust to move to L.A., he had gone there and been hired as a dancer. He claimed it was to reunite with me. Several of my dancer friends had told me the same. If he had wanted to reunite, he could have found me easily. It didn't matter. It was long over. I had a wonderful new life unfolding in Las Vegas and planned on making the most of it. I had incredible friends and many exciting people to enjoy life with. I didn't need anything dragging me down.

Several days later, I went into the show and loved "Allez Lido." Mindy asked me how things were with Vince. I shared what had happened since our last talk. "As hot as he is, he's not worthy of our hearts," Mindy claimed.

"I agree," I told her. "Thanks for being honest with me." Mindy and I bonded over Vince. I knew I'd done the right thing, but her information confirmed my instincts.

Two weeks later, Mindy and I had the great pleasure of dancing on *The Merv Griffin Show*. Merv was doing his talk show from Caesars Palace. Part of his show's format was to feature dancers and showgirls from each of the big productions on the Strip. Our line captains offered us the opportunity to appear on Merv's show, and it was an AFTRA gig!

It was great fun. I worked his show with Shirley, Mindy, Marian and Ellen. We were nudes wearing rhinestone bras for TV. We rehearsed with Merv and did a little dance with him on air. We also worked with Wayne Newton and James Darren, both huge headliners in Las Vegas. I concluded that Merv loved having the dancers and showgirls on the show. He enjoyed dancing as much as we did. A fantastic soul, he resonated with the beautiful showgirls.

After the shoot, Wayne invited us to a little soiree at his private suite at the Sands Hotel. Marian Palmer and I accepted the offer and went to have some fun. Once we were at his suite and had a drink, I could see Marian and Wayne chatting. I was left with his bodyguards, and one of them started coming on to me. I told him I had a boyfriend. He was nice enough and backed off.

I told Marian I was ready to head home a short time later. She was, too, and since she was driving, we announced our goodbyes and left.

This is what Vegas was about: footloose and fancy free, which suited me perfectly! That was my first multi-celebrity encounter in Sin City, with many more to come.

The next event was the Beaux Arts Ball at the Riviera Hotel on Halloween. The fun-loving Lido cast was abuzz regarding this upcoming bash, which featured a huge costume contest that everyone wanted to participate in. That was right up my alley, and I had a fabulous costume from Puerto Rico, where I had slayed at the gay bars with Errol.

Diane in stage makeup and Tarantella costume in "Allez Lido" at the Stardust, 1981.

We all began planning for this event, which was to be hosted by comedian David Brenner. He was headlining at one of the huge hotels on the Strip and would be doing so on air for this well-publicized shindig.

Halloween was quickly approaching, and we knew they saved the costume judging contest until after all the dancers were off work around 1:30 a.m. We kicked into high gear after our last show that night, got into our costumes and makeup backstage to go across the street to the Riviera for the ball. I painted makeup on Neil Letham to look like David Bowie *à la* Ziggy Stardust.

We were all dressed up and ready to go. I'd done my makeup, including a creepy yet sexy witch theme. I had a green face with a spider web made of black pipe cleaners jutting out from the black skull cap over my face. I wore a large black cape covering black fishnets, boots, bat G-string and pipe cleaner spider pasties on each breast. I had long black gloves, and when I went onstage during the costume contest, I flashed open my cape so that David Brenner and the audience saw my minimal costume underneath. I let out a dramatic cackle! I worked it! I was rewarded with a giant roar from the excited audience. I loved every minute of it!

The costumes were individually displayed by various participants during the next 20 minutes. Then we were invited one more time to come to the stage and strut our stuff. Each costume received applause from the lively crowd, and the loudest of all would be awarded Best Costume by David Brenner. Guess who brought down the house and won that trophy? Yours truly! I have a photo with David Brenner in *Playboy* magazine for winning that night. Of course, I had the loudest entourage in the whole casino! I was having a ball in Las Vegas and felt welcomed wholeheartedly.

Diane in her Halloween costume at the 1979 Riviera Hotel's Beaux Arts Ball.

34

Win-Win, 1979

One of the great things about living in Las Vegas was how close I was to Los Angeles. I had friends there, one whom I had stayed in touch with since my days on tour with my ex-husband Arnold and Sonny Turner. Her name was Ramona, and she had been married to Jeff, the sax player in the group. I had known Jeff since the beginning in the Bahamas, and when his gorgeous East Indian wife Ramona joined us on the road, we had so much fun together. We were the same age and, like me, she liked to enjoy life to the fullest! Eventually, Jeff and Ramona relocated to Atlanta, and Jeff did some studio work with Arnold at Melody Recording Studios. We spent a lot of time with them even after Arnold left the group. I'd say we had a close relationship. Once we all had moved away from Atlanta, Ramona and I stayed in touched.

While I lived in Puerto Rico, Jeff and Ramona split up around the same time I left Arnold. Touring killed relationships. Ramona had moved to Beverly Hills and shared a four-bedroom home with her mom, sister and young niece, all originally from Sri Lanka. Since we had corresponded constantly through all our moves, Ramona was anxious to get together as single women in Los Angeles. She insisted I come to visit now that I lived in Vegas.

I was especially excited to see Ramona when she told me who she was dating: none other than Maurice White, lead singer of Earth, Wind and Fire. I told Ramona about my encounter with them in L.A. and how attracted I had felt to Maurice's brother Monte, the famous group's road manager.

"He's single," she mentioned. "Why don't you come visit, stay with me, and we can go out?"

"I'm not sure Monte would even remember me," I said. "Our meeting was brief, although he and I had a deeply spiritual discussion that day."

"Well, let me find out!"

The great thing about my job at the Lido was that there was always a swing person for every group of dancers in the show. We could ask for vacation time at any time and be covered. It was easy. We were free to enjoy vacations and time off whenever. It certainly helped me when I started booking feature film jobs as an actress, which I did quite a bit in the three years I worked at the Lido. Barbara and I could plan vacations to the exotic places we loved so much, and we did. A weekend excursion to Los Angeles was very doable.

Ramona got back to me quickly. Monte White remembered me and wanted to know if he could call me. I insisted she give him my phone numbers, at home and backstage.

About two weeks later, I got a call out of the blue from Monte at home. He wondered if we could get together for lunch or dinner when I came to L.A. We chatted for a while and began getting reacquainted. He was so spiritual; that part of him appealed to me very much. He was also charming and light-hearted. A fun Libra. I liked him.

We hit it off as naturally as we had originally. We talked about traveling, my breakup with Arnold, my new job at the Lido, and his life on tour. We also discussed my friendship with Ramona.

There was heat between us in a *good* way, not a lusty, "gotta have you now" way. It was a mellow current of energy. I liked this guy. I hadn't met anyone in Vegas I liked this much. In fact, I hadn't met many guys besides those in the show, and most of the straight ones were married. Slim pickin's for us gals.

"Ramona has asked me to come visit soon," I told him.

"I'd love to take you to dinner and have you over to my place in West Hollywood when you come. Why don't you call me once you've planned that?"

He let me know his schedule. It was insanely busy, traveling on tour, and we agreed it would be sometime a few months from now when they would be spending two whole months off in L.A. for a break. That suited me just fine. My life in Vegas was bustling and full as well. I could wait a while to see him.

Something about Monte was very appealing. He would call me occasionally, and I would call him when I knew he was in L.A. We developed a warm friendship. The attraction was there, too, and I looked forward to consummating that soon in L.A. Anticipation was half the fun, and this worldly man seemed to embrace it with ease and grace.

I liked the way neither of us felt the need to hurry anything. It felt mature, sweet and respectful. A more spiritual connection than a lustful one. I did, however, fantasize about him after our phone calls.

Now that I had Monte's schedule, I could plan my first trip to Los Angeles to visit Ramona.

The "Fashion Show" Mall was opening, and we showgirls were the runway models of choice for the designers being introduced in every new department store. The work was abundant, and Barbara insisted I get some modeling photos done. She wanted me to meet her modeling agent to do daytime runway shows. Opportunity was coming at us from every direction.

It may seem like I had just moved on without a blink from Vince. I hadn't. I had numerous opportunities and distractions in this fabulous town, which always helped alleviate a broken heart, but I had one.

For one month solid after I lied to Vince at my front door, I cried tears into my pool every day. I wept deeply for that loss. I don't know if my heartbreak was more for the end of the relationship or the lack of closure. I missed Vince. We had fun, and he loved me in some fashion. Was he good for me? Was he honest? Did I regret what I did? *No*, no and no! I gave myself the time to lament my loss.

I not only wept for the loss of love but for my inability to choose better men. I doubted my choices. I wondered how I couldn't recognize a cheater and a liar by now. I was fed up with womanizers. I wanted someone wonderful to fall in love with and vowed I would never settle again! At least until the Universe brought me smarter people.

They say we choose in each relationship whatever we didn't have in the last one. This seemed true in my life, but was I blind to bad boys? Was Monte White a bad boy in disguise? He lived on tour with one of the most famous groups in history. What did that say about me at this juncture?

Could this be a win-win? Would I be the high roller in this game? I was living in Las Vegas. Maybe I'd get lucky.

35

Living Large in Sin City, 1979

Barbara's birthday was approaching in September, and her parents and mine were anxious to pay us a visit.

We decided to have them come at the same time for Barbara's 30th birthday. Her parents would drive in from Los Angeles and mine would fly in from Illinois.

Tickets and dates were secured. Complimentary family tickets were reserved for our show, and birthday plans were tossed around. Trying to get Barb to lock down what she wanted to do was not easy.

I discussed Barbara's birthday party options with our dear friend Kim Cornell, aka Kimbo. We devised a plan. We decided to have a surprise party after the show on her actual birthday. This was genius because it would be a potluck with all the people in the show, and we would have our parents at the house to set up while we were at work. Kimbo pointed out, "Barb is very popular, and you will need a lot of booze!"

It turned out perfectly! Kim detained Barb after the show since they shared a dressing room, and I rushed home to help our dedicated parents prepare. We decorated and set up our "bar" outside around the pool. The neighbors were notified and invited to stop by.

It worked! Our parents loved being part of it and getting to meet everyone in the show. Barbara was completely surprised. This was a bash for the books! She loved it and we decided after that we needed many more parties.

Our parties were epic and became even more so when Barbara bought a bigger house and we moved into it. With such a large, close cast, we did lots of bonding at our house parties and had lots of fun to boot.

While my parents were in town, Jerry pulled an all-nighter one night in the casinos without my mom. He couldn't control himself. Phoebe was pissed, but at least he had the decency to stay away once he got tanked. It was embarrassing for my mom. It didn't surprise me. He just hadn't had enough excitement in his life, I suppose. I'm just glad he didn't come back to our home drunk! He showed up fairly sober around noon the next day, claiming he was winning at gambling. Yeah, right, Dad!

Barbara (left) and Diane backstage at the Lido with Siegfried & Roy's tiger White Gold, five weeks old, in 1980.

When Barb and I moved into the bigger house, we really spread out with our three dogs and infamous parties. Barbara's dad and older brother lived in Vegas and were on hand to help us paint and settle in. We had so much fun at that house!

One of the boy singers in the show, Michael Gallagher, asked me to come to acting class with him in Vegas. He'd been studying with Joseph Bernard and thought it was time I got my feet wet again. I was excited about the idea of training with Michael and agreed to register for an eight-week session. Joseph Bernard had moved to Vegas from New York, where he had taught at the Lee Strasberg Institute. I had always been curious about method acting and decided to try it out. Unfortunately, my scholarship was no longer valid. I'd waited 13 years to use it. But no worries, we made good money, and I could easily afford to pay for training.

Michael chose a scene from *Same Time, Next Year*. He wanted us to play the couple during their hippie era, and I fell in love with the script. We had the advantage of rehearsing between shows at the Lido. I was hooked from my first class and felt confident in my renewed ability. Most of my acting talent had lain dormant, just waiting to emerge from hibernation. I flourished in class and committed 100 percent. Within a few months, I

35. Living Large in Sin City, 1979

was ready to take headshots and modeling shots and booked a session with a popular photographer in Vegas, Ron Tomlin. I wanted to pursue this career I had shifted to the back burner years earlier. Acting was and always will be my first love, and it felt good to prioritize it.

With new photos, I went to Barbara's modeling agency, as she had encouraged me to do. Lenz Models, my modeling agency in Las Vegas, and I met with several reps there. With gorgeous new Zed cards and a portfolio to show, I was signed right away, and before you knew it, I was working the runway with Barb for the designer shows. One of the first gigs I booked was a fur fashion show at Caesars Palace. I modeled luxurious fur coats, sold exclusively at Caesars. Next came shows for Saks Fifth Avenue, Neiman Marcus and the big designers in the new fashion show mall. I was honored to do runway for Bill Blass, Halston, Carolina Herrera, Oscar de la Renta, and many more. There was no shortage of daytime work for us, and we managed to do several weekly. The money was outstanding, and Barbara and I were often lucky enough to book shows together.

While speaking with my modeling agents, I asked about film and TV representation. They picked up the phone, called the best agency in Vegas on my behalf, and arranged an interview with Jaki Baskow. Jaki was a young go-getter with a new agency, and after I interviewed, they signed me. I loved them, and they loved my new head shots! I attended many

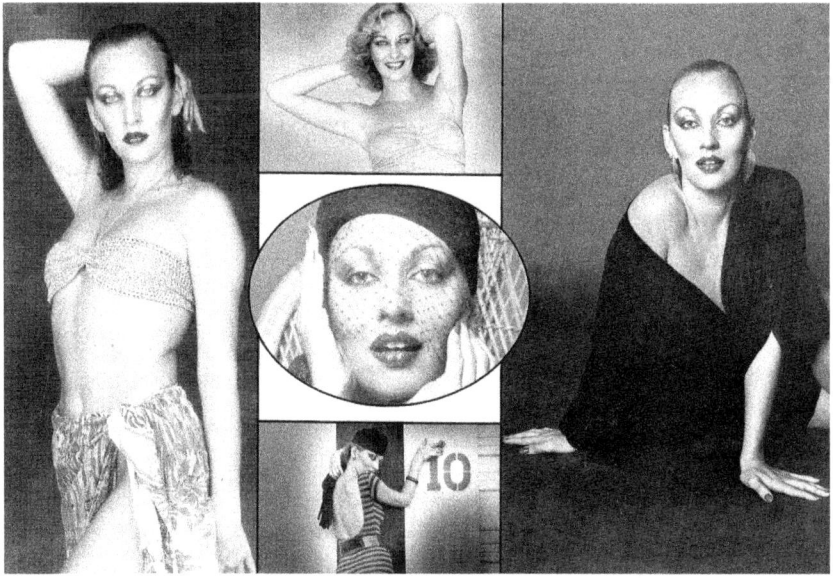

Zed card with new "Diana Mann" stage name—model and actress (photos by Ron Tomlin, 1980).

local and regional commercial and voiceover auditions. I was practically working two jobs as an actress and full-time dancer. There were dozens of opportunities for actors and models in Vegas.

I forged a strong bond with my acting coach, Joseph Bernard. Joe was truly a treasure. One of the wonderful perks of training at his studio was the many celebrities who came to study with Joe. Whenever headliners were in town to perform, Joe would invite them to speak to our class. This meant we had the great fortune to meet Joan Rivers, Alan King and Dom DeLuise. Joe also knew directors. When they were in town to shoot movies, he invited them to speak to our class as well. Director Matt Cimber, casting directors Lynn Stalmaster and Buck Flower and numerous professionals seeking actors for their productions.

I was always the first to get to know them after class. That is one of the reasons I loved Joan Rivers so much. She came to our class most often because that beautiful, generous soul loved helping young people. She was one of the sweetest, most brilliant, savviest dames I have ever met. She spent hours of her time after class explaining the ins and outs of the business to us. She was incredibly encouraging and helpful, and I was so very grateful for her input. She really inspired me.

Joseph Bernard went above and beyond for his students, and I will always be grateful for all he did to further my career.

I wound up auditioning for one of the first films that Matt Cimber was set to direct for another sizzling local, Pia Zadora. Young Pia was married to the owner of the Riviera Hotel, Meshulam Riklis. Her debut film *Butterfly*

Headshot (photo by Ron Tomlin, 1980).

was set to start shooting in Vegas that spring. In 1981, Pia won the Golden Globe Award for "New Star of the Year." I auditioned for and landed my first role in this huge feature film! Matt Cimber had once been married to Jayne Mansfield. He was well-known as a writer-director for the films *The Black Six, Fake-Out, Femora, Peace for Profit, Mariam, Glow, Yellow Hair and the Fortress of Gold, Tiger Man, Hundra, A Time to Die* and *The Witch Who Came from the Sea*.

I had an affair with Matt Cimber when he shot another Pia Zadora film in Vegas months after *Butterfly*. Once he was hired to direct *Fake-Out* in Vegas, his casting director called me directly and said, "Matt definitely wants you in this movie. Will you come audition?"

Matt was 16 years older than me, and I loved spending time with him. We had a lot of laughs, and when I moved to Los Angeles to act full-time, he took me to all the private clubs and introduced me to many industry people. It wasn't until my move to L.A. that I came to realize that Matt drank too much. When a car unexpectedly arrived at my house at midnight to pick me up to go out with him, I stopped seeing him. That didn't work for me. I had moved there on a mission to become a working actress. I had responsibilities and couldn't be expected to just jump in his limo and party at midnight with him. I had my artistry to protect. After everything I had been through, my feelings about drinkers were clear. No, thank you!

The endless opportunities for work outside our show continued for all of us. I learned to refrain from discussing these opportunities backstage at the Lido, even though many came to us directly via our company captains or Siegfried & Roy.

I mentioned an upcoming feature film audition to Shirley. Another girl overheard and expressed her desire to audition for the same role. She was upset that her agent had not approached her about it. I realized that not everything backstage was a constant lovefest. I learned to keep my callbacks and acting gigs quiet, to avoid stirring up jealousies or igniting competitive behavior. Keeping those opportunities to oneself encapsulates the energies and our focus on booking them intact.

It didn't make the possibilities any less potent.

A huge project came our way when Siegfried & Roy had an NBC special set to shoot at the Stardust. Our entire cast was to be in it as dancers! Many of the dancers were union and wanted AFTRA day player rates. A lot of emotion circled around backstage during company meetings regarding our pay rate. For most of us, it would be our first TV special, and we wanted to accept any rate in order to have the credit and be seen dancing on national television. Two NBC specials starring Siegfried & Roy were shot while I was there, in 1980 and 1981.

Another big one was a Hal Ashby feature film that used the Lido

The poster for Diane's first film, Pia Zadora's *Butterfly* (1980).

show as its backdrop. *Looking to Get Out* with Jon Voight, Ann-Margret and Burt Young. Ashby was best known for his huge hit film *Harold and Maude*, one of my favorites in the '70s. Lynn Stalmaster, the master caster, was set to cast the movie. The entire Lido de Paris cast was hired to perform in the background of the main actors' scenes while they were sitting in the audience at our show at the Stardust in the movie. White tigers and all!

Ashby was known for doing numerous takes. He sometimes would shoot *hundreds* of takes to get the shots. A week or two after the dancers' segments were completed, they began shooting Siegfried & Roy's act. I wasn't present that day, but apparently they shot a portion of the act over and over. White Gold became exhausted and lurched into the pit and onto a woman.

Ashby learned that you can't do extensive takes with wild animals not accustomed to performing repeatedly over long stretches of time. They still had to perform two shows each night. After that scare, Siegfried & Roy no longer permitted Ashby to do an immense number of takes.

In 2003 came the harrowing incident at the Mirage Resort Casino where another tiger mangled Roy and severed his spine. Roy was left immobilized with impaired motor and verbal abilities. It's incredible what wild animals can unpredictably do. Roy's recovery was better than expected through many years of physical therapy. He passed away in 2020 from Covid-19.

36

Cha-Ching, 1980

Vegas! Not one month went by in this ever-expanding town that I wasn't making bank. Everyone in our show seemed busy with endless opportunities for success. I had three commercials airing on regional TV and radio for clubs, bars, restaurants and casinos. TV credits started growing beyond my initial *Merv Griffin* appearance. I booked locally-shot shows like *Vega$* with Robert Urich and Tony Curtis. As my local persona as an actress blossomed, so did my bank accounts, and I began to manifest merging my gifts mainstream into the L.A. and New York markets.

I enjoyed studying and feeling inspired by my acting classes at Joe Bernard's twice a week. I absolutely loved it! I booked more work as an actress in Las Vegas in the three years I worked there than in Los Angeles when I eventually moved. I made more money in one year than I had ever earned doing anything anywhere. I made plans to spend a little of it when I finally went to visit my friend Ramona in L.A. After all, I had been working a lot since day one. Time for some fun! Work hard, play hard, I always say.

I had been talking to Monte White occasionally by phone and knew he would be in town when I planned my first road trip to Ramona's.

Los Angeles, the City of Angels, felt different to me since Arnold and I had been there. It now felt inviting, brighter, more fun, more luxurious—but so spread out! It was good to have close friends there. That made all the difference. I now had connections, friends and a possible romance brewing.

Ramona and her family, all great beauties, had a big 1940s four-bedroom house in Beverly Hills. We hadn't seen one another since Atlanta, so this was truly a happy reunion, filled with catching up, delicious Indian curry that her mom made, and a little wine on the side. Soon after my arrival, Monte called and asked if he could take me to dinner the next night. I couldn't wait to see him.

Monte picked me up, looking very cool. He hugged me tightly, then we hopped into his chocolate brown Mercedes and went to dinner at a fun

36. Cha-Ching, 1980

West Hollywood café. We laughed, shared stories about our adventures, spiritual beliefs, jobs and the exciting things happening in our lives. We bonded over dinner across a table in candlelight at the charming, busy little café. He suggested I come to see his place once the evening began to wind down a bit. It was a beautiful date.

"It's very close to here, and I want to turn you on to some incredible music we recently discovered," Monte said.

"That sounds perfect," I agreed.

"The artist I want you to hear has just released his second album. You might not know him yet. Wait till I play his music for you. We heard him in the studio, and I have his new album at the crib."

Once we arrived at his hip, one-bedroom, somewhat masculine, well-appointed West Hollywood apartment, we decided to chill. Monte didn't smoke weed or drink. None of the members of Earth, Wind and Fire did. We forgot all about that cassette until much later. We were sidetracked with our first physical union. And that was delightful, to say the least.

Monte and I had waited quite a while and built up lots of anticipation for this coupling. I hadn't been with anyone since Vince. The sexual tension started when I first met Monte while I was married to Arnold.

Making love with Monte was a sweet, sensual, sensitive and spiritual exchange of fulfilling energy. Not lusty and full of firecrackers, but soulful and deep. Precious moments of discovery and passion. It felt good to be with someone I respected and cared for. We had a dreamy evening, and he asked me to stay the night with him. "I'll have to call Ramona and let her know since I am their houseguest this week," I told him.

"Of course." Monte brought his long-corded telephone to me from the living room into the bedroom. "You do that while I find the music I promised you!" He went in search of it. Naked.

I called Ramona at around 10:30, and she laughed, knowing what had happened. "I can't wait to hear about your night," she giggled.

"See you in the morning," I chuckled in return.

Monte placed the tape in a small cassette player on the dresser. He dimmed the lights and held me. A sexy and masterful dance tune came on: "I Wanna Be Your Lover," by a budding young artist named Prince. I loved it! That was the name of his second album, *Prince*.

Monte told me all about being in the recording studio at the same time as Prince, and how blown away he and Earth, Wind and Fire were, listening to this talented young guy. Monte played several of the songs from his newly released album. I loved every tune, agreeing that he was a promising artist.

"I love his sound," I told Monte as we listened to several cuts. The night wound down listening to this exceptionally cool artist, while Monte and I really connected and made sweet love once again before falling fast asleep in one another's arms.

The following morning, Monte went to a meeting and dropped me off on Gayle Ave. in Beverly Hills. I floated on air into Ramona's house. We were giddy all day, sharing last night's secrets and very special moments with one another. We were young girls blushing and flushed with the thrill of romance. With superb taste in men, I might add.

Once back from my first trip to L.A., I continued auditioning, dancing in the show with all my beloved gypsies, acting in TV and film, and training with wonderful actors. We had all kinds of entertainers training at our classes at Joseph Bernard's Studio, including country singer Alan Jackson and Olympic champion gymnast Mary Lou Retton. The opportunities were abundant when these people came to shoot and perform in Vegas. Not just for them, but for everyone. This town was the entertainment capital of the nation. I loved seeing my fellow actors and dancers flourish.

In addition to performing six nights a week, our husband-and-wife co-workers, Karen and Neil Letham, were doing fabulous hair and nails for everyone in the show. We called them "Mr. Snips" and "Mrs. Tips." Several of the boys and showgirls became highly successful real estate agents; for instance, Shirley, Ellen and Michael Lyle. Because dancers' careers don't last forever! Small groups of us often rented a cabin for a single night in Mount Charleston and hiked in nature, then partied heavily into the wee hours. We needed our nature fix to keep it all in balance.

Lots of nights were spent out after work winding down at the discos which I had concluded would never die. Our favorite place to dance after work was a club called The Gypsy. Though it was a gay bar, lots of straight guys wound up there, especially out-of-towners. I met some cuties on that dance floor.

Mindy Hall and I felt like going out to dance one night after work, but it was a weeknight, and The Gypsy was closing early. So we showered and hurried to the club, leaving our stage makeup on, and went to boogie. We were shocked at how dead it was at 1:30 a.m. It was not your usual night at The Gypsy, but we stayed and danced. While standing, chatting by the dance floor, all of a sudden, from behind us, this short, wild-haired guy with scarves tied to his wrists and wearing only a fringed vest with ripped bellbottom jeans grabbed Mindy and me by the hand and dragged us out onto the dance floor. We looked at one another like "Ewwww!" He was very odd, but we danced with him to a great song that sounded somewhat familiar to me. It was an incredible dance tune, but I couldn't place where I'd heard it.

After we finished and walked off the dance floor, the wild dude said, "That's a tune from my new album."

36. Cha-Ching, 1980

"Oh really?" I questioned. I doubted that since the guy looked homeless. "What's your album called?"

"*Prince*" he told me.

"Oh!" I blurted out, "so you're Prince?" I recalled the tunes Monte had played for me several months prior.

"In the flesh!" he grinned.

"I've heard your music," I said. "In L.A., while visiting with Earth, Wind and Fire, and I love your sound."

"Thank you," Prince answered.

"Yeah, they were very excited about you," I told him.

"No one did shit for me, baby!" he exclaimed, "I did this myself!"

"Well, they certainly are supportive of your work," I answered, not allowing myself to respond to his ego.

Prince swung his scarves, turned and fluttered away.

I turned to Mindy, saying, "Weird dude!"

"No kidding!" she winced.

This was long before "Purple Rain" happened and Prince was rebranded from his wild hippie vibe into the Royal Purple Prince he became. Damn, he was talented, though. Many years later, I worked as a sweater designer for Sheila Raymond in downtown L.A. when my assistant asked me if our sample makers could do 14 sweaters for Prince and his entourage. And we did them!

His original sweater, drenched in Italian cologne, was expensive. He wanted 14 replicas for his girls! My, my, my, how times had changed! This was during his reign in the mid-'80s. I gave him a fair price, especially compared to what his original designer one had cost. We made a deal and delivered early. Pleasure doing business with you, Your Purple Highness.

I wanted to tell Monte I had met Prince. I waited to hear from him, but he didn't call me. I wondered why. We had spoken just after our dreamy night together, and then they were back on tour and away from L.A. again. I wasn't upset, but I did kind of miss him. I wondered if I had limited my interest in Monte, knowing it would be another long-distance relationship.

It wasn't until several months later that I called Monte at his apartment one day when I was off. Surprised to hear from me, he reported they had just returned from touring. We had a little catch-up chat, and I slipped in this question: "Did you know that Prince played in Vegas a few months back?"

"No, we haven't talked much since he declined to have Maurice produce his album," he stated.

"I accidentally met him at a Vegas disco after work one night. He seemed to have just played somewhere and dragged me and a friend onto the dance floor to dance!"

"How was he?" Monte asked.
"Kinda weird!" I laughed.
"He's something else!" Monte agreed, "And such a huge talent!"
"I really miss you, Monte!"
"I'm surprised at that," he commented.
"Really?"
"Yeah, I didn't know you cared!"
"I do!" I said, shocked at his comment.
"I never knew," he said blandly.

I was confused because I felt I had expressed how much I liked him. Had I never shown how much? Or had he become accustomed to women fawning over him? I was confused after that conversation, but I realized that as much as I liked Monte, there wasn't much time to develop a relationship with him, especially with our career commitments.

That was the last time we spoke until several years later when I lived in Los Angeles. I introduced him to a good friend of mine who was a vocalist in and around L.A. We attended that friend's showcase one summer evening and had dinner afterward. I realized then that we were friends. That was fine with me because, by that time, I had met and fallen for my second husband, actor Craig Christiansen.

We had so much freedom for traveling while working at the Stardust. Barbara and I were planning a trip to Puerto Rico. One of the boys in our show, Herbie Chorn, had left the Lido and taken a job at my former show in Puerto Rico with Miller-Reich. Barbara also had one of her closest friends, Suzie Hiett, in that show, and wanted me to meet her. Herbie insisted we stay at his place, so we agreed and began planning our one-week trip.

Just before we left, our new company captain, Dawnie Gulbranson, announced that Cher was currently performing at Caesars Palace and had invited all the dancers on the Strip to a roller disco party next week. Roller disco was very popular, and almost everyone attended that event.

I got out my disco drag, which I'd kept tucked away since my Le Clique days in New York City, and dressed the part. We had a wildly fun time. Naturally, the boys in our show instantly met the boys in her show, which was a lovefest. Cher was adorable and somewhat shy, yet I wanted to talk to her.

I waited until I could connect with her at the roller disco party, but it seemed when she wasn't skating with her boys, she was skating alone. She never stopped! She must have loved roller skating at the beautiful Caesars indoor rink. I never got a chance to talk face to face with her. Before I knew it, it was time for the gypsies to scamper off to their shows to work, and Cher was swept behind the scenes to get ready for her own performances that night.

36. Cha-Ching, 1980

James and I decided to buy tickets to her show for the following Thursday. We both had Thursdays off and went out together often. Cher's show at Caesars Palace was extraordinary. She had long ago separated from Sonny and had her own TV show, *The Cher Show*. Her boy dancers were excellent, and James and I recognized so many of the boys we had met at the roller disco bash.

Cher and Diana Ross had two of the finest live productions I had ever attended at Caesars in the late '70s. These were truly breathtaking presentations from two of the era's most magnificent divas. Their names were on the Caesars marquee regularly. I was so grateful I got to see them both perform in Vegas.

Our Puerto Rican vacation was fast approaching. We decided to stretch it into two weeks, spending one in Puerto Rico and the next at an exotic Club Med in Eleuthera, Bahamas, a small island not far from our old Paradise Island stomping grounds. Club Med was quite different. It was French and known worldwide for its all-inclusive resorts.

We had a blast in Puerto Rico and played Scrabble the entire plane trip there and back. I met Barbara's adorable dancer friend, Suzie Hiett, and we hit it off. She was a firecracker! Over time, she, too, became one of my besties. We call one another "Ya Ya" sisters.

Herbie and one of the girls in the show insisted on booking a day tour of the rainforest in Puerto Rico. It was pure Heaven, laden with monkeys, frogs, bamboo and sloths. I relished every moist moment.

Rainforests and Old San Juan by day, and discos by night. Boy, did we have a good time! We went sunbathing topless on the roof of the El San Juan.

Arnold had left the island at least a year earlier and was now singing with a hit *a cappella* group called the Nylons. He was back on world tour, as they had just released a hit song called "The Lion Sleeps Tonight." They were quite good. I guess it was inevitable that he lived on the road with his phenomenal singing voice. We had kept in touch but had not yet arranged a divorce.

Once our time in lush Puerto Rico ended, we said goodbye to our friends and flew to Eleuthera. It was my first time on the little Caribbean island and my first visit to a Club Med resort. We thought Paradise Island was gorgeous, but wow! Eleuthera was beyond exquisite. On one side of the long, narrow island was the Atlantic Ocean, and on the other the Caribbean.

Club Med was in the sparkling, sleepy and sunny Governor's Harbour. I don't think I've ever loved an island more. I have been back at least a dozen times since. I fell in love with the island founded in 1648, the birthplace of the Bahamas. We enjoyed swimming, skiing, snorkeling, sunbathing and endless exotic buffets and drinks.

People from all over the world were there, and we danced the nights away. We met lots of guys who competed to spend as much of their time as possible with us.

I fell for a French-Tunisian club employee named Raouf, who was adorable. A nice guy. We spent a large portion of our week together in his cottage, making love and smoking weed. He was so cute and so sweet to me.

You know what I do with nice guys by now, right? Why am I always choosing long-distance lovers on tropical islands?

37

The Big Apple or Lala Land?, 1981

My acting teacher, Joseph Bernard, began speaking to me about the many acting opportunities in New York. He said that he felt I would do well as an actress there. I can't say I missed New York City, but having my coach encourage me to consider going there inspired me.

"You could hold your own against any New York actor," he said. He was very supportive of me and often made me feel like I was the best actress in our class.

"Plus you can do as much theater as you want while auditioning for film and TV," he added.

I trusted him. He knew how well I had been doing in Las Vegas. I had recently earned my SAG card in Pia Zadora's second feature film, *Fake-Out*. I became excited about returning to the Big Apple to pursue acting. It was my third year in Vegas and acting was moving into the forefront of my ambitions. I was nearly 30 and never wanted to be an "old" showgirl. I saw so many careers become dancers' entire lives. Many of us were burdened with heavy work commitments and insufficient relationship material in Sin City. In fact, most of the guys I met were tourists and gamblers, or only in town briefly. There was a never-ending string of unavailable men in many of our lives.

I did date a few dancers, actors and musicians in town, but no one I wanted to spend my life with. After our vacation, auditions were pouring in. I was consumed with my big, beautiful, happy, creatively fulfilling life. I began to believe that long-distance relationships were perfect for me in some weird way. I could fully fling myself into my career and still have a heart full of love for someone miles and miles away. After everything I'd been through, it now didn't seem strange that this would be the case.

I came home to my biggest audition yet, the audition for Pia Zadora's second feature film, *Fake-Out*. Initially, I was asked to audition for a significant role by the director, Matt Cimber, and the casting director, Buck

Flower, who really loved my work. Buck was ready to present me to the director for this role at a callback. But before that callback, Buck called my agent and had me read for three smaller roles. One of them was a lesbian rapist in a women's prison scene.

When I finally arrived at my callback with Matt one afternoon, I walked into the room and said, "I don't know if I'm Arthur or Martha!"

Matt and Buck laughed so hard.

"You remind me of a young Eve Arden," Matt claimed. "I really wanted to give you the larger role right off the bat, but a favor got in the way!"

He and I had discussed my initial audition for Pia's first film, *Butterfly*, at the acting studio when Joe Bernard had invited him to speak to us. After that class, when I introduced myself to Matt, a handsome, fun-loving Italian-American in his 50s, he told me he'd be casting several roles in Las Vegas. I said I would love to audition. He said, "Pia insists that no young, attractive blondes audition."

"I'm actually 52 and I have a dazzling collection of brunette wigs," I insisted. Matt laughed then, too. I couldn't dye my hair because all the wigs, falls and headdresses I wore in the Lido show were blonde.

We began to talk about the roles available to me in *Fake-Out*. Matt later told me they had committed to a Greek L.A.-based actress for the larger role. That actress was a friend of Telly Savalas, who had recently starred in the TV hit *Kojak*. He was attached to *Fake-Out* and he brought along his friend. Those things happen!

One day, my agent, Jaki Baskow, sent me on an audition with a local photographer seeking showgirls for covers for *Las Vegas* magazine. "I'm not sure I'm cover girl material?" I said.

"Just take your portfolio over and do the interview. This photographer pays really well!" she instructed. "You would be great!"

I don't think Jaki really knew how gorgeous most of the girls in the shows were. I was attractive and captivating onstage, but magazines were different. Jaki represented more actors.

The photographer was Jeff Kogan, and we tossed around some creative ideas. But when he described what he was looking for on this shoot, I said, "You need to meet my roommate, Barbara Beverly. She is exactly what you are seeking. May I send her over?"

"Sure," he said, "I'd love to interview her."

I went home and told Barb, "I just had an interview with a photographer who is seeking a legendary Las Vegas showgirl who is a dazzling beauty and the epitome of glamour. It's for a *Las Vegas* magazine cover. I am sure he is looking for you!"

"If you say so," she said. "I'll call him."

"Call him now. I told him you would call today. The job pays really well, and you are perfect."

Barbara was exactly what Jeff was looking for. He took fantastic photos that wound up on that magazine cover. Jeff pursued her with everything he had! He sent hundreds of roses to her backstage and, once they started dating, picked her up in his Rolls-Royce after the show. He didn't stop until she agreed to go to Hawaii with him.

I longed to be in love but hadn't met my one and only. This sent me into a spiritual growth period, and I poured all my emotion into acting. It felt good.

My dear friend Michael Gallagher was planning to move to L.A. to pursue acting full-time. He was 33 and knew he wasn't getting any younger. He was doing great work in class, and I supported him entirely in pursuing his acting dream.

Joseph Bernard and I continued discussing my move to New York and the endless connections he could help me make via Lee Strasberg's. I was beginning to get antsy to go and pursue my true love, acting.

At this point, Barbara had taken up with Jeff and was falling for him. Jeff brought a lot to the party and wooed her nonstop. She was smitten with him, and he had a substantial life to offer her. (Barbara and I never liked the same guys. I'm confident that contributed to our prolonged friendship.)

I hadn't met anyone interesting enough to date long-term. I had little flings, one with an actor from class after we shot Pia's movie and another guy called Disco Dave from Hawaii, whom I met at a disco. Can you guess what we had in common besides great sex? I continued to see director Matt Cimber occasionally, but he lived primarily in L.A.

I had started working with Vimmi doing makeup for his photoshoots. He was still with Roy Vanoy, and they were quite happy together, when Vimmi began talking about leaving Las Vegas. I was bummed. Vimmi was one of my beloved besties, and I couldn't stand the thought of him and Michael Gallagher leaving the show. I adored them both.

My agent called with an offer I couldn't refuse. A major casting director from L.A., Mike Hanks, was in town and asked my agent to send over her best two guy and best two girl actors for a G.I. (general interview) with him. General interviews were few and far between in the industry and were coveted because when casting directors did G.I.s, they would consider you for everything they were casting. I researched and found that Mike Hanks was fond of scouting new talent nationwide and bringing them onto *The Young and the Restless* in L.A. His casting office was at CBS.

I was flattered beyond measure that my agent had even considered me one of her two "best." In the last few years, I booked roles in three major features, several TV series, voiceover gigs and half a dozen local and regional commercials while she represented me. Not to mention working at the Stardust and as a runway model as much as I wanted. There had been so many runway shows in town that I had become selective and only worked for top designers. I did swimwear collections, gowns, furs and even a hair show. I couldn't possibly act, dance and model all the time! The best part was that most of those fashion shows were done with Barbara.

Portfolio in hand, I arrived for my interview at Mike Hanks' Caesars Palace suite. He was great! He was in his late 30s, attractive, personable, relatable and professional. We discussed my résumé and several projects I'd recently completed. Mike had me cold-read sides from *The Young and the Restless*. He gave me a few re-directs, and I did the scene again. Then he asked what my plans were once my Stardust contract ended.

I told him I had been discussing moving to New York to pursue my acting career, but that I was open to either New York or L.A. An actor needs to be in one of those places if they're serious about an acting career. And at this point, I was as serious as a heart attack!

Mike told me he would be in touch and gave me his CBS card and home phone number, saying I could contact him anytime. He said he would let me know if I'd made the cut for the soap opera after he finished interviewing in Vegas.

I was elated, but the only person I told was Barbara. I'd learned to hang onto my auditions until I was in or out and never share it backstage. I felt like that would jinx it.

Two days later, my agent called and said, "Well, you must have been incredible, like always, because Mike Hanks would like you to come to LA for a callback at CBS for *The Young and the Restless* in two weeks. Can you do that?"

"Of course. I can get off work and go anytime."

"He'd like to see you on a Tuesday at the end of the month."

And it was scheduled. I was going to Los Angeles, for a callback with Mike Hanks!

I got time off work at the Stardust and called Ramona to make arrangements to stay with her. Their house in Beverly Hills was less than ten minutes from CBS. She was thrilled for me. I also called Matt Cimber and told him the news. He insisted on taking me to dinner while I was in L.A. He was excited for me, too!

When I shared the news with Joe Bernard, he said he felt I was more of a New York actor and that L.A. was too huge. "But, Joe, it's a callback for an under-five on a soap!" I exclaimed.

37. The Big Apple or Lala Land?, 1981

An under-five, as they were called back then, was a role with five or fewer lines. We now call them co-stars. Many actors did under-fives to launch their TV careers.

"I know," he said. "But that's only one job, then it's about pounding pavement, and I think you are more talented than the actresses in L.A."

"So you think I should keep my focus on New York and ignore this opportunity?" I asked.

"No, I think it's a great credit for you, but then go to New York," Joe suggested.

"I'll think about that between now and July," I promised. But L.A. was calling. Not just because of my callback with Mike Hanks but because I had friends and beaus there.

Barbara and Jeff had been dating for about eight months. Jeff had proposed, and she said yes. Barbara was getting married! I was thrilled for her.

There were many moving parts in our lives at this time, and they were all pretty big and exciting.

Ramona said that if I booked the *Young and the Restless* job, I was welcome to room with them for as long as I'd like. That was huge because rent in L.A. was astronomical. I could share a lovely home with my friend and her family, who welcomed me with open arms. The Universe conspired to have me move to L.A.

Two weeks passed, and I began to prepare to drive to L.A. again. I wanted to have my car with me. As I was packing one afternoon, Barbara told me that Jeff wanted her to move into his house with him. She wanted to know what I would do if she rented out our house.

I told her not to worry about it and make her move to Jeff's. I could always find a place to stay before I moved to either L.A. or New York.

I drove to L.A., stayed with Ramona and had my callback at CBS. Mike Hanks had me read for a nurse on the show and told me there would be a lot of nurses in an upcoming hospital segment.

After I read for him, Mike told me he loved my work and would like to hire me for *The Young and the Restless*. He asked if I would move to L.A. to do this. I told him, "I have been offered a place to live, so it will be easy to do. It's just that I don't end my contract at the Stardust until July 1."

"Perfect. Just call me when you're in town, and we will find a role for you when you're here!"

There it was! A reason to move to Los Angeles. I loved L.A. Everything about it appealed to me now. I felt as though I had made my own connections and had friends there. And I loved, loved, loved the beach! Plus, I was dating a well-known director, Matt Cimber! We went to a private Beverly Hills club called Pips for dinner and drinks while I was there, and we celebrated my new upcoming soap opera gig in July.

I couldn't wait to move to L.A. All things New York suddenly disappeared from my mind.

Back in Las Vegas, I told Joe Bernard my plans. He said, "You must train with Milton Katselas at the Beverly Hills Playhouse when you get there. He was trained by Lee Strasberg and Elia Kazan in New York City before he opened his own school in Beverly Hills."

There was another connection for me in L.A.

Back in Las Vegas, I managed to somehow survive my good friend Michael Gallagher leaving the Lido and moving to L.A. in May 1981. "I promise to show you all around once you come in July, and we can study acting together once you arrive," Michael suggested.

"I love that idea. I'm thrilled we will be pursuing our careers together in L.A.!"

"Me, too. It will be great to have my good friend to do that with!"

Neil McGee, my adorable, funny dancer friend, needed a roommate. So Sasha and I moved in to finish out our last few months in town. Living with Neil was easy, as we were both extremely busy navigating our lives. He was a doll!

Before you knew it, June rolled around. Barb and Jeff were married in a beautiful hotel suite on the strip in a small ceremony. Kim Cornell and I attended. It was lovely, and we celebrated with a wonderful dinner afterward and toasted the happy couple. Knowing that Barb was loved and taken care of made my heart swell as I planned my escape from dancing into my new life in Los Angeles as an actress.

Ramona and her family began rearranging their home to include me as a roommate. I felt blessed in every way and started socking away as much money as possible for my transition to L.A. I started getting referrals for agents from numerous sources, including Joe Bernard, classmates in acting class, and friends. Everything was lining up for my success in L.A. Every step of the way, I felt guided by Divine intervention.

At last, I was headed into the life I had always dreamed of, and the Universe seemed to be on my side.

38

The Big Move, 1981

The closer I got to retiring as a showgirl, the more excited I was about the next phase of my existence. I felt I had worked my entire life for a shot at being the actress I knew I was born to be. It was a break worth moving for and the perfect next step. I began lining up interviews with L.A. agents. I was determined to do this right. I had my first feature film, *Butterfly*, coming out this summer, and it was to premiere in Los Angeles. That couldn't hurt.

Though excited about moving, I would miss my Vegas friends terribly, Barbara most of all. Yet I knew Barbara and I would always be friends. We were more like sisters by now. I missed her already now that she had moved in with Jeff. Barbara and I had gotten into the habit of ending our nights after work at the same time and walking out to our cars in the Stardust parking lot together. Having been roommates for so long, we always made time to stay up-to-date on each other's loves, lives and dreams. We also spent time together between shows when possible.

One night, we were doing just that, catching up before heading home. When our conversation ended, I went to my car and Barb went to hers. That was around 1:00 a.m., after our second show.

Jeff called me around 2:30 a.m., asking if Barb was with me. "No, she isn't, Jeff. She left the Stardust around 1:00, and I did, too!"

"Did you see Barbara leave?" he asked, sounding slightly concerned.

"No, I went one way to my car in the parking lot, and she went in another direction. I got to my car and left right away. You haven't heard from her?"

"Not since between shows, and she said she was coming straight home. I think I'll drive over to the Stardust lot and just look around."

I was worried. Something felt off. I hoped to hear back from Jeff and stayed up waiting. I must have dosed off around 4:30.

I awoke to a phone call from Jeff saying Barb had been found in the trunk of her car around five a.m. by Stardust parking lot security. She was alive, safe, and at the hospital for treatment of her wounds. Jeff told me solemnly, "Barbara was kidnapped in the parking lot, driven in her own car to the desert, beaten, raped and stuffed in her trunk while her assailant peed all over her car and then drove the car back to the Stardust lot and left."

I was in shock. I started to cry. "Jeff, is she okay?"

"I don't know. She's doing a police report with the doctor right now," he heaved.

"Who would do this?" I asked him, shaken and horrified.

"I'll damn sure find out!" Jeff swore.

"How did Barbara get away?"

"The kidnapper drove her car back to the Stardust and left it there. She kicked out the taillight lamps and screamed for help until a security officer heard her and got her out."

"Oh my God, Jeff. If you need me, call, and I'll come right over," I told him while weeping.

I couldn't believe something like this could happen here in Camelot and to Barbara Beverly, of all people! One of the sweetest humans on Earth. I felt creeped out and horrified for my best friend.

The police questioned me privately since I had been the last person to see Barbara that night. They interviewed everyone else in a group meeting backstage and gave us the "Be aware of your surroundings" speech, asking us to be on the lookout and to call them if we saw anything.

The criminal had stolen Barbara's wallet and address book and left her purse. That was even creepier. That meant this person had my number and address and everyone else's that Barb kept in her little address book. I started to cry at that meeting. I needed to do something to relieve my own fears and care for my friend.

I struck up a fundraiser and food drive for Barb backstage. Joanna and her husband would buy groceries, and I'd take them over. Everyone chipped in, so she didn't have to go out until she was better.

Joanna's husband, a waiter at the Stardust, took up a fund as well. We took everything to her home. I had been there earlier that day, spending time with Barb, and she shared the details of her assault with me. We both wept, and I hugged her. She had bruises on her face, arms and shoulders.

Barbara needed to get her story out: "This guy pushed me into my car as I opened the door in the parking lot and drove to the desert. He beat me with rocks, which really hurt because he hit my face, and then he raped me. But the rape was the least of the assault because he was very nervous and had a hard time staying hard. After that, he threw me in the trunk and peed on the car, then drove back to the Stardust parking lot where he had first abducted me. He was a young guy in his 30s and didn't exactly seem crazy as much as distressed. I guess I was vulnerable in the parking lot, not looking around while unlocking the car."

38. The Big Move, 1981

I was in tears. It broke me inside. I took her hands and held them. My heart shattered, seeing my closest friend so vulnerable, distraught and hurt. It broke the illusion that my stint at the Stardust was perfect. It broke my trust in the world. After that, I armed myself with mace and carried it at the ready.

I went over to be with her at her house numerous times during the next few days. Jeff had assembled what seemed like an arsenal in their upstairs office-loft area facing the front door. That freaked me out, too. I'd never seen him so tense.

Jeff was tightly wound and on constant vigilance. He was acting incredibly paranoid, as would be expected. But he was hard to be around. Barbara seemed somewhat agitated with him. She shouldn't have to deal with that too!

It took Barbara about a week to return to work. In one more week, I'd be moving to Los Angeles.

My rose-colored glasses had come off. The excitement I had once felt was replaced by hyper-vigilance and fear. My dream was blemished and tainted. I had to use every ounce of Zen I could muster to go confidently ahead with my plans, and it wasn't easy. I was leaving so much behind, and now I was extremely anxious to go away, petrified about living in a bigger city.

Hollywood certainly had its share of crime in 1981.

I had to get Sasha ready to send home to Illinois,

Barbara Beverly on the 1978 Lido de Paris program.

where my parents had offered to take my sweet little terrier while I set forth on my new adventure. I couldn't bring a dog into a friend's house where they had a cat. Another reason to feel bereft. My little Sashita wasn't getting any younger, and although I could gallivant across the world like a gypsy, she couldn't anymore. She was now nearly 13.

I knew it might be the last time I ever saw Sasha. My heart broke a little more. I kissed her tiny face goodbye through my emotions and got her on her flight to Illinois.

I can't say I was headed to LaLa Land and my dream of acting with the same enthusiasm I'd felt a few weeks earlier. However, I was still close enough to Vegas to attend events and parties and to visit if I missed them too much. I found that comforting.

My time to depart had arrived. The night before I retired from the Lido, my pals pulled some "going away" pranks, like hanging a sign on the largest feather backpack of my finale costume that said, "Hollywood or Bust!" I wasn't even aware of it until I was offstage.

I knew someone would take some heat for that, but it felt like love when I found out. I'm pretty sure Joanna made that happen. Only a line captain could pull that off.

The girls made a champagne punch and we had a little party backstage. I received cards, gifts, promises and hugs. The boys in the show somehow muscled their way into the costume vaults and created a fabulous silver lamé and jeweled choker, and all signed on the inside for me. I felt so loved. I promised to let them know when my *Young and the Restless* episode aired.

James Maxwell insisted on driving me to L.A. He confided in me on the way that he, too, was inspired to move to L.A., where he had other career possibilities to pursue. I was thrilled that he, Michael and Vimmi would all be there soon. My three best guy friends were all about to be in L.A. at the same time as I was! That was a generous dose of comfort for my transition.

I felt as if I had an entourage. I didn't, we were just dancer friends casting our nets into a larger pond, expanding our careers before we got much older. Most of us were in our late 20s or early 30s. This was typical in Las Vegas. Older dancers finished up their dance careers in the best shows on the Strip.

Dear, sweet, beautiful Blase had gotten wind of my big move and called me, promising to show me around Hollywood as he'd promised so many years ago.

Sometimes, I think that entire experience with Barbara's assault prepared me for the disappointments I would inevitably encounter as an actress in L.A. It shrouded me in a cloak of vulnerability that wasn't the

38. The Big Move, 1981

norm for my confident nature. That vulnerability may have been precisely what I needed to become the actress I intended to be after my move. A force to reckon with, whole, complete and hardly one-dimensional.

I decided to take Hollywood by storm. I began exploring all the casting offices and dropped in to introduce myself to many of the prominent casting directors. No stone was left unturned. I invested in my career.

I had fulfilled my promise to myself to never be an "old" showgirl. I would move into my destiny as an actress and a much larger life, keeping my gypsies close to me—forever!

La fin

Epilogue

Upon my arrival in L.A., I contacted Blase. Sure enough, he introduced me to everyone in Hollywood, took me everywhere, and claimed to have always loved me even though he lived with his boyfriend, just as he had promised a dozen years ago.

A month after moving to L.A., I signed with an agent. Two months later, I booked my first job: two roles on a series for the all-new Playboy Channel. The series, *Getting Sexy*, was the Canadian equivalent of *Love, American Style*.

At my first audition for that show, I met Craig Christiansen—soon to be my second husband. He was a charming and extremely good-looking Italian-American actor who had moved to L.A. from the Bay Area because of casting director Mike Hanks. The same man "discovered" both of us, and Craig was on *The Young and the Restless* in a recurring role when we met.

I was cast in lead roles on two *Getting Sexy* episodes. I worked with and fell in love with Craig in one of them. I played his therapist. We had two children (now adults) together: Maximilian and Tess Christiansen.

Sound like a fairy tale? Not exactly. When I reported for duty to Mike Hanks at CBS to work on *The Young and the Restless*, I was disheartened to learn he had been fired the day before I arrived. I didn't get to work on the show as a new casting director hadn't yet been hired.

Yet Mike was the reason both Craig and I had moved to LaLa Land! The catalyst for me and Craig to meet. Though we didn't work on that soap opera together, we did work together in every other way. We began training with an extraordinary coach at Strasberg's, Oscar-nominated actress Sally Kirkland. She affectionately referred to our class as "The Faces of the '80s." It was there that several lifelong friendships were forged, including our best friend and our son's godfather, Will Corrado. Will is a true renaissance man, having served as an actor, producer, talent manager, gallery director and now psychiatrist. He is the best male friend I've ever had.

I became a member of the West Coast Actors Studio. While pursuing a career in Hollywood and booking some work here and there, I also became Sally's personal secretary. Craig became her driver, as she was wary of driving in L.A. She officiated our wedding in 1983 in the hills of Ventura overlooking the beautiful Pacific Ocean. She was a minister for the spiritual organization Movement for Spiritual Inner Awareness. We became devotees until Will introduced us to Self Realization Fellowship, which soon became our church and our spiritual path. The Lake Shrine in Malibu is home to a portion of Gandhi's ashes as guru Paramahansa Yogananda had instructed Gandhi to meditate in India.

Much of that sounds like pretty smooth sailing, yet I was confronted with a very harsh beginning while living with my dear friend Ramona and her family. After living with them and paying rent in their home for six months, they reported that the entire family would travel to their original home in Sri Lanka for three months starting in December of 1982. They asked if Craig would like to live with me there while they were away.

Although Craig was renting a room in a lovely home in Palos Verdes, we decided, after four short months of dating, that we were ready to move in together. So we struck a deal and paid three months' rent in advance. Craig and I moved in together as Ramona and her family jetted off to Sri Lanka.

A few days after their departure, a young married couple whom we had met at Ramona's family parties a few times, Doc and Sushila, knocked at our door with luggage in hand. "We're here!" they announced.

"Oh, hi," I replied curiously. "Come on in. It's nice to see you. Were you here for something specific?" I asked as they brought in their luggage and belongings.

"Didn't they tell you? We rented the house for the next three months from Olga, Ramona's mother."

"Really?" I was shocked. "So did we. Didn't they tell you?"

"They did tell us," added Doc. He was a tanned, handsome California boy in his early 30s. "They told us we would rent along with you two."

"It is a big house, and there are four bedrooms. I'm just amazed they didn't tell us," I told them.

We shared some wine and enjoyed the evening as Craig played the grand piano in the living room. As surprised as we all were at the lack of communication from Olga, we were all delighted to spend time together. Sushila, a darling young woman from India, was a phenomenal cook who generously taught me to make Indian food. She'd been a friend of Ramona's family since her childhood in Sri Lanka and assured us with a measure of caution that Olga was not always the most forthcoming. Three weeks later, my American Express card statement arrived, and much to my dismay, there were four round-trip airline tickets and three sets of luggage from a department store listed on my bill. I had been ripped off.

This broke my heart. Did Ramona know? Had she been a part of it?

Once I told Doc and Sushila the story, we began to refer to Ramona's family as "the barracudas." My devoted housemates insisted I call American Express and report the theft and fraud. It took about a month, but I finally had the Amex lawyers involved and pressed charges against Olga. I knew it was her because of her signature on the Amex charges. Upon her return several months later, she was apprehended at the airport. I can't begin to tell you how violated I felt having had my card stolen from my purse at home and used this way.

Needless to say, we all found homes elsewhere. Doc and Sushila stayed our dear friends, and none of us ever saw "the barracudas" again. It was a rough rollercoaster ride and a wake-up call for me, learning not to trust so easily.

Craig and I found a lovely Beverly Hills apartment and part-time jobs. Our apartment was on Oakhurst Drive, across the street from Sally Kirkland's godmother, Shelley Winters. We were just down the block from Richard Simmons, who we regularly saw walking his two gorgeous Dalmatians.

Most interesting of all, one block over from us was Blase, who lived on Doheny. I never doubted that destiny was at play in my life and that Divine orchestration was playing its concerto for me by bringing me to L.A., despite the disappointment with Ramona's mother and Mike Hanks.

The day I met Craig, I knew beyond a shadow of a doubt that I was destined to have children with him. We *both* knew this. We shared a deep feeling of knowing one another, perhaps from a past life connection. I had never wanted kids, and he told me he felt the same. We knew it was Kismet.

We brought a son, Maximilian Miles Christiansen, and daughter, Tess Lauren Christiansen, into the world. They are the light of our lives. Though Craig and I wore many hats and were challenged several times with financial and marital issues, we always adored and cherished our incredible kids.

We raised them in the Valley for a time, then moved to a mountain community called Pine Mountain Club when Max was nine and Tess was three. Living in a National Forest off the Grapevine at 10,000 feet was an alternative lifestyle with four mild California seasons. I had been working as a knitwear designer and Craig worked at Warner Brothers Studio in production control.

Once settled into the mountain community, we recognized a desperate need for entertainment there. Our hearts longed to continue acting, even though we had mostly given it up, so when we met actress Pam McGee, we decided to start a community theater, the Rainbow Theatre Guild. We produced, directed and starred in some outstanding and very successful shows for the next seven years. Our efforts were so well received after our first show, *Peter Pan*, that we continued to engage and entertain the community with delightful shows for as long as we lived there. We included our kids in all aspects of running the theater.

I began teaching dance and acting classes in the community and owned a studio for a long time.

Craig and I split up in 1998. I left him. I was broken and devastated. A few years later, once Max graduated from high school and Tess finished elementary school, I moved to Santa Clarita and began teaching acting full-time at several locations. Tess became a working child actress, and Max forged his video game career during college.

Over the next ten years, I worked very hard to become Hollywood's #1 acting coach. I now have a 33-year-old business that is wildly successful. Tess grew tired of her professional acting career, although she was extremely gifted as an actress, and began teaching 14 years ago, joining me in running the Christiansen Acting Academy in Los Angeles. We have had the honor and privilege of coaching some of the hottest talent in Hollywood.

Max became "Maximilian Dood," a content creator and streamer of video games, holding the *Guinness Book* record for "largest fighting game channel in the world" since 2020. In 2022, *Fortune* magazine listed him as one of the "Top 25 Creators in the World."

Both of my children have married their soulmates. Tess and her husband, Matt Sklena, met in my acting class and tied the knot 17 years later. Max and Jessica met when he was studying video game design in college. She had seen his online gallery and set out to meet fellow artist Max.

I am the proud "Glamma" of Max and Jessica's Ripley, and of Tess and Matt's Gwenyth. They are the brightest beams in the Universe and the lights of my life.

I have remained close to Craig and his new family. I poured myself into my acting academy and have been awarded year after year as the #1 acting coach in Hollywood. I love what I do and will probably teach until the end of my days.

In the meantime, I plan to be the best Glamma in the world and continue to spend my happiest moments with my family. I travel often, especially with my best friend ever, Barbara Beverly-Crockett, and I stay close to my brothers and immediate family in Illinois.

Once again, I'm a happy jet-setter and an even happier matriarch of my family. I'm blessed to be able to spend my exquisite life with my best friends nearby. Barbara and I live only 30 minutes from one another. Knowing I have my loved ones close only deepens the gratitude of this Last Real Showgirl.

Diane (left) and Barbara in Malibu, 2023.

Index

abortion 30
abuse 20
acting 13, 14, 22, 24, 26, 33, 39, 40, 47, 73, 80, 82, 83, 90, 106, 118, 145, 200, 204, 219, 222-225, 228, 235-241, 244-246, 249
acrobats 26, 37, 67, 73, 85, 96, 106, 107, 180
Adair, Jeff 204
addiction 74, 110
Ado Annie 13, 22
Africa 120, 187
AIDS 25, 204
Aimes, Hardy 180
alcoholism 17, 18, 19, 20, 32, 104, 110, 193, 225
Allen, Barbara 25, 26, 29
Allen, Shirley 203, 205-207, 210, 211, 215, 225, 230
Allez Lido 148, 150, 193, 195, 201, 206, 215, 216
Amazons 72
American Express 247
amphetamines 74
aneurysm 20
angels 29, 41-43, 45, 49, 53, 55, 89, 90, 95, 135, 155, 157, 166, 181, 186
Anita 13, 15, 22
Ann Margret 24, 227
Arc de Triomphe 119
Arden, Donn 72, 120, 124, 194, 205
Arden, Eve 236
Ashby, Hal 225, 227
Aspen 98
Astaire, Fred 124
Atlanta 1, 114, 115, 134, 135, 138-148, 151-153, 160, 167, 169, 192, 218, 228
Atlantic Ocean 153
Atlantis Hotel 5, 8, 11-14, 26, 61, 67, 71, 99, 114
audition 1-3, 95, 96, 98, 99, 155, 157-159, 224, 225, 230, 235, 236, 238, 246
Australia 27, 29, 30, 32, 33, 39, 67, 72, 75, 87, 97, 106, 107

backstage 10, 11, 27, 30-32, 47, 49, 57, 62, 70, 79, 90, 92, 97, 102, 103, 106, 107, 111, 121, 148, 157, 168, 170, 172, 174, 177, 180, 181, 203, 207, 208, 211, 216, 219, 225, 242
Backstage Dance Studio 99
Bad Boys 49, 107, 177, 192, 220
Bahamas 1, 3, 4, 7, 26, 39, 40, 59-61, 72, 73, 82, 91, 97, 98, 105, 107, 113, 122, 153, 218
Bailey, Pearl 8, 4
Bailey, Philip 151
Baker, Josephine 122
Baker, Michael 203
Baldwin Hills 150
Baltimore 29, 30
Barbizon 10
The Barn 96, 98
bartender 138, 145, 154, 155, 163, 168
Basie, Count 195
basketball 17-20, 23, 159
Baskow, Jaki 223, 236
beach 71, 72, 74, 75, 77, 79, 105, 110, 111, 153, 154, 156, 161, 163, 168, 173, 239
The Beatles 41, 75, 97, 106
Beaux Arts Ball 216, 217
Bedazzled 207
Belafonte, Harry 61
Bellagio Hotel and Casino 204
Ben 146, 147, 150, 15
Bennet, Pearl 121
Berghof, Herbert 10, 14
Bernard, Joseph 204, 222, 224, 228, 230, 235-238, 240
Bettencourt, Jose 155, 156, 166, 168, 172-176
Beverly, Barbara 1, 2, 62-70, 72, 75, 79, 85-87, 90, 116-125, 127-133, 148, 193-195, 199, 200, 202, 208-210, 212-214, 219-223, 232, 233, 236, 237, 239-244, 249
Beverly Hills 141, 218, 228, 230, 238, 240, 248
Beverly Hills Playhouse 240
The Beverly-Mann Hotel 200

251

Big Bands 195
Big Ten 18
Birch, Ellen 215, 230
birth control pills 48, 49, 57
birthday 44, 58, 107, 172, 175, 221
Black Beauties 74, 75, 77-79, 83, 84, 94
black light 187
The Black Six 225
Blass, Bill 223
Blue Ridge Mountains 96
Bluebell girls 119-124, 210
Bobbi 30-34, 37-39, 60, 62, 67
body paint 122, 123, 125
bodyguards 215
Bonjour la Nuit 123
Boston 195
Bowie, David 216
Boyd Gaming 3
boyfriend 25, 29, 30, 38, 41, 48, 64, 71, 82, 83, 87, 90, 99, 138, 188, 216
Brazil 138
breasts 33, 35, 38, 71, 84-85, 105, 116, 217
Brenner, David 216, 217
Brian 138
Brice, Fanny 6, 32, 35, 69
Britannia Beach Hotel 1, 61, 62, 64-66, 107, 111
Broadway 8, 10, 13, 96, 186
Brown, Charlie 91-93
Bruce, Lenny 84
Brynner, Yul 155
Buckhead 141, 142
Buddhism 110, 111
Burke, Sonny 195
Butterfly 224-226, 236, 241

Cable Beach 107
Caesars Palace Hotel and Casino 98, 150, 215, 223, 232, 233, 238
Le Caf Conc 27, 31, 40, 63-65
California 25, 30, 65, 178, 181, 209, 211-215
callback 238
Calloway, Cab 8
Camelot 242
can can 6, 28, 31, 32, 35, 37, 38, 57, 67
Canada 1, 45, 49-51, 55-58, 61, 203, 246
Canoga Park 150-152
Capricorn 113, 145
cardiovascular problems 74
Caribbean 65, 77, 105, 106, 153, 233
Carnegie Hall 187
Carol 211, 212
Carroll, Jean 93
Carter, Jimmy 141
Carter, Roselyn 141
casino 62, 72, 73, 80, 82, 97, 107, 111, 148, 150, 154, 168, 169, 199, 206, 217, 221, 228

Casino de Paradis 1, 59, 62, 68-70, 78, 80, 86
Casino de Paris 208
casting 97, 225, 227, 235, 237, 245, 246
Catalina 165-167
Catskills 86
CBS 237-239, 246
Central Park 187
"C'est Magnifique" 154, 155, 159, 167, 174
chakras 82
Champs-Elysees 120, 125
Charleston 70
Chateau Champlain 27, 31, 37
cheating 83, 145-147, 190, 193, 213, 220
Chelsea Hotel 188
Cher 151, 232
Cheryl 72, 75, 233, 85
CHIC 185
Chicago 7, 18, 19, 45, 46
choreography 15, 27-29, 37, 64, 67, 69, 96, 98, 105, 120, 123, 124, 126, 128, 133, 148, 154-156, 158, 168, 179, 185, 187, 194, 206-208, 210
Christiansen, Craig 232, 246-249
Christiansen, Jessica 249
Christiansen, Maximilian 246, 248, 249
Christiansen, Ripley 249
Christiansen, Tess 246, 248, 249
Christiansen Acting Academy 249
Christine 128, 129
Chorn, Herbie 232, 233
cigarettes 27, 50, 53, 55, 56, 67, 72
Cimber, Matt 224, 225, 235-239
Cinderella 23, 24, 174
Cirque de Soleil 3, 4
Clark, Sterling 124
claustrophobia 184
"Le Clique" 179-181, 183, 185-187, 189, 192, 193, 195, 198, 232
Club Med 233, 234
cocaine 98, 132
comedy 32, 44, 48, 77, 80, 81, 84-86, 90, 93, 94, 108, 141
Community Theatre 20, 21, 23, 25, 26, 249
company captain 72, 73, 105, 155, 159, 161, 163, 168, 193, 200, 225
contract 61, 86, 90, 104-106, 118, 119, 135, 144, 146, 148, 161, 163, 164, 169, 185, 186, 193, 200, 238, 239
Cornell, Kenny 203
Cornell, Kim 203, 221, 240
Corrado, Will 246
costumes 5, 6, 26, 70, 124-129, 169, 180, 182-187, 194, 207, 210, 216, 217, 244
Cote du Rhone 131
Cotton Comes to Harlem 73
Court of Law 18

Index

The Cove 105
covered dancer 32, 37, 63, 67, 197, 207, 210
Covid-19 227
craps table 80
"Crazy Girls" 133
Crazy Horse Saloon 4, 125, 130, 131, 133
Curtis, Tony 228
CVS Pharmacy 4
Czechoslovakia 29, 32, 33, 59

Dakota 187
dance class 7, 13, 15, 21, 23, 26, 35, 71, 106, 155, 156, 166, 168, 172, 173, 209, 249
dancer 1, 5, 13, 21, 22, 24, 26, 28, 31, 32, 37, 38, 40, 44, 45, 47, 52, 59, 62, 64, 65, 70, 71, 81, 83, 87, 96–100, 103, 104, 107, 111, 114, 116, 121–124, 126, 132, 133, 145, 148, 149, 154, 155, 157, 159, 162, 168, 172, 175–178, 182, 183, 185, 193–196, 199, 200, 202, 203, 206–209, 215, 216, 218, 224, 227, 230, 231, 233–235, 240, 244
dancing nude 32, 33, 37, 67, 68, 98, 104, 121–126, 129, 155, 157, 158, 180, 194, 195, 204, 206, 209, 210, 215
Dangerfield, Deborah 186, 187, 189, 195
Danny 99–103, 133, 134
Dark of the Moon 26
Darnall, Karen 7, 9–11, 15, 25, 23, 25, 32, 44, 71, 72, 75
Darren, James 215
dating 24, 25, 107, 111, 112, 134, 182, 192, 198, 205, 218, 237
The Dating Game 24
Dave 91, 92, 94–96
David 145, 147
"Dead Man's Curve" 64
Debbie 51–55, 206–211
DeGaulle, Charles 136
de la Renta, Oscar 223
Deluise, Dom 224
DeNiro, Robert 148
Denise 155–158, 161
Dennhardt, Larry 11, 12
Dennhardt, Mary Lou 1, 5, 7, 8, 10–13, 15, 16, 20, 22, 26, 34, 35, 38, 39, 67
depression 79, 80
Desert Inn Hotel and Casino 207
diet pills 73–79, 86, 91
Dietrich, Marlene 122
disco 1, 37, 124, 128, 129, 131, 159, 172–180, 184–189, 195, 197, 200, 202, 230, 231, 233, 237
divorce 19, 55, 182, 193
Dixie 147, 148, 150–152
D.J. 32, 38, 172, 176
Doc 247, 248
Doheny Drive 248

Don 45–47, 49–54
Donghia, Angelo 146
Donny 172
Doorman 188
Dorsie, Tommy 195
dressing room 11, 27, 32, 48, 49, 80, 86, 91, 94, 99, 111, 116, 122, 123, 125–127, 129, 170, 181, 221
drugs 74, 84, 160, 169
Dubonnet 82, 107
Duckworth, Diane 204
Duckworth, John 107
Dunes Hotel and Casino 4, 98, 208, 209, 211-213
Durkee, Deonna 5
dust storms 99

Earth, Wind & Fire 151, 210, 218, 229
East Coast 211
East Village 188
Eastern Asia 120
Echelon Place 3
Eiffel Tower 118
El San Juan Hotel and Casino 154, 159, 162, 164, 167, 179, 233
Eleuthera 233, 234
Emerald City 180, 185
Emmy Award 141
Eric 119, 126, 130, 134
Estefan, Gloria 153
estrangement 61
L'Etoile Verde 120
Europe 102, 120, 133, 146, 179
Eva 32, 33, 59
Everette 187, 189
Excalibur Hotel and Casino 211, 214
eye high kicks 9, 11
eyelashes 38, 97–99, 174, 175

Fake-Out 225, 235
Fantasy Players 79, 184–187, 195
fashion design 15, 144, 146, 180, 220
fat doctor 73, 74, 79, 82
fatherhood 18
feathers 26, 31, 37, 38, 123–125, 169, 187, 207
feature films 201, 219, 225, 226, 235, 241
featured dancer 67, 68, 98, 104, 128, 168, 180, 194
Feinstein, Marlene 179, 185, 186, 193, 197
Feinstein, Stewart 179, 185, 186, 193, 197
Femora 225
Ferrell, Lynda 203
Filipino 46, 47
finale 125, 168, 169
fire eater 64, 180
Fire Island 25

254 Index

fireworks 198
fishnets 26, 27, 38, 99, 157, 216
Fitzgerald, Ella 195
Flamingo Hotel and Casino 199
Flip 46–49, 51–55, 57, 58, 64, 65, 188
Florida 172
Flower, Buck 224, 235
flower children 32
"Folies Bergere" 96, 98, 99, 120
Fonda, Jane 72
Fort Lauderdale 60
Fortune magazine 249
Fourth of July 198
France 4, 38, 50, 118, 119, 121, 133, 146
francs 128
Fraza, Cheryl 203
"Le Freak" 185
freak flag 119
free love 32, 37, 38, 59
free spirit 190
freebasing 84
Fremont Street 96
French Cabaret 1, 3, 4, 31, 121, 122, 124, 130
French Quarter 148
fundraiser 242
Funny Girl 6
furs 67, 69, 238

g-string 26, 27, 38, 68, 98, 216
Gail 85
Gallagher, Michael 204, 222, 237, 240, 244
gambling 154
Gandhi 247
Gay Paree 27, 117, 119
Gemini 24, 182, 198
general interview 237
George 73, 106
Georgetown 77, 86, 91
Geri 91, 92, 94, 95, 96
getaway 210
Getting Sexy 246
Gina 73, 74, 86, 87, 10
go go girl 6, 114
God 31, 55, 74
Golden Girls 5, 6, 35
Golden Globes 225
Gosse, Peter 133
Governor's Harbour 233
graduation 13, 15, 18
Grammys 6
Grand Prix 123
Great Depression 19
The Great Pretender 111
Griffin, Merv 215, 228
grunge 188, 189
Gulbranson, Dawnie 232
guru 113

The Gypsy 230
Gypsy Peacock 141, 142, 145, 146

Hair 8, 96
Hall, Mindy 203, 211, 212, 215, 230
"Hallelujah Hollywood" 194
Halloween 216
Halston 223
Hanks, Mike 237, 238, 246, 248
Happy Hour 192
Harlow, Jean 69, 70, 71, 77, 87, 98, 104
Harold and Maude 227
Harrera, Carolina 223
Hartford, Huntington 66
Hawaii 114, 133, 237
Hayden, Liz 203, 206–209, 211, 213, 215
Hayward, Susan 106
head dresses 26, 37, 38, 125, 126, 127, 187, 207, 236
headliners 31, 44, 45, 64, 116, 123, 172, 179, 180, 187, 215, 216
headshot 86, 223, 224
health 67, 71, 74, 78, 79, 89, 104–106, 157
Hefner, Hugh 12, 115, 116
Hello Dolly 8, 10
Hemingway, Ernest 79
Hendrix, Jimi 45
Herb Alpert and the Tijuana Brass 6
heroin 160, 169
Hiett, Suzan 232, 233
high roller 220
hippies 37, 42, 43, 49, 50, 75, 92, 98, 222
Ho, Pearl 29, 30, 34, 38, 59
Holiday on Ice 177, 179, 180, 183, 188, 190
Hollywood 4, 22–24, 243–247, 249
Holmes, Clint 74, 77, 86, 91, 94
house dressing 141, 142, 146
Hughes, Howard 64, 66
Hungarian 73
Hyatt Regency Hotel 138, 139, 141
hydraulics 9, 123, 126, 199

I Can't Give You Anything But Love 67
I Ching 139
I Wanna Be Your Lover 229
Ice Capades 203, 211
ice skating 123, 124, 145, 177, 178, 188, 193, 197, 199, 203, 208, 209, 211
Ikettes 100
Illinois 4, 12, 20, 22, 40, 59, 61, 103, 104, 141, 182, 195, 197, 221, 243, 244, 249
impersonations 81
improvisation 70
India 37, 218, 228, 247
The Inferno 180
insomnia 77–79, 87
Instamatic camera 10

Index

International Hotel and Casino 97
Iowa 45
Isla Verde 152–154
islands 27, 62, 72, 77, 78, 82, 86, 87, 105, 112, 113, 153, 154, 162, 164, 165, 172, 182, 234
Italy 42, 71, 72, 108, 137, 150, 199

Jackson, Alan 230
Jackson, Jerry 96, 98, 99
Jagger, Bianca 80, 180
Jagger, Mick 80
James, Harry 195
Jamie 172–174
Jan and Dean 64, 65
Japan 29, 154, 187
Jeanne-Marie 49–53
Jeff 218
Jeri 84, 85, 106
Jerry 96, 97, 103
Jewish Princess 81
Jimmy 65, 187, 188
jitterbug 21
Joe 138, 139
Joey 85
John, Elton 122
Johnette 86, 104
Johnson, Mrs. 173
Joie de Vivre 133
Jones, Grace 180
Juan 172, 174–176
Jubilee 4
jugglers 180
Juicy Fruit 23, 24
jukebox 21
Julianna 29, 30, 40, 44, 46, 47
Junkanoo 64, 85
Junito 155

Kahlua 40
karma 103
Katie 107
Katsales, Milton 240
Kazan, Elia 240
Kelly, Fred 8
Kelly, Gene 63, 65
Kelly, Margaret 120, 121
Kendricks, John 204
Kentucky 134, 137
kidnapping 242
King, Alan 224
Kirkland, Sally 204, 246, 248
Kismet 111, 248
kiss 25, 78, 101, 103, 109, 119, 133, 178, 188, 198
Kitt, Eartha 122
Klineline, John 204

Klute 73
Kogan, Jeff 236, 237, 239–243
Kojack 236
Korn, Herbie 204
Krishna 37
Krogman, Blase 22–25, 64, 73, 182, 244, 246
Kruger, Vimmi 204, 210, 237, 244

Lady GaGa 196
Lake Mead 194
Lake Tahoe 194
Las Vegas 1, 3, 26, 27, 31, 63–65, 68, 96–98, 100, 104, 138, 139, 148–150, 154, 155, 193–195, 197, 199, 201, 202, 204–206, 208, 213, 215–220, 222, 223, 225, 230, 231, 235–241, 244
Las Vegas magazine 236, 237
Las Vegas Review-Journal 208
Las Vegas Strip 3, 4, 97, 100, 197, 200, 210, 211, 213, 232, 240, 244
Laugh In 6
Laurin, Corky 26, 197
Leah 67
Lebanon 133
Lee 31–33, 38, 67, 69
Lee, Barry 44–49, 57
Lee Canyon 208
Lefty 149
Lenny 141, 146, 152–154, 159–165, 168, 169, 173
Leo 49, 189
Letham, Karen 203, 230
Letham, Neil 203, 216, 230
Lewis, Ron 96
Liberace 31
Lido de Paris 3, 116, 118, 120–126, 129, 133–137, 149, 150, 193–195, 200, 202, 204–206, 216, 218, 219, 222, 225, 227, 232, 236, 240, 243, 244
Lincoln Ave. 37, 41, 59
line captain 27, 32, 60, 67, 72, 84, 97, 103, 106, 204, 206, 215
Linda 51, 52
The Lion Sleeps Tonight 233
lip sync 63, 67, 69
Lipshitz, Shirley 42, 10
Little Old Lady from Pasadena 64
Lockhart, Calvin 73, 74, 82, 83, 87, 88, 107–110, 145, 178
London 180, 181, 183, 185, 189
Lonsdale, Kim 203
Lopez, Lizbeth 153–155, 157, 159, 163–166, 168
Lopez, Vincent 195
Los Angeles 24, 25, 47, 55, 58, 62–64, 66, 146, 147, 150–152, 194, 204, 215, 218, 219, 221, 228, 232, 236–241, 243, 246–249

Louann 197
Louboutin, Christian 131
Louisiana 144
Louisville 134
lounges 4, 71, 74, 80, 84–86, 90, 99, 100, 111, 157, 169, 174
Louvre 130
Love, American Style 246
LSD 25, 37, 43, 51–55, 71, 75
Luigi 8
Lyle, Michael 230

MacLaine, Shirley 71, 77, 122, 125, 128
Madonna 29, 30
Mafia 4, 97, 131, 132, 134, 137, 149, 150
Maggie 200
Maharishi 75
Malibu 247, 250
Mama Leone's 8, 11
Mandy 126, 129
Mann, Diana 200, 211, 223, 224, 226
Manoff, Errol 172, 179, 180, 184–187
Mansfield, Jayne 225
Marando's 22
Maria 15
Mariah 138, 140
Mariam 225
marijuana 37, 41–43, 71, 74, 75, 112, 118, 119, 153, 160, 175, 178, 189, 233
Markert, Russell 4, 5, 8, 9, 11
marriage 134, 135, 137, 140, 143, 145–147, 149, 157, 158, 162–164, 167 170, 172, 199, 213, 224, 225, 239, 240, 247–249
marriage counseling 19, 20
Martin, Ricky 154
Max 146, 147
Max, Peter 74
Maximilian Dood 249
Maxwell, James 203, 233, 244
Mazlow, Kenny 203
McGee, Neil 203, 240
McGee, Pam 248
McSwain, Carolee 29, 30, 32, 38, 96–101, 103
meditation 106, 110, 194
menage a trois 102, 190
Menudo 154
Mercedes 228
MGM 194
Miami 81, 85, 154, 195
Michael 49, 56, 58, 64, 147, 148, 150–152
Michaels, Bob 203, 210
Midwest 4
Mikey 62, 64, 67, 69, 72
Miller-Reich Dancers 3, 154, 161, 166, 180, 182, 232

Millett, Jane 203
Mimi 140
Mimi's Restaurant 144–146
Minelli, Liza 30
Minner, Prentice 80–82, 85
Mirage Hotel and Casino 227
misogyny 128
Miss America Pageant 106
Miss Bluebell 3, 72, 116–118, 120, 121, 123–129, 134, 135, 205
Mississippi 198
Mod 23
modeling 22, 24, 119, 145, 194, 200–202, 219, 220, 223, 236–238
Modesto 29
Moline High School 17
mononucleosis 103, 104, 133, 148
Montreal 26–30, 37, 44, 45, 49, 51, 56, 59–61, 63–65, 96, 97, 101, 118, 155, 197
Moreno, Rita 175
Morocco 132
Mother Nature 52, 161
Moulin Rouge 4, 27
Mount Charleston 194, 230
movies 24, 32, 42, 72, 73, 83
Mudd Club 189
music 23, 42, 45
Mustang 198, 199, 209, 212, 213
Myra Breckinridge 73

Native American 113, 195
Navarro, Nick 96
NBC 225
Neil 119, 120, 134
neon 187, 189
Neon Museum 3
Nevada 148
New Jersey 73
New Orleans 144, 146, 148
New Rochelle 183, 193
New Years 187
New York City 1, 3–5, 7–9, 13, 15, 16, 20, 22, 24, 25, 40, 44, 81, 83, 85–87, 108, 134, 136, 139, 155, 172, 179–180, 182–187, 189, 190, 192, 193, 195, 200, 222, 228, 232, 235, 237–240
Newton, Wayne 31, 215
newlyweds 18, 180
NFL 180, 206
Nino 203
Nirvana 4
NOLA 148
Normal Ohio 141
North Carolina 113
Nureyev 203
The Nylons 233

Index

Oakhurst Drive 248
objectification 206
Office Lounge 154, 157
Oklahoma 13
Old San Juan 233
Olga 247, 248
Olympics 178, 230
Omni International 144–146
"Only You" 111
Onstage 27, 33, 40, 67, 70, 101, 104, 120, 125, 126, 181, 205, 206, 217, 236
L'Opera 133
opium den 131–133
Oz 132

Pacific Ocean 150, 194, 247
Palmer, Marian 215, 216
Palos Verdes 247
Papaver Somniferum 132
Paradise Island 26, 39, 59–62, 64–66, 68, 71, 72, 74, 80, 84, 88, 89, 93, 97, 104, 105, 108, 110–112, 233
Paris 1, 3, 4, 27, 118–125, 128, 130–136, 138, 155, 157, 194, 205
Parks, Bert 106
pasties 26, 33, 37, 38, 68, 217
Patrick 134, 135
Patsy 188–192, 213
Patty 114, 135, 136, 138, 139, 197
pay phone 48, 90, 178, 181
Peace, Larry 43, 45, 56, 58
peace for profit 225
Peachtree Street 141, 142
Pecitto, Joanna 204, 242, 244
Perth 29, 67, 97, 101, 107
Peter 172–174, 179, 180, 183, 187
Peter Pan 249
photos 24, 26, 117, 185, 204, 220, 236, 237
Piaff, Edith 122
piano 71
Pickles, Carolyn 121
Piero 72, 79, 148, 150, 193, 199
pimp 160
Pine Mountain Club 248
pink hats 207
Pinky 126, 127
Pips 239
Pirates 4, 72
Pirmann, Albert 18
Pirmann, Diane 8, 13, 32, 38, 68–71, 85, 200
Pirmann, Jerry 17–21, 24, 25, 29, 32, 35, 58, 59, 90, 103, 104, 107, 116, 182, 183, 193, 197–199, 221
Pirmann, Lois 18, 121
Pirmann, Tom 20
Pit Boss 71, 107

Place Charles de Gaulle 120
The Platters 111, 137
Playboy 66, 114–116, 122, 135, 141, 217, 246
Playboy Bunny 1, 12, 114–116, 122, 138
Playboy magazine 116
Playboy Mansion 116
Playcrafters Theatre 26
Playground in my Mind 94
Poitier, Sidney 61, 17, 30
Poust, Carter 204
Preminger, Otto 24
Presley, Elvis 31, 97, 205, 207
Prince 174, 229, 231
principal dancer 59, 67, 68, 116, 122–124, 128, 150, 187, 193, 211
Pryor, Richard 84
psychedelics 44, 51–57, 74, 131
psychic 139, 157, 165, 166, 167, 170
Puerto Rico 1, 3, 4, 152–154, 157, 165, 167, 172, 175, 177–180, 199, 209, 216, 232, 233
punk rock 188, 189
Puppet People 172, 177, 179, 180, 183–187
Purple Rain 231

Quad City Music Guild 13–15, 20, 22
Quebec City 48–50, 55
Queen of Disco 195
queer 24, 25

racism 114, 140
Radio City Music Hall 4, 5, 8, 10, 11, 13, 22, 26
The Rainbow Theatre Guild 248
Ramona 218, 219, 228–230, 238–240, 247, 248
Randy 187, 189
Raouf 234
rape 242
Rathafel, Roxy 8, 9
Raymond, Sheila 231
real estate 204, 230
Reba 114
recording studio 135, 140, 142, 144, 218, 229
Red Baron 138
rehearsal 27, 29–32, 37, 64–69, 81, 82, 98, 99, 103, 104, 107, 122, 126, 152, 154, 155, 157, 159, 161–168, 173, 178, 180, 183, 187, 195, 197, 200, 205–207, 209–211, 213
reincarnation 121
Reno 194
Retton, Mary Lou 230
Rick 212
Ride the Wild Surf 64
Riklis, Meshulam 224
Rio Grande 148
RIU 61

Rivers, Joan 224
Riviera Hotel and Casino 133, 199, 216, 217, 224
Rizzo, Rich 148
Robbins, Jerome 14
Robby 192, 193
Robinson, Arnold 111–114, 117, 134, 135, 137–157, 159–167, 169, 177, 182, 199, 213, 218, 219, 228, 229, 233
Rock Island 13, 14, 20, 22, 23, 25, 29
Rock Island High School 6, 17, 22- 24
rock stars 44–47, 51–55, 57, 72, 74, 90, 92, 106, 114, 141, 144, 146, 151, 152, 155, 193, 235
Rockettes 4–10, 13–16, 22, 25, 26, 40
Rodeo Drive 25
Rogers, Ginger 10, 124
Rogers, Kenny and the First Edition 97
roller disco 232, 233
Rolls Royce 237
roommates 28–30, 38, 44, 68, 71, 87, 101, 114, 119, 135, 136, 139, 187, 188, 193, 194, 240, 241, 248
Rose, Felipe 195, 213, 214
Roseland 180, 195
Rosenthal, Frank 148, 149, 206
Ross, Diana 233
Roxy Theatre 8
Roxyettes 8, 9
Rudas, Tibor 29–32, 35, 38–40, 49, 59, 62–64, 67, 68, 69, 72, 73, 78, 86, 87, 90, 97–99, 104, 107, 128
Rudas Dancers 3, 26, 27, 31, 35, 63, 64, 67, 96, 154
Rue Pergoles 119, 132, 133

Sachs, Al 150, 206
SAG/AFTRA 215, 235
Sands Hotel and Casino 4, 99, 208, 215
Sandy 85, 107
Saint James Theatre 8
Saint Louis 8
Salvation Army House 186
Same Time Next Year 204, 222
San Francisco 75, 195
San Juan 152
Santa Paula 178, 180, 197, 198
Saturday Night Live 141
Savales, Telly 236
Savoie, Leo 42–45, 56, 58
Sax Fifth Avenue 223
Scarlett O'Hara's 138
Schnallinger, Maximilian 145, 146
Scotland, the Yard 187
Scrabble 233
self realization 89, 247
"Send in the Clones" 180

senior prom 13–15, 18, 20
Señor Wences 31
sex 38, 44, 47, 48, 57–59, 73, 75–77, 82, 91, 102, 103, 109, 110, 113, 145, 146, 174, 180, 190, 192, 229, 237
Shangri-La 65
Shelly 99–103, 133, 134
Sheraton Hotel 61, 141, 152, 154, 157, 182, 183, 186, 192, 193
Sherman, Emily 7, 9, 11, 15
Sherman Oaks 151
Shindig 47
Shriner, Kathy 203
Shull-Pirmann, Phoebe 17–22, 24, 25, 28, 29, 35, 39, 44, 54, 58, 59, 90, 103, 104, 106, 111, 182, 183, 197, 198, 199, 221
Siegfried & Roy 3, 31, 193, 194, 201, 222, 225, 227
Simmons, Richard 248
Sindra 186, 187
Sklena, Gwenyth 249
Sklena, Matthew 249
sleeping pills 73, 79
Sly and the Family Stone 46
Smith/Smitty 74–79, 81–83, 86, 91–94, 112
Smithsonian 96
Smoke Gets in Your Eyes 111
Sound Limited 111, 112, 114, 134
South Africa 172
Spain 4, 10, 133, 156, 170
Spanglish 153, 167
"Spanish Flea" 6
Sri Lanka 218
Stallone brothers 25
Stalmaster, Lynn 224, 227
standing ovation 85
Stardust, Ziggy 216
Stardust Hotel and Casino 3, 148–150, 193, 194, 197, 199–201, 203, 206, 208, 212, 215, 227, 232, 238, 239, 241–243
stimulants 74, 76–79
stoned 42, 48, 72, 75, 97, 100, 101, 119, 153
Strasbergs Acting Studio 204, 222, 246
Streisand, Barbra 6
suicidal tendencies 79
summer replacements 15, 25
sunbathing 98, 104
Sunset Blvd. 151
Surf City 64
Sushila 247
Sutherland, Donald 72
swag 73
swami 74, 89
Swarovski Crystal 12
Sweden 180
Sweet Charity 125, 128

swing girl/boy 99, 125–129, 158, 200, 210, 218
Sylvester 195

tan lines 98
Tarnatella 216
Tegano, Sharon 203
Teri 85, 87, 104
Texas 148
Thanksgiving 183
That '80s Show 141
That '70s Show 141
Third Rock from the Sun 141
Tiger Man 225
A Time to Die 225
Tita 172, 174–176, 181
tits and feathers 3, 4, 154
Tobman, Herb 150, 206
Tomlin, Ron 223, 224
topless 26, 32, 33, 98, 121, 197, 206, 207, 233
Touchstone 65
Toulouse-Lautrec, Henri de 31, 64
Tracy 67–70
Treasure Island Hotel and Casino 4
Tropicana Hotel and Casino 26, 96–100, 104, 133
Turner, Bonnie 141
Turner, Ike 99, 100
Turner, Sonny 111–113, 134, 137, 157, 218
Turner, Ted 141
Turner, Terry 141
Turner, Tina 99, 100
The Turtles 23
TV 73, 238, 239
Twilight Time 137
Two Tons of Fun 195

Uncle Sam's 180
under-five 238, 239
understudies 22, 68
Union Plaza Hotel and Casino 96, 97
United Airlines 7
United States 14, 22, 47, 57, 113, 118, 133, 136
Universe 49, 61, 71, 107, 110, 166, 187, 220, 239, 240, 249
University of California–Los Angeles 18
University of Nevada–Las Vegas 202, 207, 209
University of Texas 20
Upshaw, Victor 133
Urich, Robert 228

Valentines Ball 180
Valerie 153, 159–162, 164, 169
Valley of the Dolls 73, 87, 106
VanDyke, Dick 141

Vanoy, Roy 237
Vega$ 228
vegetarians 71
ventriloquist 31
Vest, Buddy 124, 128, 129
video games 249
Vietnam 26
Village People 195, 208, 209, 211
Vince 177–182, 185, 187, 189–193, 197–200, 208, 211–215, 220
Virginia 94
virginity 25, 30, 38, 44, 45, 47, 48, 54, 55, 57, 59, 91
voiceover 224, 238
Voight, Jon 227
volcanoes 123
VW Bug 138

Walker, Ron 29, 65, 67, 69, 70, 96, 105, 107
Warner Brothers Studios 248
Washington D.C. 76, 77, 81–83, 86, 87, 90, 92, 93, 95, 96, 97, 108
Watts, Alan 105, 110, 111
The Way of Zen 110, 111
Webb, Chick 195
weight 40, 41, 49, 60, 67, 72–74, 77, 79, 86, 127, 128, 155, 157, 168
West, Mae 42
West Hollywood 150, 151, 219, 229
West Side Story 13, 14, 175
Whirlwind 162, 164, 166
White, Maurice 151, 218, 231
White, Monte 151, 218–220, 228, 229, 231, 232
White Gold 210, 222, 227
White Shoulders 41
wigs 67, 81, 84, 98, 125, 131, 236
Wikipedia 8
Wild West 151, 205
Winters, Shelley 248
Wilson, Colin 26, 30, 32, 33, 38, 59, 61
The Witch Who Came from the Sea 225
Wits' End Dinner Theatre 141–143, 146
Wonderful World of 30 Girls 63
Woodbridge 94
Woods, Doug 203
The World of Sid and Marty Krofft 145
Wright, David 193, 195
Wynn Hotel and Casino 4

Yellow Hair and the Fortress of Gold 225
Yin-Yang 205
yoga 41, 74, 75, 89, 106, 110
Yogananda 247
Yolanda 157, 158, 170, 176
You Make Me Feel (Mighty Real) 195

Young, Bert 227
Young, Loretta 42
The Young and the Restless 237, 238, 239, 246

Zen 105, 106, 110, 111, 243

Zadora, Pia 224, 226, 235
Zarro, Jim 203
Zed cards 223
Ziegfeld, Florenz 32, 35
Ziggy 74, 77, 81, 86, 90–94, 97

www.ingramcontent.com/pod-product-compliance
Ingram Content Group UK Ltd.
Pitfield, Milton Keynes, MK11 3LW, UK
UKHW041933140426
5217IPUK00014B/456